P9-CEP-688

BIG THICKET LEGACY

BIG THICKET LEGACY

Compiled and edited by

Campbell and Lynn Loughmiller

Foreword by Francis E. Abernethy

University of Texas Press, Austin & London

Library of Congress Cataloging in Publication Data

Main entry under title:

Big Thicket legacy.
    1. Big Thicket, Tex.—Social life and customs.
2. Big Thicket, Tex.—Biography. I. Loughmiller,
Campbell. II. Loughmiller, Lynn.
F392.H37B53   976.4'157 (B)   76-46329
ISBN 0-292-70716-9

Set in Korinna by G&S Typesetters, Inc.

Printed in the United States of America by
Kingsport Press

*Photographs on pages 148 and 224 courtesy
Larry Jene Fisher Collection, Gray Library,
Lamar University.*

To Alice Cashen

in the house by the side of the road

CONTENTS

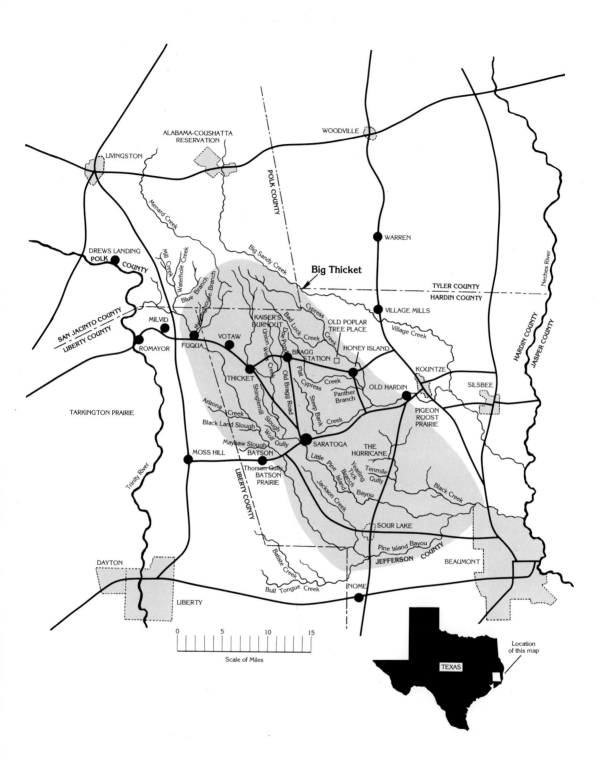

Big Thicket Country

*Campbell
Loughmiller in
the Pine Island
Bayou*

FOREWORD

Few books are able to catch the spirit as well as the sound of a place, especially when that place has as strong an identity and personality as the Big Thicket has. But Campbell and Lynn Loughmiller have, and they have been able to catch the speech patterns and figures and rhythms without resorting to cracker-barrel dialect writing. They have also kept honest. They haven't tried to make the people corn-pone folksy nor have they laundered the language for polite society. They wrote down what these old settlers said in the way that they said it, so if some of the terms used jangle the sensibilities, remember that they are writing fact not fiction.

The people in this book come from a real dimensional and historical place also, an area that is as much a part of them as they are of it. The Thicket is a part of the creative process of one way of life. Those who are native to the area have a share in the humanity that is common to all mankind, but their ancestors' generations in these woods have molded them to a slightly different form.

In spite of alien historians and biologists, of dollar-eyed land promoters and chambers of commerce who among them have stretched the Thicket to cover every county in East Texas, the old timers generally agree on its location. At the outside, the Big Thicket is about forty miles long and twenty miles wide. It is flat land, gray clay and sand, that is a part of the Pine Island Bayou drainage system. It begins in the southern parts of Polk and Tyler counties where the creeks flow out of the red dirt hills. It ends in the south below Sour Lake where the dense woods thin out in stands of pine and in the rice farms of the coastal prairie. The eastern and western boundaries were easier to define in the old days before the loggers got hold of it, but east of Cypress Creek the elevation is higher, the land is sandy, and there used to be great climax stands of yellow pine, five and six feet in diameter. The western boundary of the Thicket was marked by big open pine stands along the spoil banks of the Trinity River and by Batson Prairie on the southwest.

The land that holds the Big Thicket has been born and reborn through the last million years and has continued submerging and emerging with the ebb and flow of the great glaciers of the Pleistocene. During the Ice Age the shore line that eventually was to hold the Big Thicket rose and built, taking soils from the overflow of some great ancestral Trinity River to form layers of its land. As it grew higher and away from the sea, the marsh grasses and salt cedars gave way to pines and hardwoods drifting down from the north; and the animals that roamed and hunted the rich new land were the old ones, the ones we know only through their bones—the mastodons and elephants, the American horse and Taylor's bison, camels, tapirs, sabre-toothed tigers and the dire wolf, and giant versions of present-day sloths, beavers, and armadillos. That part of Texas that later settlers were to call the Big Thicket was rich in life, and perhaps some early man lived off its riches, but so far no one knows.

The earliest people that we can associate with the Thicket were the Indians, the Caddos to the north and the Atakapans to the south. Other tribes, some from as far away as Colorado and Kansas, came to the Thicket to hunt bear for the meat and the tallow and to meet peacefully around the springs of medicinal water that flowed near what is now Sour Lake. The Thicket became the meat house and common hunting ground for many tribes. Toward the end of the eighteenth century the Alabama and Coushatta began drifting in from Louisiana and the Thicket became theirs for a few decades.

But the Indians didn't own the land; it was a part of them as was the air they breathed. The first man to own the Thicket lands was Lorenzo de Zavalla, who held a personal claim to that area through an 1829 Mexican land grant. No Mexicans came, however, nor did any settlers come under his grant. The first to come were white Anglo-Saxon Protestants, who began settling on the fringes of the Thicket in the 1830's and living off the bounty of the land as independently as the Indians who preceded them.

As time passed, settlers began pushing into the Thicket to build their cabins on the islands of high ground and to hunt the buck and the bear as had their predecessors and to raise corn and sweet potatoes and cane. The generations that were shaped by their lives in the Big Thicket were as rugged as the Thicket itself.

The core of the Thicket population is still white, Anglo-Saxon, and Protestant. The Negro population within its boundaries is small. The Thicket did not lend itself to plantation farming and the slaves and field hands that went with it. There are a few Cajuns on the southwestern edge, in the Batson Prairie area. There are a few Slavonians left over from the days of tie cutting and stave making, and some "foreigners" stayed behind after they drifted in to work for the big sawmills or during the oil boom. But the natives, the ones whose roots are generations deep in the

Thicket soil, are Southerners by sympathy and migration, they
are conservative politically and socially, and they are Protestant
fundamentalists in religion.

The strength of these sympathies is increased by the fact that
the blood lines of the old families have frequently overlapped.
The family trees have grown close together with limbs entwined.
The old families loaned and borrowed seed among themselves,
and the result is a kinship by blood as well as a kinship in the
common bond with the land and the way of life it has nourished.

Through the 1930's the Big Thicket way of life remained pretty close to what it had been for a hundred years, and the family
unit was traditionally centered around a small subsistence farm.
Some extra money was brought in from sawmilling or working in
the oil fields. During prohibition moonshine was a money crop
for some. But for the most part, they lived off their land, sweetening the pot only a little from the outside. They were—and still
are—proud of their independence.

World War II economy and the Gulf Coast industrial develop-
ment were major factors in changing the old way of life to what it
is now. In the early 1940's the shipyards sent out their call for a
labor force. Many of the Thicketites, smarting from the sting of
the Depression, left the area for Houston and the Golden Tri-
angle never to return. At the same time a generation of soldiers
and sailors moved off to new hunting grounds. The accelerated
progress of the war years and the population explosion that followed inevitably caused the old ways to change. Those souls that
returned after the war boom and those that never left watched as
an increasing number of cars, paved roads, and power lines
invaded the heart of the Thicket, and television funneled in mas-
sive doses of the outside world.

Except for the most confirmed woodsmen, the population is
now located in the small towns in and around the Thicket, in
Kountze, Honey Island, Sour Lake, Saratoga, and Batson. Life in
these towns and in other crossroads settlements is much like
small town life elsewhere. It is a slower world than most urbanites
are used to, and fast traffic and time clocks are pleasantly absent.
The people live casually with time and one seldom gets the
notion that they live to work. A part of the sense of independence
one finds in the Thicket results from the rural tradition of working
enough to live and of not asking too much from life. There is
work enough in and near the Thicket—in the lumber, oil, or
coastal industries—to go around, but there is still no bustling
ant-hill economy. Many of the energized young people find this
speed of life too slow, and they mark time until they can leave for
more exciting urban pastures.

One consequence of this casual pace of life is that conversation is still a cultivated art form in the Thicket. People have time,
or they take it, to sit around and talk, and the social centers are

the cafes, barber shops, and filling stations where talkers and listeners are provided with a regular flow of people. They analyze the political and social world in the light of old prejudices and a fairly absolute Hebraic morality. The world's problems are simply solved. They discuss the weather in detail, with ancestral references and a personal concern that reflects a life governed by the elements and unused to air conditioning and central heat. They savor a vintage episode or experience as one would a mellow wine. They value and re-evaluate the past and the people in it as a connoisseur views a precious antique. Their main topic of conversation is each other and they share a community of information that leaves no one out.

The present-day Thicket population has been considerably diluted by urbanites fleeing the press and pollution that they have created in the coastal industrial complexes. Lumber companies and other outside interests control most of the land and have fenced it and leased it to city-born hunting clubs. Open range was over during the fifties, and barb-wire fences lattice-worked the Thicket into well-posted plots of mine-and-thine. Old woods have been logged and new ones have been planted in their space, and the result is a modern picture.

In spite of multifarious division, invasion, and dilution much of the old spirit is still there. The hunting gene is as strong as it was a hundred years ago, and hound dogs and shotguns are a natural part of their way of life. In spite of modern game laws and posted signs many of the old settlers still have the frontiersman's feeling that time and place should be no hindrance to hunting, that the time is when they need meat and the place is their ancestral hunting ground. The old clannishness can still be felt, along with a general distrust of outsiders. There is the usual woodsman's snobbery toward a tenderfoot and a mild amusement directed toward the urban bird watchers who regularly tour the Thicket. And because they are very satisfied with their own ways, they are distrustful and sometimes antagonistic toward philosophies and fashions brought in from the outside.

Those natives of the old cloth are still the soul of the Big Thicket and the common denominator for their way of life. They move with a confidence that is born of the knowledge that in a nomadic world they belong by birth to the land that they live on. They still walk the land their fathers watered with their sweat and finally nurtured with their bones. The grass and the myrtle bushes and the deer that feed on it are all a part of an interminable past that they still participate in.

Francis Edward Abernethy

PREFACE

When westward-moving pioneers crossed the Sabine River in southeast Texas they found a forest so thick they could not get through, so they settled on its fringes or went around. It was described as a forest so thick it could not be traveled even by foot. Indians, attracted by abundant game, could penetrate portions of this primeval wilderness only by canoe along the many streams that laced its three to four million acres. This land became known as the Big Thicket, and, though the origin of the name is unknown, no man living can remember when it was called anything else.

A few families probed their way into the heart of the Thicket and established isolated homesteads. For those who stayed it was a congenial wilderness. The climate was mild, the rainfall adequate, the loamy soil was rich, and game was plentiful in the forest. The "land of milk and honey" would have seemed poor by comparison.

Most of the settlers came from the southern states. From the Carolinas to Florida they came in wagon trains pulled by oxen. Many came in family groups, the father and mother and their married sons and daughters, younger children, and other relatives or friends; and single families came in single wagons. Ruby Herrington gives this account of her family's move to Texas: "The Herrington family, along with several others, moved from Alabama to East Texas in the fall of 1853, in two-wheel carts drawn by oxen. The men rode on horseback. They crossed the Alabama, Tom Bigbee, Pascagoula, Pearl, Mississippi, Red, Atchafalaya, Calcasieu, Sabine, and Neches rivers by log floats and ferries. The trip consumed three months. Another son was born on the road in the oxcart carrying grandma. She was attended only by her husband and the oldest girl, Elizabeth, who was then only seven years old."

The Thicket contains the greatest variety of plants of any comparable area in the United States—a sort of biological island with many species not to be found within hundreds of miles in any direction: desert cactus and giant palmetto, tumble weed and tupelo, yucca and bald cypress, mesquite and magnolia

Neches River

Giant Palmetto

exemplify its contrasts. It has trees of spectacular size, including
state and national champions. Wildflowers are unsurpassed.
From the commonest varieties to the rarest orchid, they seem to
reach their prolific best in this favorable habitat.

The difficulty in crossing it was due to many things, any one of
which might have been surmounted, but the numerous streams,
swamps, bogs, and the thick matted undergrowth, that sometimes stretched for miles, made travel impossible. It is a wilderness composed of a mosaic landscape, with lowlands, hammocks, sloughs, bayous, pine forest, hardwoods, ti ti thickets,
and baygalls, and these merging one with the other. The heart of
the Thicket lies within the broad "V" formed by Village and
Menard Creeks, which originate within a mile of each other in
Polk County on the north, and the rivers they feed into, the
Neches on the east and the Trinity on the west.

Yank Collins tells us this: "When the north and east lines of
Hardin County were surveyed and established in 1858 my father
was one of the chain carriers. They were out on this surveying
expedition for several weeks, and crossed only two or three dim
roads. The story he told me of what he saw and heard would rival
the most thrilling stories from the jungles of Africa. In many
places it would require hours to cut through the palmetto, vines,
and underbrush a distance of a hundred yards. A large hack
knife was used to open a path for the surveyor and chain carriers.
All kinds of wild animals were encountered, and bear tracks in
the mud were as numerous as hog tracks in a hog pasture. Many
herds of wild, unmarked, and unbranded cattle were seen."

Progress leaped over the Thicket. The oil boom that hit
Saratoga, Batson, and Sour Lake in 1903 was a short interlude
that left not a mark on the lives and customs of the few settlers
who lived there. At the peak of the boom they were hunting bear
and wild turkey in the depths of the Thicket three miles away,
indifferent if not oblivious to a life of inconceivable contrasts
closer, in some cases, than their nearest neighbor.

For nine years Lynn and I explored this country, photographing and camping for weeks in its woods, by its ponds, and on its
streams, canoeing hundreds of miles on the Neches, the Trinity,
and the creeks and bayous between them.

One's fondness for the area is hard to explain. It has no com-
manding peak or awesome gorge, no topographical feature of
distinction. Its appeal is more subtle. It must be experienced bit
by bit, step by step. One can neither see far nor go fast. A
hundred yards off the road without a compass and you are lost,
and the dense understory of the ti ti thicket could give one claus-
trophobia. What is left of the Thicket is as wild as ever. Its wilderness character was, and still is, its essential appeal, the major
interest that took us there in the first place.

A thousand things compete for one's attention, from the color-

Slave Lake

*Little Green's
Bayou*

Brushy Lake
Rookery

ful fungi to the pileated woodpecker. It is simply impossible to go
far without stopping for something that captures one's attention. I have never walked through woods with a greater sense of expectancy.

Finally, the people themselves became our chief interest. Any wilderness puts its own stamp on the people who live there, shaping their lives and culture by the physical demands it imposes. Big Thicket people love their country and derive daily enjoyment from it as no other we have known. They mention hardships but never complain about them, and, for all its provincial flavor, one gets the feeling that life has been good to them. They have an unquenchable optimism. Their days are not filled with odious tasks from which they seek a respite; instead, they seem to savor the vital but commonplace experiences of everyday living.

The stories that follow tell about them—their own stories in their own words. Lynn and I began taping them for our own use, because we liked the stories and the people who told them. It was six years before we ever thought of compiling them for publication. Some of the words the people use, such as "nigger," might offend some readers, but we felt it was important to give an accurate rendering of the speakers' vocabularies. These words and what they meant to the people of the Thicket are a part of oral history.

Many people encouraged us to compile the tapes for publication, especially Archer Fullingim, editor of the "Kountze News." I had known "the printer," as Archer is called, long before he went to Kountze, but I had not seen him for years. We found him supremely satisfied as editor of the weekly newspaper which is read in all parts of the nation and was recently selected as one of the three most unique weeklies in the United States. Archer was raised in West Texas but fell under the spell of the Thicket as he lived in a cabin on Village Creek after World War II. He calls it the most beautiful creek in America, and he has not strayed far from it since.

From the stories that follow, and others we could not include, a few impressions gained increasing emphasis; for instance, women enjoyed life in the Thicket as much as the men. Often they helped cut logs for the cabin, dressed the hogs, went on the hunt, and danced all night at the logrollings. They were full partners with the men in meeting the requirements of the times and could shoot just as straight.

Many of the people who speak in this book were related. The population was small and settlements were few. Randolph ("Dolph") Fillingim recalled that in order not to marry kinfolks the boys invaded other settlements looking for wives. It would not be far from the truth to say that at the beginning of the century, or even up to now, half the population of the Thicket from Pine Island Bayou to Village Creek was related.

A single family might constitute a "settlement," and, if there were more, the closest neighbor could still be three miles away. Each brought its own culture, its values and traditions, and these might vary widely between settlements less than ten miles apart. Whiskey drinking, for example, might be accepted as normal in one community but rejected in another.

Dogs! No place on earth has so many dogs per person as the Thicket. Ten times as many people will show up at a meeting of the Dog Hunter's Association as would be found at a political rally or a school bond election. Dogs are to the Thicket what horses were to the range. It would have been hard to survive without them.

The three hundred thousand acres that are left of this tight little pocket of wilderness are much like they always were. People are basically related to the land they live on, their immediate environment; and, as Leak Bevil said, "The good old days are right on up to now."

ACKNOWLEDGMENTS

We interviewed many persons whose accounts could not be included but which were nonetheless helpful in giving us a fuller understanding of the area and its people. We are deeply grateful to the following for many pleasant hours and for the information they so generously provided: Martha Sultana Jacobsen, Margaret Amanda Ayres, Susie Overstreet, Corbitt and Delphia Brackin, Hale Johnston, Bud Overstreet, Ebbie Cotton, Ruby Herrington, W. A. (Bill) Warren, Carl Richardson, Mamie Vickers McKim, Bill Brett, Annie Moye Hendrix, Ruth Lee Hooks, Peter Mihelich, Jean Batiste ("Uncle Bat") Charpiot, and Ethel Osborne Hill.

Our thanks is also extended to those who suggested persons we might interview, who helped us locate them, or who provided historical perspective for some of the stories we obtained: Dwayne Overstreet, Brown Wiggins, Archer Fullingim, Maxine Johnston, Alice Cashen, Ludie and Veston Oliver, Cecil Overstreet, John Blair, Harold Nicholas, and Durwood ("Rocky") Richardson.

Martha Sultana Jacobsen

We did not meet Mrs. Jacobsen until she was ninety-three, but we were fast friends five minutes later. She lived alone in a small frame house off a dirt road south of Pine Ridge Baptist Church, of which she was a member. 1879–1973, interviewed 1972–1973.

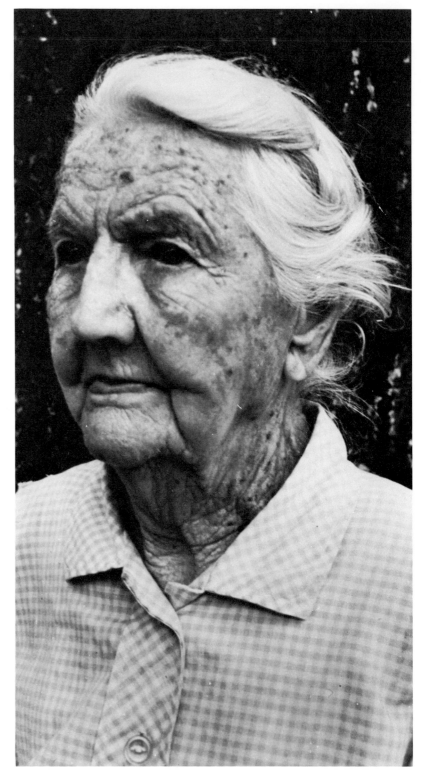

Amanda Margaret Ayres and Bragg Hotel

By preference and necessity Mrs. Ayres has lived in the woods all her life. Her father was a "turpentine man" and worked the southern pine forests from his native North Carolina to Georgia, Florida, Alabama, Mississippi, and Louisiana. He moved to Texas about the turn of the century. Since 1910, Mrs. Ayres has owned and operated the Bragg Hotel, a two-story frame building, at what used to be a siding on the Santa Fe Railroad. The line was discontinued and the tracks removed in 1935. When we interviewed her at age ninety she had not had a paying guest in seven years, and her closest neighbor was miles away; but in times past she had a full house and a yard full of tents to handle the overflow. Born 1885, interviewed 1969–1975.

*Jean Claud Justin
Batiste Charpiot*

*"Uncle Bat" was
considered a su-
preme optimist
when, at 95, he
planted a peach
orchard because
he liked peaches,
but he ate many
baskets of his
favorite fruit be-
fore he died at
105. His father
came from France,
settled on Pine Is-
land Bayou, and
lived to be 106
years old. "Uncle
Bat," a skilled car-
penter and black-
smith, could build
a house, shoe a
horse, make a
fiddle or a wagon
wheel—just any-
thing a person
needed. Turkey
hunting was his
favorite sport.
1869–1975,
interviewed 1968–
1974.*

Ethel Osborn Hill

Mrs. Hill was born November 3, 1878. She is not a native of the Thicket but has spent more than fifty years there, writing about it, talking about it, helping preserve it. She lived alone in a log cabin in the woods northeast of Woodville but, in recent years, has spent the winter in an apartment in Orange. At ninety-five she still wrote a weekly column for the Woodville newspaper and had published a small volume of her poems. Born 1878, interviewed 1965–1975.

BIG THICKET LEGACY

Ellen Walker

Introducing Mrs. Ellen Walker

"Aunt Ell" Walker, as she was affectionately known, lived ninety-nine years within seven miles of where she was born. She never wanted to live anywhere else. After her husband died she lived alone and regularly walked six miles—to Saratoga and back—for her mail and occasional groceries, until she broke her hip at ninety-two. She remained active until her death, though one of her daughters and her husband, Mr. and Mrs. Shortie Jackson, lived with her the last four years.

Aunt Ell loved the woods. She never let the commonplace become common but retained a positive appreciation of her environment, which she knew like the back of her hand. She was neither surprised nor concerned at the scream of a panther in the draw behind her house, which she continued to hear till she died. Her favorite flower was the wild honeysuckle, though in her yard she nurtured a burr rosebush from a cutting her mother brought from Alabama when the family headed for Texas over a century ago.

Mrs. Walker worked in the woods with her husband until she was fifty-three, when an injury to her husband forced them to quit. Most people would think of it as hard, physically demanding work, but she said, "No, I wouldn't say tie-hacking is hard work. I enjoyed it."

Despite the demands of a rugged environment, the years dealt kindly with Aunt Ell. She was interested in life and people till the day she died. Diminished hearing was the only noticeable impairment of her faculties. Her gnarled hands that gripped the broad ax in years past served her reliably as she moved about the place with her walking cane. On our many visits during the last eight years of her life, we never saw her when she was not pleasant and cheerful. She was widely known as "Ma Thicket," a title that seemed to fit, and certainly one that she earned.

MRS. MARY ELLEN WALKER ("AUNT ELL")

My grandmother and grandfather come from Alabama to Texas in a ox wagon. They stayed one year in Mississippi and then come on to Texas and located about five miles from Old Hardin, on Big Cypress. Old Hardin was the county seat. There was my grandmother and grandfather, three aunts and one of my aunt's husband, Charlie Flowers. He was my uncle on both sides. My grandfather was William Brackin, and my grandmother was Ida Snelder before she was married. My father was Irving Flowers and my mother Lottie Brackin. Bud Brackin was my own uncle. My ma and pa married durin' the war. My daddy got a furlough and come home and they married over there on Cypress Creek at the old Brackin place. I was born at Honey Island, October 10, 1874, but when I was ten years old we moved from Honey Island down there, five miles from Saratogie and six miles from Honey Island, right in the middle of the Big Thicket.

My daddy built our house out of pine, hand-hewed logs, notched and fitted and leveled. The floor was three inches thick and hewed out of logs. The kitchen wasn't built on to the rest of the house but was connected by a shed. It was built out of round logs, not hewed. The floor was red clay, built up about twelve inches higher than the ground. They'd always have a mudcat chimney, take about a day to build, neighbors help. Women would cook and men built the chimney. I stayed right there till I was twenty years old, when I married and moved to Saratogie, and I've been here ever since.

Uncle Bud and Uncle Jim was our closest neighbors, six miles to their house. Uncle Bud hunted a lot. He called me to the gate one mornin', said, "Come here, I got a purty for ya." I went out there and he reached back in his saddle pocket, and he had a little old bear about ten inches long. The old mama bear had one of his dogs hugged up and about to kill it. He run in and jabbed his gun in her mouth and shot her, and the print of her teeth was on each side of his Winchester. She had two little cubs in her bed and he carried 'em home and raised 'em. They was about a year old when he sold 'em to Ben Hooks. They'd walk on their hind feet and hold up a broom just like somebody.

When I was a girl there was big timber on the high ground, virgin pines five feet through, and just a little underbrush. In other places it was so thick you couldn't get through without a hack knife, and ever' kind of animal you ever heard of nearly. Turkey go in herds, just like a bunch of chickens. Deer aplenty, and bobcats and wolves, and bear and wild hogs and wild cattle. And I've seen wild horses that didn't belong to nobody, couldn't catch 'em. They used to be over here at Batson, plenty of 'em. If you could catch 'em, they was your'n.

There was plenty of blackberries and mayhaws and worlds of black walnuts and chinquapins. There was worlds of wild flowers in the woods. Wild honeysuckle was my favorite. I got a bouquet in there now.

Over yonder, that big cypress brake was just covered in palmettos. Ma used to make fans out of 'em. Sometimes she made 'em out o' turkey feathers, from the wing and tail. That made a good 'un. Sew turkey tails together and made 'em round, and sew a little piece o' cloth over 'em; made a nice fan.

We raised what we eat, had a garden. Always had a patch o' corn and sweet potatoes, sugar cane and maybe some peanuts. We'd raise peas and when they'd get dry ma'd put somethin' in 'em to keep the weevils out. Had all kinds of meat: venison, turkey, squirrel. We'd cure bear meat. You can cure it just as good as you can hog meat, and you can season with it, too. You can eat all you want of it and drink the lard, and it won't make you sick. Now old summer bear, they ain't fit to eat; they're pore; they stink. But in the wintertime, they're big and fat and they're good. I liked bear meat, but in the summertime, I wanted venison. We could get that any day we wanted it, and turkey too. I loved squirrel just any time, and we eat rabbit, and sometimes coon in the wintertime, when they was big and fat. We'd cut venison up in strips and dry it on a scaffold in the sun, jerky. When it dried, put it in a sack and hang it up.

We had a old handmill and ground our own cornmeal, and we made good hominy. Made it with fireplace ashes. We'd make our soap out of hickory ashes. Make you a hopper and put the ashes in it and let it stay four or five days. Pour a little water on it and after a while it'd go to drippin'. Put a pot under it to catch it. Put your grease in there and go to cookin'. It'd make good jelly soap, never very hard. When we killed hogs we'd make enough lye soap to do all year, stored it in big old gourds, sugar gourds, maybe eight inches across.

I have my mother's iron skillet, has legs and a lid. We'd cook our bread in it, put the lid on and put a little fire on top and on the bottom. That's where I learnt to cook, on a fireplace. I don't know

what become of ma's other cook vessels. She had ovens and
pots. She had a big old high pot that we always cooked greens in,
and they're good too.

Nearly everybody had fruit trees and we'd preserve our
peaches, use homemade sugar, made it ourselves from sugar
cane. We always growed enough cane to make our own sugar
and syrup. We growed nearly everything we needed except coffee. We'd buy a big sack of green coffee beans and roast it
ourselves.

There was some salt licks where people got their salt, and
there was salt springs where people would go and camp out
maybe for a week and get enough salt to last all year. When it got
damp it'd stick together in great big old lumps. Have to beat it up
with a maul. I can remember seeing daddy beat it up to salt meat
with, in a dugout trough, about three feet long and deep enough
to beat it up, built special for that. Then you had to keep it dry or
it would stick back together, be a great big old hard lump and
have to beat it again.

We'd pickle our pork. Kill our hogs, kill about three, cut them
and throw 'em in a barrel of water to soak the blood all out of
'em. Then we'd put 'em in 'nother barrel of cold water and let
'em set all night. We'd take 'em out and salt 'em and put the
pieces down in a barrel. The brine would make on top. It was
good then. That pickled meat and collard greens was shore
good. We didn't farm but a little. We had a horse and plow, but
we done it mostly by hand.

Made our shoes out of wild cow hide; used a wooden trough
for tanning. Soak the hide in alum water and red oak bark, bark
turn it yellow. Lay the hide on a log and beat it with a club, while it
is wet, to get the hair off and make it soft. Don't dry it in the sun;
this would make it stiff. Daddy made the sole first and then put
the top on with wooden pegs. Had a awl, punch a hole and put a
peg in there, and them pegs didn't come out neither.

Ma made all our clothes, the thread, the cloth, all by hand.
Made cloth on grandma's old loom, made it out of cotton or
wool. They'd dye it different colors. Get bark off trees to dye it.
And they raised their indigo bushes, and you let 'em get about
three feet high and they'd ring 'em, pack 'em in a barrel and pour
water over 'em. Let 'em set there in that water till it begins to
foam on top. They'd take a hoe then and churn it, then after
while the indigo mud would come up just like butter on milk.
They'd take that out and lay it up and let it dry. They'd dye blue
with it, the prettiest blue you ever did see, and it wouldn't wash
out. Indigo grows in the Thicket now. Another dye, you get the
bark off'n trees and boil it, squeeze the juice out, take the bark
out and then put whatever they're goin' to work with in the dye.
Some of it has to be cold, some of it hot. They'd put the cop-
peras in while it was hot and stir it in there till it melted. It made

dye stick. I've got a old quilt in there that was dyed with red oak bark. I reckon I've had it forty years, but still I can use it. We used to have revivals in the summer, last a week or two, and the girls would dye their dresses two or three different colors during the revival so it would look like a new dress.

We raised our own cotton and picked the seed out with our fingers, then carded it. I've got the old cards in there now, worn out, but I still got 'em. Then I spun it on the spinnin' wheel. We'd buy our wool, raw wool, or trade for it. We had a neighbor that had a bunch of sheep. We'd pick our wool up, card it, spin it, weave it into cloth like we did cotton.

I guess there's been wild hogs in here always, and wild cattle. Anybody could go and kill one when he wanted to. Be wild just like a wild fox. They'd go out and kill a wild beef, kill one and divide it with the neighbors. Didn't everybody have a gun, and a lot of 'em that had guns didn't have enough money to buy lead to make bullets.

I've seen pigeons in here by the thousands. I know it to be the truth that there would be so many pigeons they'd break the limbs off the trees. That was over here at Honey Island on Cypress Creek. My two brothers would go over there and bring pigeons by the sackful. Just knock 'em out of the trees and bushes.

Didn't never call a doctor when we was born. Used a old lady, Grandma Patterson. She lived 'round among the neighbors. She was a old widow woman and she just lived where anybody would take her. She was a good old soul. She stayed with us a long time. We thought as much of her as we did our own grandma. We called her granny. When a woman had a baby and her breast rose, why they'd soak mullein leaves in vinegar and put 'em to her breast, and that brought the fever out. And we used mullein leaves to put on sprains.

We had a neighbor where we used to live and I went to see her one morning, and she had a little baby in a basket sittin' on a stool by her wash tub. It was just born the night before, and she was a'washin'. It wasn't customary, but she had it to do. Her husband worked at a mill and he'd gone on to work. Didn't seem to hurt her, neither.

When one of us get kinda puney, why daddy would fix us up some old rusty nails in water and make us drink it; gave us iron. 'Nother thing, you've seen a tar kiln haven't you? They'd fix a hole in the ground and get some fat lighter pine and put it in there and get some pine straw and cover it up, and fire them lighter splinters, and after while the tar go to runnin' down in the ditch, like pitch runs out of rich splinters, well, that's the way that was—run into a pot. And pa'd put a big old lump of tar in a bucket of water and make us drink water off it. In the spring of the year they did that to clear up our blood, and the rusty nails gave us iron. We never had much sickness, neither.

Now and then somebody'd have a logrollin'. They'd pile logs all day, then have a big dinner and dance. Some of 'em would get drunk and fight, fight worse than dogs. I was at a logrollin' one time and just before dinner two of the boys got in a fight over a girl and one knocked the other in the head with a hand spike and killed him just as dead as a doornail, right there in the field. He was drunk, how come him to do it. Made their liquor out of peaches and apples and corn. Had plenty of peach and apple orchards. I was small, but I can still remember seein' that man lie there dead, just as good as I can see that chair now. It was McMillan that got killed and Ainsworth that killed 'im. The families didn't get mad at each other, like they do now; they stayed friends. The other boy run away from here and went to Mexico and got killed. They sent his body back here to his parents, but his parents was both dead, but his uncle took him off the train and brought him home and buried 'im.

We had dances about once't a week, at the neighbors' houses. I've plowed all day long, get ready and walk seven miles to a dance, and dance every set all night long, walk home next mornin', go to the field and go to plowin'—no sleep. One brother hunted every day, but my youngest brother and me worked in the field with my daddy. I was about fifteen years old then, and it was seven miles to my brother Joe's place. His neighbors, the Suttons would be there, and his mother-in-law. My brother, Pres, his name was Calvin, went with me. I was a good dancer. I could out–two-step a nigger. I had a boyfriend that always danced with me. Me and him won the prize ever' time we went to a dance for being the best dancers there was in the house. He was Sherrod Sutton.

For music at the dances we used fiddles. Some of them was made out of gourds and some out of cigar boxes. They put a neck in it to put the strings on, and they'd make 'em a bow and put strings on it just like they do now.

Sometimes my mother didn't want me to go and she'd hide my starched dress, but I'd take one of my other 'ns and go on. My youngest brother, Josh, would hide them for me sometimes. I remember one time I had a new wool dress, wool challie, and I was goin' to wear it. It was Christmas time, and I'd never had it on. I was goin' to take it with me to my sister's and dress over to her house. And ma took my dress and hid it in a sack of cotton, and got it all full of cotton. And my brother got me 'nother 'n, one of my Sunday ones, just a plain calico dress, rolled it up and put it under his coat. "Come on, Ell," he said, "we'll go anyhow." I said, "Go like I am?" He said, "Yes, we'll get a dress from Tink." That was my sister. So we went, and when we got away from the house, he said, "I got this old dress. I couldn't find 'nare 'nother 'n." I said, "Well, good! That's just as good as I'd have!" It was a black and white striped calico dress. Daddy said, "Let her go."

Ma never did want me to go nowhere. I went to the dance that night and danced all night long.

That wool dress was a mess. Ma had a time gettin' the cotton off'n it. I told her she could burn the damned thing if she wanted to, I wouldn't pick a speck of it off.

I never went no place till I got old enough to take care of myself; I was fifteen. We used to get together at a neighbor's house and have singin's, see which one could sing the prettiest love song. We had a time! Boys would sing some and the girls would sing some. They were "One Cold Snowy Day," "Bring my Blue-Eyed Boy Back to Me," "Molly Darlin'," and lots o' other 'ns. Oh, I know'd a lot o' songs. Can't sing no more; ain't got breath enough to sing. And we'd go to Josie parties and sing and play games: "You swing your sugar and tea, and I'll swing my candy; You swing your sugar and tea, and I'll swing 'round my brandy; You eat all your sugar and tea, and I'll eat all my candy." You'd change partners. Like you and I was partners, we'd lead them up and down the "shoodall," and then you'd take a girl and I'd get ahold of a boy's hand. We'd square-dance and two-step and waltz.

I used to love to dance. I'd rather dance than eat when I was hungry. But I quit dancin', j'ined the church, tried to live a Christian life. I don't think there's any harm in dancin', but I quit when I was eighteen, when I j'ined the church. Wasn't s'posed to dance then and I quit, and ain't danced since.

We went to Saratogie to church, six miles each way. Go at night, too, walk, never light a light when we got home, go to bed. Had a nice church house right side of the graveyard. Just me and ma would go, wade water ankle deep to knee deep from our house to Saratogie, five miles through that cypress brake. Take our shoes in our arms, tie up our dresses, hit the road and go to church, ma and me would, but the boys wouldn't never go. We went summertime, wintertime, anytime we got ready, but our feet never got cold, don't seem like. The go was what we wanted.

We'd see packs of wolves, and I seen lots of bear and deer and bobcat, but nothin' never did bother us. There was lots of snakes and we always toted a stick to kill them snakes with. I never had one bite me, but one bit ma. She had on her shoes though, bit her right on the instep. She was half a mile from home but she come on back, and Daddy got on a horse and got some medicine to put on it. It was a ground rattler. Her foot and leg swelled awful bad, but never hurt her much, just made her sick for a little while. But one bit my brother and it like to killed him. Bit him on the leg. Daddy got the doctor and brought him down there and he cupped it. He put some paper in something like a jar he had with him, and he fired that paper and turned it over that snake bite and drawed that poison out, called it cuppin'; did that, and give him some medicine, and he got all right.

My husband, Jim Walker, was born March 1, 1858, in Alabama. We's married in 1897. He grew up in Florida, and was just a boy when he come to Texas. He come by hisself and left his parents there. He was a saloon keeper, but he went broke. We was glad of it because he might have stayed with it, and we liked farmin' much better. After we married, we farmed and made crossties for the railroad. He hunted deer quite smart till they got to where they wouldn't let you kill 'em, go out and kill one whenever he got ready. After the law come in, he wouldn't hunt. He was a good citizen.

We lived in a old house; it was eighteen by twenty, two rooms, and we bought it and paid for it by cuttin' wood for a man. When we got this land down here, we tore that house down and moved it to this place. There was a pinepost shed out there, and we moved in it till our house was ready. We tore that old house down and brought it down here and put it up, and we didn't spend one penny. We didn't have it. We drawed the nails out of the lumber and out of the shingles, and put the same shingles back, put the same old lumber up, and used the same old nails, old square nails. We moved it about a mile and a half, toted most of it on our shoulders, but a neighbor brought the heavy pieces on his wagon. Bought a old outhouse, cut two ricks of wood for it, and put us up a little shed room to cook in, and we lived in that house for thirty-seven years. It had a fireplace, and we built a mudcat chimney, mixed the mud with pine straw.

Me and my husband cut crossties on the Blake Survey. It was three-and-a-half miles from our house to where we cut. We had a baby then, and I had to take the baby with me. Took my old coat, spread it down and put her on it. She'd set there, and I'd watch her. I'd score hack and my husband would take his broad ax and bust the slabs off, and level it up. It was a while before I learnt how to score hack, but I finally learnt it, and he'd bust the doubles out, hew 'em up. Still got that old measurin' stick. We made about twenty a day. They was nine by ten, ten by twelve, and six by eight. We made switch ties out of oak. They had to be eighteen feet long, had to use S irons in 'em to keep 'em from splittin'. We got ten cents for the regular ties and twenty cents for them long 'uns.

Cut ties all day, walk home, cook supper, wash clothes, and tie up all them old dogs of a night. Had to tie 'em up to keep 'em from runnin' off and huntin' things.

We's afraid they'd get killed. Wolves would kill 'em; used to be worlds of wolves here. We had bear dogs, deer dogs, hog dogs, and a little old feist for squirrels and coons. You could sell coon hides for a good price. We'd ship 'em someplace to a fur factory, and in a few days there'd come a big check. That helped out, 'specially a tie hacker.

We'd just bought a brand new saw to make them ties with, and he got disabled and had to quit, then I had to quit. Makin' ties ain't hard work, just takes time. You cut your tree down, measure 'em end to end, measure 'em in the middle and score hack 'em, then take a broad ax and bust it out. I enjoyed makin' them ties. We sold 'em to the Santa Fe Railroad and they paid off good. Paid once a month. I was fifty-three years old when we quit makin' ties.

Been in good health all my life, held up pretty good. Done all kinds of work, made crossties, mud sills, walking beams, ox yokes, split board, split rails. But I enjoyed it. I love the woods.

1874–1973, interviewed 1964–1972.

Introducing Brown Wiggins

If one listens very long to Brown Wiggins tell a story he gets the feeling that he is listening to a gifted historian. He supplies a wealth of detail without becoming tedious. His restrained enthusiasm and interest in the things he tells are obvious, for he tries to make clear any event or process he describes. He tells his stories deftly.

Brown Wiggins is tall and thin, soft-spoken, mild-mannered, his large eyes twinkling with humorous recollections, hair parted down the middle; it is hard to imagine him wearing a six-shooter as he operated the loader on a tram line in a logging camp. He didn't usually wear it, only when it seemed appropriate. "I'm made aware," he said, "of the advance we've made in that we don't have to shoot and fistfight like they did fifty to a hundred years ago."

Brown's mother died when he was nine, and he lived with his father and sister until he was fifteen. He attended business school in Houston but came back and spent years in logging camps, usually operating the loader, a job he always preferred. He ended his active career as a longtime operator of a grocery store in Votaw, a short distance from where he was born.

Brown liked music, and his resonant voice equipped him for singing. His favorite entertainment for years was group singings on weekends at church or at someone's home. He was instrumental in getting a music teacher to work with the Alabama-Coushatta Indians and, according to Brown, with great success. "They had some of the best quartets in the country."

From reading Brown's story one gets the feeling that he was a part of the fun and mischief of the times. He knows many of the old timers and was most helpful to us in locating persons who could supply information on unusual aspects of Big Thicket life. The only time I ever saw him even mildly impatient was when he went with us to see one of his friends who answered my first question for two-and-a-half hours.

Mrs. Wiggins died in 1971, and Brown lives in a large house trailer near the home of Ludy and Veston Oliver, in Saratoga, and enjoys Ludy's fine cooking. Ludy is his niece.

BROWN WIGGINS

I was born and raised down here about three miles from Votaw. I'm eighty-two. At about nine years my mother died, and me and my sister and my father kept house at this old place right on. So when we broke up housekeeping, we turned the place over to my sister and her husband, Eli Collins. My grand- father's name was Ed Wiggins; my grandmother was Josie Wiggins. Her maiden name was Clark. My father was Henry Wiggins, born in 1854, and he married Sapphire Davis at Big Sandy. Came from Mississippi about the time all the rest of them. These old folks filled up this country; that was about 1840.

My grandfather didn't die until I was about sixteen or seven- teen. He very often told me of the journey. He said they bunched up, probably a dozen wagons, and their milk cows and their saddle horses would follow after they traveled a week. They all had ox wagons, generally two yoke of steers to each wagon, with a cover on it. Some had a little tent packed away in their wagon. He said they'd come a piece and camp, and the young men would get out and work a while, if they could find something to do. At times, along these rivers, they'd cut timber and float it down the rivers—about the only way of logging they had. He said when they came to the Mississippi, it was just level banks, and the kind of boats they had them days it was dangerous to tackle it. So they just camped till the river went down before they'd risk crossing—crossed in ferry boats and came on by old Town Bluff on the Neches River. They landed up here at what we call Big Sandy. It was a mighty pretty place, nice little stream run through there with springs all over it. It was open pine woods as far as you could see. They decided that would be a good healthy country— lots of mosquitoes in the low country, lots of malaria. While they didn't know the mosquito caused it, they thought that old green water was the thing they had to dodge. But they would tell you, "If you live on a river, you better get on a big bluff where you get the breeze both ways. Malaria will kill you if you don't." Well that is the reason they stopped out at Big Sandy.

After they stopped there, the men saddled their horses, exper-

Brown Wiggins

imenting, took a compass and they went seven miles west of here. They forded the river and went across to where Dayton is, then they set their compass and turned north on the other side of the river and traveled north till they got to Camillar, a little old settlement there about three or four miles west of the Trinity River, west of Swarthout Ferry. They crossed there and headed back to their camp on a due east course. They didn't easily find it, but they did. The Moyes stayed there and there's some of them still there. The Wiggins and the Moyes are kinfolks. The Wiggins didn't like that, no game, so they came on into the Thicket.

I think it took them about a year to come from Mississippi. They had their cattle so well trained, where they camped, they'd turn loose those steers, everything else, and they wouldn't leave the wagon. They didn't know anything else but those wagons. Boys would work for feedstuff for their cattle; anything the folks had they worked for it. They'd rest a while, wasn't in any hurry, milk the cows on the way. Fed the cows every night, and next morning when they pulled out, the cows would be right there. This was after the war and the slaves was freed and so they had no slaves. That disgusted the old folks, and I think that was the reason they were huntin' a new country.

They had just small farms, but year by year they'd take in more. In the river bottoms was the biggest farms, closest to the river. We had about twenty-five acres, but all we'd raise was feedstuff. Then we had a woods pasture.

If you went and settled on a place and went to livin' there, anywhere in these woods, if you paid taxes on it and they didn't bother you for ten years, the court would give you a title to 160 acres. Timber wasn't worth anything, wasn't any way of gettin' it out of here, and they didn't watch it very close, and some of these squatters would get 160 acres off of most any big land owner before he would know it. They didn't stir around on their holdings.

When they settled that way they generally built them one of those board houses. You could split a big board out of the timber we had then, and they'd build a mudcat chimney, made out of mud and pine straw. They'd cook on the fireplace. Everybody cooked on the fireplace then. They'd fix hooks there to hang the iron pots on.

A family named Barneycastle came to our place, and had a small tent and a wagon sheet over his wagon. Now they didn't mind that. They'd come from Alabama, Georgia, someplace over that way. After the war, they wanted to examine Texas to see what kind of a place it was. They crossed the Neches River on a ferry right there at Town Bluff, and crossed the Mississippi somewhere close to Jackson. Half the time they was traveling by compass, you know, and little wagon roads. Barneycastle came

in an ox wagon, one big yoke of steers, a saddle horse, and a
milk cow following. He had three sons and his wife. They were
middle-aged and they made a pretty good work team. They
came to our house and me and my father led them through the
woods, and my father picked out a level place to make a good
farm. That's what he wanted. Well they made a good farm there,
and one of his sons, Tom, stayed there.

We came back later to this old man's house to see what he'd
done, probably six months. He'd cleared him up a place there
and raised some sweet potatoes and was diggin' them. He had
built a furnace out of clay and called it a dirt oven. He'd build a
fire in there and wait till it got good and hot, and then drag nearly
all that fire out and put a couple of bushels of sweet potatoes in
there and shut the door, and go on to work, and he'd have baked
sweet potatoes for three or four days. So when we rode by the old
man give us a big one right out of the oven.

We had all kinds of animals that was eatable, but I preferred to
hunt turkey and ducks. Ducks were all over this country! There
were big ponds here, shallow ponds that would cover ten acres
or more. They were full of these pin oak trees, and those ducks
would float on that water and dive down and get the acorns. You
could sneak up to the edge of the pond, through the bushes, and
holler one time, and they'd all throw their heads up, and you
could kill a mess of ducks, more than you could carry home if
you was afoot, at one shot. You couldn't carry over ten big ducks.
They were all fat, regular old mallards.

We trapped quail. In this good-splittin' timber, we could rive
out any kind of a little strip you wanted. We'd take 6-foot strips
and build a pen about 2-1/2 feet high and dig a trench under it;
start it on the outside, and let it come to about the middle of the
pen; put a board over the trench on the inside next to the wall,
and bait it with corn. The quail would trail the grains of corn till
they got to the pen, and they'd go under the pen, and when
they'd come up in the middle, they'd go to runnin' around the
edge. They wouldn't go back through that opening out in the
center. Sometimes you'd leave that pen there two or three days,
sometimes catch a hundred. We'd carry them to the house and
put them in a big pen, and when we didn't want to eat 'em, we'd
sell 'em. At the time we was catchin' so many, there was a loggin'
camp nearby, about twenty-five families, and they'd give us ten
cents apiece for 'em.

Some folks didn't have a gun, and some didn't have the
money to buy powder, or lead to make the bullets, and they'd set
snares, especially for deer. If you had a garden, the deer was bad
to get in it. They'd walk up to the fence, maybe six feet high, and
jump right over. They didn't take a runnin' start, just jumped
from a standing position. And they'd always jump from the same
place and land in the same place in the garden, wouldn't be but

just a little place where all four feet hit the ground. You could depend on that, and people would sharpen a pole and stick one end in the ground and aim the other end so the deer would hit it when he jumped in the garden, and it would kill him right there, and that's the way they'd get fresh meat.

It would surprise you the number of things we boys would have fun with. Sometimes it was riding yearlings, all the way from yearlings to grown steers. Other times it would be horses, and we'd go swimming, too. Other than church, we'd have our socials and play parties. Sometimes we'd have a bunch of plays wrote out, and each one perform his part. This would be in somebody's home. They had certain places in the country they'd have singin's. They generally lasted two days, all day Saturday and all day Sunday. They used what we call now the "Old Book." Just had four notes, called Sacred Harp. I took up music when I was young and pretty well mastered the regular music. Quite a lot of the Indians study music. I helped put a man in the village to teach them and it turned out good. They've got as nice a quartet and as good piano players there as you'll hear anywhere.

When I was small some people would go down here on the Batson Prairie and catch those prairie ponies, feed them up and break them and work them to a double buggy or a hack. Those little fellows would trot twenty-five miles on these dirt roads and not be hurt a bit. You couldn't hardly kill 'em. They were just almost any color except the pinto; we didn't have that among them. We had a white horse and a blue dapple, and a buckskin with black mane and tail, and when you fed them they were really pretty. But they didn't look like anything when you got them off the prairie. They were small, wouldn't weigh over five hundred pounds, maybe six, but they could carry you in a buggy all day. We didn't use them for anything else. We had good horses to use working our stock. There were men down there that would gather up about fifty head of those prairie ponies and drive them up through the country—down around Devers, Daisetta, Hull, that was pony country—and swap them for yearlings. When they got shed of their horses, they had a bunch of cattle to drive back.

My uncle, John Wiggins, at Hyatt, had a butcher shop and guaranteed meat to Rice's sawmill, and had worked with them a long time. One of the Rice brothers gave Uncle John his own house, forty acres of land, and several smaller houses when they closed the sawmill. It was a big beautiful house. Best rich men in the world, Rice brothers was.

The Rices liked to hunt up here, and we'd carry them and show them the best places. At that time you could charter a boxcar for forty dollars and keep it ten days. They'd load their horses, camping outfits, and enough food to do 'em, come up to Kountze and hire somebody to bring them to the Thicket. They'd stay a week or ten days, charter them another car if they wanted to stay longer. When they got ready to go back, they'd generally give us what they had left, except the horses.

I remember one time they were over here in the Thicket about six or seven miles from here, and Fred Rice had bought him one of those double-barreled, hammerless shotguns. They saddled their horses next morning and started out to hunt deer. Fred Rice and another man got on their horses about the same time and Fred Rice let that gun go off, and it killed the other fellow's horse, just did miss the man. And he walked out to a big log and he just bent the gun over that log and throwed it down. He had laid it just across his lap, had a safety, and they weren't used to that; had a hammer in those days.

The Rice brothers had old Dr. Dubose with them on one of their hunts. They was on a little old meandering road, moonshiny night, and they was all sitting around the camp talkin' and old Dr. Dubose got up and went to walkin' that road back and forth. Some of them got kind o' stirred up about it, and Baldwin Rice asked him, said, "What's the matter with you, Doc?" He said, "Well, I thought I maybe wouldn't have to tell ya, but when I was young a hydrophobia dog bit me, and my folks liked to not noticed it in time to save me, and on certain times of the moon I get nervous, and if I just get up and walk about an hour, I'll walk it off." And he kept walkin', and Baldwin said, "That damn doctor is liable to bite us." But after a while he came back to the camp, sat down and went to talkin', seemed to be all right. He was a doctor at the old Rice mill.

A lot of the Indians came into the Thicket after their meat. They lived at the Indian Village, east of Livingston, and they'd come about twice a year when I was small. They'd generally come in the spring, along in April, and in late September. The main game they wanted was deer, and they knew where all the springs and water holes was. There was only one in the bunch that could talk. The men would ride the little ponies and the squaws would walk. If they had babies they'd carry them on their backs in a sack. And quite a lot of poor little dogs came along, so poor you could count the joints in their tails.

They wouldn't bring salt with them or grease, hog grease was what they wanted. And they'd come and line up crossways in our front yard and go to humming, no tune to it, sort of a chant. This was their way of announcing their presence. This was when they'd be on their way to hunt. If we had a dirty potato patch or cotton patch or something, they'd grab the hoes and hoe it out, and they'd do it good. Then my father, we had a smokehouse about twelve by fifty hanging full of cured meat, and my father would give them two or three of the shoulders, and we had lard put up in buckets. He'd give them some of that and a sack of salt, and they'd pull out. This old Indian would say, "You come." He wanted us to come to his camp, and the only way you would ever find his camp, about every fifty yards he'd hack a bush and just let it fall over, but as a general thing they went pretty straight.

And those old Indians, before they started back, they'd get that deer meat and put it on a scaffold and build a smoke under it in the sun. And the women would watch it while the men would hunt. That venison is all lean meat and it will dry as hard as a piece of wood. They'd put that in a sack and carry it back home. We fixed a lot of it that way. If you want to cook it tomorrow, you throw it in a pan of water tonight, and tomorrow it makes the best hash you ever had almost; it's mighty nice. They couldn't handle the bear meat. It wouldn't dry, too oily. They'd eat the bear at the camp and take his hide. They valued the hide very much. They'd make their beds out of those bear hides.

When they came, they'd bring little baskets of all kinds. They'd take the switch cane—it growed mighty high—and they'd peel that stuff and make their baskets. One strand would be one color and one another. They get their dye out of different things in the woods and they were mighty pretty. They just had any size you wanted from little ornament baskets on up. They had them with handles you could hang on your arm for feeding the stock or picking up the eggs. They just had a basket for everything. They were all prices and very reasonable, twenty-five cents up, to a bushel basket for a dollar. That was their money crop, and they sold to every house almost.

They also made saddle blankets out of Spanish moss. They were about three quarters of an inch thick, and when you put them on a horse's back, they were worth lots of money. It was placed between the horse's back and the saddle, and regardless of how hot it was or how hard you rode him, his back never scalded. In the Trinity bottom there would be places this moss hung so thick from the trees you'd have to part it to get through. You could just pull down any amount of good, nice moss and it was free of any sticks and trash. They'd kind o' twist it into rolls and lay them in sections. They'd hem it up, stitch it up on the edges, and it would last you a long time.

They also made hair ropes we liked. They'd save all the hair in trimming their horses' tails, long hair, and they'd twist that and make it into about a three-quarter-inch rope, and we used it for bridle reins. You'd never wear out one of those things. And they dried those deer hides and sold them, have them good and pliable. They'd make the nicest shoestrings you ever saw. And people all used black-snake whips, and they'd plait the whips out of cow hide and tail it with a piece of deer skin. Folks would look ahead to the time when the Indians would come to buy their baskets or the moss rugs or hair rope or other things. The Indians would make mattresses out of the moss, use them to sleep on. Made a very good bed, too. I've tried them. This was always done on their hunting trips. They had pack horses to take their things back—women all walked and the men would ride.

Now right where I was raised was the Indians' main hunting ground. Ten miles either way from there was where they generally struck camp. They would go to the Trinity in the fall and pick up pecans and carry them back, but there was more deer out here than there was in the bottom.

There's not too many names in the village—many of them got the same name. Now you take the name Sillistine, there was quite a lot of them, and there was quite a lot of the Bullocks, and quite a lot of the Batisse Indians, and then there was a bunch of Trentons there. And that's about all the names we knew. Fulton Batisse is the chief.

You know when this country was discovered they tried to use the Indian to do their handy work around, but they never could do it. But the nigger, he come and stayed with us, and was always abidable.

We ate lots of game, but hogs were what we used most. We called them rake-straw hogs because they'd rake up a pile of pine straw to make their bed, rake it walking backwards. There'd be a pile of hogs as big as a common house, and it was hard for a cat or wolf to get in there. The little pigs would be in the center and the old boars on the outside. The woods was absolutely full of the big black wolves, and the yellow wolves, timber wolves, almost as big as a German police dog. And in them days, when you saw one hog you saw seventy-five, for protection, you know.

The older a hog gets the meaner he gets. Sometimes they'll meet up in the woods and they'll kill one another, just the leaders. They have a sideways lick that they make the cut with, and you'd find a hog with a whole shoulder cut all to pieces.

We'd round our hogs up and mark the pigs. We had one young man in our bunch had more nerve than the rest of us. We'd pen up a bunch of them bad hogs, and the way they fight, they'll back up agin' the fence on one side of the lot, and directly one of them will just come running, one at a time, and when they run by you, that's when they cut you. But that fella would just stand there, and when they got nearly to him, he'd jump right straight up and the hog would run under him. He was running so fast, seemed like that would scare him and he'd keep going. That was Lee Mitchell. If he hit you one time, you was ruined, but Lee would jump right straight up and let them run under him, and they'd just keep going.

We'd rope the pigs, had a little quarter-inch cotton rope with a ring in one end, like you rope cattle with, and we'd just drop a little loop over the pig's head and tighten up, and swing him right up in the saddle. It'll hold him anywhere you get him if it has that ring in it. If you give it slack, you can shake it and turn him loose.

Like if you're drivin' cattle and you rope a cow's foot just to see if you can, you shake the rope and she'll step out of it, but as long as you pull it tight, you've got her.

We never went anywhere without we was riding. We always carried a gun in the saddle pocket, six-shooter mostly. When we was in the woods we generally shot those twenty-two Winchesters; have one in the scabbard, under your leg, carried that all the time. We daresn't walk anywhere in the settlement, 'cause there were panther and bear. All of them wouldn't attack a man, but some of them would, and others would scare you half to death. They'd side you on the road, the panther would. You could hear them out there in the bushes. We'd camp a lot and the first thing we'd do when we got there, we'd tote up enough wood to keep a burnin' fire all night. Those varmints, they won't come to a fire, but they'll circle that camp all night. Those old panthers will holler and meow. We'd tie our dogs or the wolves would eat them up. They'd run in packs, and they were the worst thing we had to catch the dogs.

We built a pen to trap wolves. The boys would take an ax and chop little poles, and they'd start with about a twelve-foot pole at the bottom, make the pen square, and slope the sides in toward the top, about eight feet high. They'd notch those poles so they wouldn't slip, and leave about a four-foot square hole at the top. We'd put the poles several inches apart, and a wolf could walk up the side like a ladder, but when he jumped down inside he couldn't get out, couldn't jump straight up that high. If we found a dead animal we'd use it to bait the trap.

About the time I was born there was a family we knew named Dobbs. Mrs. Dobbs had about a acre of cotton she planted down in the bottom field, good little piece from the house, to make her a bed, a mattress. The man was gone somewhere and she was down there hoeing it with a big old scovel hoe. She had on a bonnet that come out ahead of her face, and she didn't hear anything, but she turned around and there was a bear about four feet from her. She was a big, stout woman, and she turned and hit him on the head with the eye of that hoe and broke his skull. She finished him. Old pore bears will sometimes attack a person.

Annie Moye Hendrix told this story. John Risinger was her cousin and he was working one day and heard a hog a-squealin', and he told his wife he'd go down there and see what was wrong. That was between Horse Pen Creek and Hickory Creek. He got down there and it was a bear, and the bear left the hog and took after him, and he went up a little tree. He didn't have much time to select a good tree but he knew he'd gone up one too small, couldn't go too high or it would bend over with him. There was a big stump right by the side of that little tree, and the bear tryin' to get up on it where he could jump out on the man. But he kept hollerin' at him and cuttin' at him with his knife until he quit tryin'

Annie Moye Hendrix

Mrs. Hendrix's parents on both sides came from Alabama. She married Aris Anson "Bud" Hendrix, and they settled on a farm southeast of Honey Island. Bud Hendrix and his brother, Cornell, hauled pine knots and heart pine which they sold for fuel to fire the boilers on the tram engines and at the mill. Born 1891, interviewed 1975–1976.

it, but he tried to climb that little tree and he could just reach Risinger, and he cut his feet up pretty bad. Risinger cut the bear pretty bad, too, with his knife, reach over and jab him in the ear or somewhere on the head, and the bear finally left. A lot of people went down there to see that tree.

Horses were afraid of varmints. If one crossed the road ahead of you, you couldn't hardly get a horse to cross. I had a saddle horse I rode in here when I was young, and when he wanted to run, I generally turned him loose—figured he caught the scent of something we both better leave alone.

One of my aunts was a-leadin' her little brother along a small branch. She said she didn't hear anything, just happened to look around and there was a panther right behind them, sittin' there. Said she had some clothes wrapped in a big piece of paper and she just whirled and throwed them clothes all over him and screamed as loud as she could. Scared him to death; he ran.

Right over here, about two miles out there north of Bragg, there was a man, he had a funny name and I couldn't call it then, much less now, couldn't pronounce it. He was a tie maker. Well, he carried a old single-barreled shotgun out to his work and leant it up agin' a stump, and he was working on the tree, and a panther caught him. Well he didn't come in that night, and no-body knew exactly where he was workin' except another man that helped him fell the timber. They'd work that way, cut enough trees at one man's place to last three or four days, then go to the other man's place and cut, and they'd work up the ties separately. So they went and found the man and learned where the timber was cut. And the panther hadn't eat him at all, but he tore him all to pieces. Couldn't figure why the panther didn't eat him, maybe going to keep him a while. They knew it was a panther by the teeth marks on his neck. Scratches were all over him, his clothes just tore to strings.

My wife's grandmother, Elizabeth Gay, was at home one night, her and the little ones, in one of these small houses they built in them days. When the first norther blowed in they killed a hog and kept a little part for fresh eatin', and they broke some little pine tops and spread just inside of the house and salted it down on that. The menfolks were gone and she had the door barred, but the door liked two or three inches of coming to the floor. There was a big ax layin' there and she seen a big panther's foot a reachin' under that door tryin' to pull this fresh meat out. She got the ax and cut off his paw. The panther left but she had his foot.

Now there's a bear here now that's workin' the garbage cans at my old place. My nephew and my niece is keepin' my sister there, and he comes there every night. They haven't got anything but two little short-legged dogs, and they just fuss with him. There's a few in here, not too many, and there's a few panther across Menard. They never could whip them all out of there. It was a bad place in there for those panthers and bear, up and down Menard.

When we killed a beef in the woods, cattle would come from all directions. There would be two, three hundred head of cattle come from all directions, runnin', hollerin', and when they get there, they'd scrape and paw and fight, nearly kill one another. And they'd stay there for a couple of hours. I remember when I was little, there was a big stooping hickory tree and we'd swing a beef up and butcher it, and when we finished we'd back the wagon under him and let him down. Well I asked my dad if I could climb up there—about as high as the ceiling and good limbs to hold to—and watch them cows. I got scared so bad till I almost turned loose those limbs. They'd bellow and paw and fight, just a solid roar of screaming and bawling. That was a scary thing. Just as many as were in hearing, they'd come. This was a rake-straw cow, the old Texas longhorn, and I think they had it in their mind that a varmint had killed that cow. They'd smell that blood, and it seemed that if one found it and hollered, just as far as they could hear, they knew what it was. When these cows had a young calf, they'd stay right with it till they nearly starved to death, and they'd make him a pretty good bed, rake the straw up for a bed. They wouldn't leave it unguarded.

I spent most of my life in the woods, working in sawmills, around the edge of the Thicket. Most of the mills were small, but I liked to work in the bigger ones, those that ran about a hundred thousand feet per day. There were about fifty houses. The white people would be on one side of the mill and the Negro quarters on the other. They just stuck the houses here, there, and yonder, no order to it, and it didn't look very good, but we made lots of lumber. They gobbled up most all of the finest timber in our country, and the sawmills didn't make very much out of it, and we didn't do too well either.

They had just one company store that carried everything. They would have the meat market off to one side in a separate building. They never had a saloon in the community. They didn't have much place for recreation, not much time either. They'd have a school and a church house. We mostly had Methodist and Baptist, and I have seen them split the time—Baptist one Sunday and the other the next. The Negroes had just the same as we did, had their church house and school. School was about four months.

Usually they had one doctor at each mill. He would have a druggist and that man generally helped him if he had a light surgical job, but if it was a big job, they'd send him to Houston or Beaumont. Sometimes they'd have to give him first aid, and it would be next day before they'd get to Beaumont with him. Just almost anything that could happen to a man, happened to us. Big sawmills would pay their doctors so much a month and then he got all he could make on the outside, after quittin' time.

Doctor get up and make his rounds every morning, and then go back to his office. He didn't leave the sawmill till night. Accidents happenin' all the time on some part of the job, and they wanted the doctor to be there. People came to his office all day, but if he had a company patient, they'd have to wait till he got through. He took care of the whole family of the mill folks and didn't charge them anything, except each family contributed a dollar a month. They had to pay for the medicine in the office, but it was very cheap.

Generally on those jobs they had about six locomotives. They'd have a skidder to skid their logs up to the tram road and they'd have a loader to load them, separate machine. There were the timber cutters in the woods, and then they had the track men, and they just had all kinds of accidents. The loggers would fell the timber and top it, and the skidder would pull the logs up to the track. Then the loader would put the logs on the train. We generally skidded logs for nine hundred feet on each side of the track, and we'd have a pile of logs as big as a house on each side of the train. Just as far as you could see we had logs up and down the track. I always run a loader as long as I worked there. We'd load forty cars a day.

Your steel gang, track gang, had about fifteen men, and you might have twenty-five men in the skidder crew, about five loaders, and the timber cutters would have twenty or more. They used a crosscut saw. If you had a good saw boss he'd have the filer give them a good sharp saw everyday, and the cutters would fell the trees so the tops would all be in one place, and the tong setters would get the logs. There wasn't much brush on that first growth timber.

A flathead is a timber cutter, logger. There was a bug in the woods called a flathead, also called sawyer, that cut into the center of the trees. Even planks would have holes in them. They'd attack a pine after the log was down, and eat the sap under the bark, then bore into the center. The bug is 2 to 2-1/2 inches long. Good fish bait.

There used to be a lot of Irishmen here, working on tram road construction jobs. When there was so much logging being done here, there was a lot of shovel work, building up the beds for the tracks, and laying tracks, and this was about all they wanted to do. And they were the best hands you ever saw, as long as they worked, and you didn't have to watch them. The railroads would have section houses ever so often for them.

These Irishmen, they called them Paddies, would work two or three months, have forty, fifty dollars, have his bar picked out. Lots of them come to [Sam] McGovern; he was Irish, too, and they trusted him. They'd give their money to him and he'd look after them, feed them, and give them liquor. When [their] money was about gone, he'd tell [them], "You're going to have to slow

up now," and [they'd] sober up and go back to work. Some of them just keep drinking until their money was all gone, and they'd do anything for another drink.

You know we used to catch bear cubs and keep them till they were grown. They're easily trained—make the awfulest pets in the world, just into everything. Well, McGovern trained one of these bears, had a big full-grown bear, and he kept him in a cage in an enclosure he had built onto his bar. He took eight-foot-long plank and built a quarter-acre enclosure. You couldn't get in there or see in there without going through the bar. When one of these Irishmen get too drunk, he'd just put him back there to sober up. But when one just had to have another drink, he'd tell him, "You box this bear and I'll give you a pint"—and they'd do it. There'd be a fight almost every day.

McGovern had some leather gloves made for the bear so he couldn't cut them with his claws, and put a muzzle on him so he couldn't bite 'em. The bear would slap at him hard enough to kill anything, but the Irishman would hold his own. Sometimes they'd hit at him and miss and the bear would fall down on him, and they'd have to get the bear off. They'd fist him, box him. When the bear whipped the Irishman, he'd give the bear a steak and the Irishman a pint of liquor.

McGovern would always hold back enough to get them back to the job, and he'd give them a quart of liquor when they left. Charlie Mitchell, Carl Richardson, and I went to these bear fights. McGovern would let it be known, and lots of people would turn out for it. Sam died and old Bill McGovern took over. When Woodrow Wilson was elected president, he put prohibition here. Before liquor went out, Sam said to Addie Moye one day, said, "Moye, I'm gonna save me a barrel of this stuff, don't you want one?" And Addie said, "No, when it goes out I'll go out with it."

Born 1889, interviewed 1970–1976.

Introducing Leak Bevil

Leak Bevil was county judge of Hardin County for eighteen years and a practicing attorney for more than half a century. He was trying a case in district court the week before he died. He came from a well-known, southeast Texas family, and his father, John Bevil, and his grandfather settled on the Neches river after the battle of San Jacinto. Although Leak practiced law all his life, one gets the impression that he could live with the law or without it. As he said, speaking of newcomers to the Thicket seventy-five years ago, "We respected them and we **made** them respect us."

You could talk to Leak Bevil for hours but you wouldn't understand him until he talked about dogs. He understood dogs, for Leak was a fox hunter, hog hunter, cat hunter, bear hunter, and he used dogs. He knew them as individuals and talked about dogs as if they were people, and he gave them people names. Folks have said that dogs understood Leak better than people did. No matter whether he was talking about hunting bear, panther, or bobcats, he was really talking about dogs.

His favorite dog was the cur. People often have a low opinion of the "common cur," thinking of them as a mixture of anything that came through the neighborhood. Leak tells us better. Although he used all kinds of dogs for one purpose or another, the cur was closest to his heart. It's the one dog that people of the Thicket could not have done without.

No one seems to know the origin of the cur dog, but Cecil Overstreet gives a plausible explanation: "What we call a cur dog was just a general mixture of dogs. They had dogs of all kinds and descriptions, took the best ones and interbred them, developed the cur dog, and the strain breeds true, the best dog in the world. Old man Ed Collins, one of my great uncles, said, 'The American people are the cur dogs of the human race. They're just a conglomerate of all the people of the earth, and they can do anything better and faster than anybody in the world.' I think he was right."

A. L. "LEAK" BEVIL

I live within five blocks of where I was born in 1887. My father lived to be ninety-seven and he was born and raised in this section of the country—so was my mother, and so were my grandparents on both sides. My daddy was born in 1854, but his grandfather, John Bevil, came to Jasper County in 1821 and established Bevilport, and he was the only white man within seventy-five miles. Bevilport was on the Neches River, in Jasper County, and right there at what we call Dam B. He raised seven sons there.

My grandfather, William Hart, and my grandfather, Warren Bevil, established residence in Tyler County up here and ran a water mill, and they had hogs and cattle.

For more than one hundred years, the people who had hogs and cattle used cur dogs. It is a special breed of dogs—short hair, either brindle or yellow, what we call dun, and some of them are black—but they are all short-haired, broad-shouldered, square-headed, black-mouthed dogs. They're not especially large, not as large as the collie or the German shepherd, just a medium-sized dog. In the early days, they were trained for most everything. They were our protectors, and the protectors of my forefathers. In this section of the country where they built their homes, the front gate was anywhere from two hundred yards to a quarter of a mile from the house, and when you passed anybody's house, you rode by gently, and if you wanted to see anybody about anything, you stopped at the gate and called. There were two reasons for that: one was to announce yourself, and the next reason was for someone to come out there and keep the dogs from biting you. Nine homes out of ten, you go to a man's house unannounced, and that dog would catch you before you got to the steps. If you had a good cur dog, you kept him chained in the daytime to keep him from biting people that might come in, but at nighttime you turned him loose. He delegated to himself the authority to protect those premises, and he'd guard them with his life.

Folks in this country had to have dogs and had to have vicious

Leak Bevil

dogs. A good cur dog, properly trained, was worth just about whatever you had to pay for him, for you used your dog every day for everything. A man used his dog to pen his cattle; he used his dog to pen his hogs; he used his dog to protect him at night; and he used him to hunt. He was used for hogs, bear, deer, cattle, panther, everything. Then the kids would get out and run rabbits with those dogs all day, catch rabbits with them. A lot of people used them to tree squirrels. Take them out at night and they'd tree possum and coon. But when the daddy took them out, it was either hog or cattle, bear or deer, and they dare not run a rabbit, or fool with a possum or a coon.

We used to have a lot of panthers in here. There was a girl here, I forget the name, but she was going to a neighbor's house and carrying a little baby girl and had a jar of milk and had on a bonnet. They had an old cur bitch they took along with them, because you never knew what you were going to run into in the woods, and they heard a panther squall. Well, she ran just as hard as she could go, and this old cur bitch would go back, would go and fight that panther until she would get it stopped and then come on up to them, then she would go back and fight the panther again, and finally the little girl dropped her bonnet and the panther stopped and tore that bonnet into shreds, and about the only thing that saved their lives was, she finally dropped that jar of milk. Well, that panther stopped and rolled that jar of milk and rolled and rolled it, and the old bitch fought him just as long as she could and finally she came on in. When the girl finally got there and told the men what happened, they found that the old panther had cut the old dog's belly wide open, and her intestines were dragging in the sand. We had what we called spinning needles at that time. They just took the needle and thread and sewed the old mama dog up and tied her. Then they gave the alarm, and fellows came from all over this section of the country with their dogs, and put 'em on the panther's trail. They ran it for hours and, way in the middle of the night, those dogs put that panther up a tree, and the men shot it out and killed it.

Just to show the loyalty of those dogs and the nerve they have, when they killed that panther and the smoke kinda cleared away, they got to looking around, and that old bitch was there, chewed the rope in two, had broken the stitches out, and her intestines were dragging on the ground, but she was there chewing on that panther. They've got all the courage in town!

My uncle used to have a pair that I thought was the best I ever saw. He kept them chained during the day and turned them loose during the night. Most all people that lived in this country in that day and time lived in a log house, double-pen log house— two big rooms with a hall between them. Well, those dogs would watch that house all night long, one of them behind, and one of

Cur dog, owned by Mr. and Mrs. Taft Miller of Ace, Texas

them in front. If the dog in front went around behind, the dog behind came up in front, and they'd just swap back and forth all night long. There wasn't any danger of anything coming in that yard. They were guarding against people, wildcats—the big bobcat—stray dogs, panthers, maybe black bear. They were guarding your cattle, chickens, just anything you had there.

We use these dogs for working our hogs and cattle. You can take a good dog and round up a bunch of hogs, and he'll hold them right there. A wild hog is very dangerous. I've had lots of dogs killed. In fact, had one killed last winter. These dogs, my dogs especially, are lead dogs. They won't work anywhere except in the lead. They lead your cattle or your hogs. You can't hardly drive cattle with your dogs behind them or on the side of them. Any bunch of hogs or cattle that you can keep together, you can drive. It's when they scatter, your dog runs out there and catches them and brings them back. I've gone down here in the woods time and time again, and I'd tell my dogs to get ahead. Maybe they'd be gone twenty or thirty minutes, and after a while I'd hear them, or maybe I'd hear the hogs first. You could hear those hogs running for half a mile. Of course they've got to fight wolves, and they've got to fight wild dogs, any kind of dog, for survival; that's natural with cattle or hogs either. I've bunched up as many as a hundred head of hogs, and if you didn't have a good dog, they'd run him out of the woods. They'd chase him. They'll kill him. I had one killed here last year, and it was simply because he wouldn't catch from behind, and that hog caught that dog and stabbed him plumb to the hollow. He got loose from him but went right back and the hog stabbed him again, and he was dead in five minutes.

I usually train my dogs to stay behind until I get to the country where I want to hunt. I'd say, "Joe, get ahead." The next time you find him, he's barking at either a hog or a cow. Then when I found what I wanted, and wanted to drive it, I'd say, "Go around, Joe," and he'd circle and lead out. And if they didn't follow him, he'd circle and lead out again. And if they still didn't follow him, he'd come in pretty close and go to fighting them and maybe nip one on the end of the nose. He'd get that animal to fighting him and then he'd run from it; and he'd come back and get the animal to fightin' him again and keep running until he got that bunch of cattle or hogs to follow him. When you got to the pen where you wanted to pen them, he went in the gate and they just followed right on in, and he'd jump out the other side and you'd close the gate.

Any dog that is well trained will catch a hog or a cow if it leaves the group. If it leaves again he'll catch him by the nose or the ear and put him back the second time, and very few will ever try it again.

A smart dog keeps circling and circling and stays out of the

way until he gets them all in a bunch. If he's a bad hog, and he's a
smart dog, he'll go in behind him and catch him right by the arm,
foreleg, and then he'll lean right against that hog, stay right
against him, and every time that hog turns to cut him, why he'll
turn with him. A little dog can hold the biggest hog in this country
if he knows how. I've seen a little dog that didn't weigh more than
25 pounds hold a hog that weighed 250 pounds, just like he was
in a vise.

If I want to take a hog in alive, I rope him and drag him to
where I can get around a tree, if I'm by myself, and then I tie him
and get him by the hind leg and throw him down and tie his
forelegs first, and then I put them right under his chin and put the
rope around his neck and take a half-hitch in his mouth, and get
on my horse and drag him.

You can take a good dog and round up a bunch of hogs and
he'll hold them right there, and you can sit on your horse and just
pitch your line out there and rope a young one and pull him up
on the saddle and mark him, and he'll keep the bunch right
there. If they're wild, of course, he'll catch him and hold him till
you get there and mark him. He'd catch him by the ear. I'm
speaking of pigs now, pigs we've never marked, not hogs.

A cousin of mine and I went down here looking for some old
meat hogs we had, and they were just as fat as they could be,
weigh 300, 350 pounds. We heard the Old Man [a cur dog] after
a while and I said, "The Old Man's got some bad ones." He said,
"That's the bunch we're looking for." Well, we went out there and
they were lying up in the bed, hadn't even got up. And there were
two especially big ones there that we wanted to kill. Carter had an
old gun that he'd used to shoot bear with for years, an old
forty-four Winchester, and I said, "Now, Carter, that old gun plays
the bullets, now don't crease that hog. Be sure you kill him. If you
don't he's going to kill the Old Man." "Oh," he said, "I'll get him."
And by jingoes, he shot that hog and didn't hurt him very bad,
and the old dog caught him, and when he did the hog cut him
from shoulder to shoulder, clear across his chest; the skin hung
straight down. The hog left and the dog went after him. Carter
killed the other hog right there, and I got my rope on him and
dragged him on down to where the old dog had stopped the
other hog, and we finally killed him and drug them both to the
camp. Then we took our knives, didn't have any needles, took
our knives and cut a saddle string off and sewed the Old Man up.
We'd puncture his skin with the knife, and we'd run the string
through there and tie it, and cut it off. He'd just lie there, didn't
squeal or whine. A dog knows when you're trying to do something for him. We tied a piece of overalls across his chest to hold
it and took him home—took him to my daddy's and left him
there. We got our other dogs and went back to camp next morning, and by jingoes, about the time we got ready to start, here

came the Old Man, all dressed up like we had him fixed, ready to go hunting again.

My daddy came to camp that afternoon. He said, "I think I'll take Old Bob"—Bob was the Old Man, he was old—"and go up here and pen me a bunch of sows and pigs." He took the old dog and found those sows and pigs, and the Old Man led them right on down and put them in the pen for him.

The cur dog is just as smart as any dog that ever lived. You can teach him anything on earth, to do anything you want him to do. We could go out in the woods and bunch up fifty, seventy-five hogs. I'd just say "Bob," or "Smith, put 'em in the pen," and they'd take 'em through the woods a mile or more and pen 'em without losing a head. Talk to 'em just like you would somebody. They worked our cattle the same way.

I have a cur dog, female, and she's all right, works fine until a cow or hog hits her. Then she becomes angry and her eyes turn green and then she'll catch the devil himself, and if they knock her around, she'll try to eat them up. I never had but two dogs get angry. I had one dog would catch anything. He worked perfectly all the time, but if he was baying a bunch of hogs, and one of them run at him and hit him, he would catch that hog just as sure as you lived before he could get back to the bunch, and then every time he caught that hog off by himself, he'd catch him again. He learned to hate him.

I used to ride in the woods a lot, had about 650 head of cattle. I'd get down off my horse and tie my lariat around his neck, turn him loose to graze. If I was tired, I'd just throw my saddle blanket across my saddle, and lay down and go to sleep. If the horse grazed off or tried to leave, that old dog would catch him and keep him there.

The main hog here is the razorback. I don't know where he came from. We call him razorback because in the summertime when they sometimes don't have sufficient forage—no acorns and maybe the blackberry crop is bad—he's all humped up and his backbone shows from his shoulders to his hips, his old back was so sharp. We improved that hog, some people by crossing with Berkshires. The best improvement we ever made was crossing with Hampshires. He's a black hog and he can forage for himself pretty well. Of course there are no more thoroughbred razorbacks, even not so much as there are longhorn cattle. There are very few original longhorn cattle left, because they're interbred with other stuff, you know, and the hogs we have now in the Thicket have been crossbred with just everything nearly.

A hog gets wild pretty soon if you don't handle him. You always carried a wallet of corn when you were riding in the woods, and when you run into a bunch of hogs you'd throw them some corn, just to make 'em gentle more than anything else. If you shoot one of them and he can go, he'll leave there and leave fast—not like the javelina, who'll fight when he's injured. But if you catch a pig or a hog and he squeals, you better get out of the way because they'll come from every direction and eat you up. They'll literally eat you up.

These wild hogs have tushes. He has that bottom tush that comes out and curves, and he has that top tush that also comes out, and he uses that top tush to sharpen the bottom one with. You can hear him click, click, click, click. When you hear him do that you better get out of the way. Once in a while one gets real mad, and he'll back up in a clay root, or against a tree or something, and he'll go to popping those teeth, and say RrrrrrrrrrU. You better stay away from him, or kill him and kill him quick. They're dangerous, especially if they've got pigs. And some of them will never quit fighting. A friend of mine, a boy, has one in a pen now, penned when she was fairly young; took a bunch of pigs away from her and that hog never did quit fighting. You walk up there and put your foot in the crack of the pen, she'll try to bite it off—come clear from the other side of the pen and try to bite you. They're just as mean as the devil. I've had cattle the same way. I've had cattle—I just sold out last year—I couldn't go in the pen with, and if I crowded them, got on my horse and crowded them, they'd try to get up in the saddle with me. But you can take a good dog, a well-trained cur dog, and you can drive them in this house; without one, you couldn't do anything.

Cholera is the only trouble we have with hogs, only disease. Ticks and lice bother hogs, too. Uncle Tom Jordan was the first man that found out about these oil pits and sour wells over in Sour Lake and Saratoga. He found hogs that had that black oily-looking stuff on them, mud, and he followed those hogs, and they led him to these oil pits and lakes. We learned that old crude oil would kill ticks and lice on them. Nearly every creosoted pole in this country has mud on it where the hogs have rubbed against them to get that creosote oil on them to kill ticks and lice. Nature taught them. Nature is the greatest doctor and the greatest teacher.

The most popular cow in this section of the country, when we had open range, which we don't have anymore, was a cross between the longhorn and the brahma. You had a rugged animal and you had to have rugged dogs to handle them. I could take two of my dogs and go down here in the Thicket and handle a hundred head of cattle and put them in a pen, just by myself. But I could take ten men down there, without a dog, and we couldn't pen one hoof. They soon learned to stay in the herd and follow the dogs. It doesn't take 'em long.

Now I had a ring-necked dog that I could handle a hundred head of cattle with. He stayed right behind my horse, and a cow would run off, and I could run that cow for thirty minutes, and he'd never open his mouth until I told him to. But I could be riding along, and one stray off, and I'd say, "Put him back, Joe," and he'd go and get that cow and bring it back. If I wanted to stop the herd, I'd say, "Go around, Joe, hold 'em." He'd go around ahead of those cattle and hold 'em. Usually they string out so long that you want them in the back to catch up, you want to bunch them. And if I didn't holler at him or make some sign to him, he'd go out and put his feet up on a log or a stump so he could see me back there, see what was going on. When I got ready for him to come back, I'd just give him a sign and he'd come back and get around behind my horse.

The cur dog is a good deer dog. Folks would go deer hunting at night with a firepan, with a headlight. That day and time, it was a firepan. You had a regular old pan that you nailed onto a board, kind of dishpanlike thing. You nailed it onto a board or small pole, six or eight feet long, and you carried that on your shoulder. Another man went behind; he carried the gun and the pine knots for your light. When you got to the spot where you wanted to start hunting, you started the fire in the pan and the man ahead carried it. You led the dog, put a rope around his neck and led him, and he'd just walk along there, slow. When he'd hit a deer trail, you could always tell, he'd stop. He'd smell it on the bushes, and he'd walk slowly along, walk right along, slowly all the time, and when he got to where he could see the deer, why he would whine softly and notify you. If you shot the deer and just wounded him, turn him loose and he'd catch him for you. In this kind of hunting the dog never opens his mouth. That's what you call a slow-track dog, one that walks slowly and you follow along walking or horseback. There were so many rattlesnakes in this country, these fellows didn't go in the Big Thicket at night time afoot, rarely ever.

When we hunted bear, we would take all the dogs we could get, all we had trained. You take Uncle Tom Jordan and my father, and my uncle, Dennis Hart, and Ben Hooks, and old man Bud Bracken and Zack Gwynes, and those fellows, they all had cur dogs—stock dogs, yellow dogs, hog dogs. When they wanted to go bear hunting they would tie those dogs up and lead them into the woods and we'd take one special dog to strike the trail. When he'd strike the trail and get pretty hot, why we'd turn another one loose, so they wouldn't be getting after hogs, and then another one, and another one, and when they jumped the bear, why we'd turn them all loose. Well, they know how to fight that bear. Some of them would be in front fighting him, and one would catch him from behind, and when the bear would wheel to catch that dog, another one would get him. And they would just keep warting him and warting him until he would finally go up a tree, or they'd hold him there until someone could get there to shoot him. We all used cur dogs.

I had one die last summer, Old Smith. He was past eleven years old. The last year that I used him, I'd just take him out,

and he'd find the cattle for me, and I'd let him work with the
youngsters, the young dogs, until they got the cattle started. It
would hurt his feelings all right, but I'd make him come back and
get behind. I'd rather hurt his feelings than have him die on me. If
something started to go wrong, I'd send him up there to
straighten it out, then make him come back. The old dog
teaches the young ones, just like the old man teaches the boy.

If your neighbor blew three long blasts on his horn—we use
cow horns—that was a signal: "There's something wrong; I want
you to help me." You answered him with one long blow, and you
then went to him as quick as you could. And when you were
hunting, why, you signal each other with your horns. If I wanted to
know where you were, I'd blow two long blows, and you answered me with one. If I killed a deer, or if I was in trouble, or if I
wanted to go to camp, or if I wanted you to come to me, I'd blow
three long blows, and you better keep your signals straight. Now,
if you were calling your dog, you simply tooted your horn, toot,
toot, toot, toot, one right after the other. You didn't blow long
calling blows.

In the good old days—and the good old days are right on up
till now—people helped each other and they got along pretty
well. When a man's house burned down, the neighbors helped
him with his work.

In the wintertime when those hogs got fat, we'd castrate the
boars, and when they got big enough and fat enough, we'd
round 'em up, mark the pigs and turn the sows and pigs out and
keep the meat hogs there, and we butchered them. And we had
our own bacon, our own lard and our own hams, made our
sausage, smoked it, have some pan sausage. Lot of us had
bacon and lard the year around. Had to do that back in the early
days. You went hungry if you didn't have plenty of bacon and
plenty of lard. Then for fresh eating you had all the deer and all
the bear that you wanted, and turkeys.

If you were getting along pretty well, you'd have cornbread all
the week and biscuits on Sunday, except when the preacher
came, and then we'd have biscuits every morning for breakfast.
We had our sweet potatoes. We had the pumpkin yam that day
and time, very productive, make four to five hundred bushels to
the acre. We put them in a bank of pine needles, and we had
sweet potatoes the year 'round. We grew our own sugar cane
and made our own syrup, and that ribbon cane syrup was the
best in the world. You take pork ribs or sausage and syrup, and I
could eat eight or ten biscuits for breakfast.

I've been practicing law for fifty-five years. They hung nine
men here before we had our first court; that's for horse stealing
and for murder and attempt to murder. We went by our own rules
and you better live by them, and your word better be just as good
as your bond. After we had our courts organized and you
brought a man into court, he went in with fear and trembling for

fear that he might miscolor the truth. They told the truth regardless of who it hurt or who it affected. This day and time they don't mind going into court and swearing to lies, anything to prevent justice. From the time we came here, we've worked hard to build respectability. We respected everybody else, and we **made** everybody respect us.

They had a riot out here and killed a nigger who raped and murdered a girl. I got a lot of friends among the niggers and I had, I guess, forty or fifty niggers hide at my house, in my garage, upstairs over my garage, and my yard full of niggers, and they organized a bunch of fellas that were going to come down there and get those niggers. There were two hundred men up there the other end of town. I just went up there and told them, "Now that's my home down there. Those niggers haven't bothered anybody; they haven't done anything to anybody. They're my friends and I'm their friend. For tonight they're my niggers, and you're not going to invade my premises and touch a one of them without trouble." I said, "Now you boys can come and get them. I know that, but I'll tell you now, you'll get them over my dead body, and I'll kill any one of you if you ever cross that property line of mine and into my yard. I'll kill many a one of you before you get me. You're not going to touch a nigger in my yard." And I just pointed them out one after the other and called their names. I said, "Where you ought to be is home with your wife and children. Now you have no business out here." I went back home and the crowd finally dispersed. That was about ten or twelve years ago, about 1960.

I've always liked to be in the woods. I would sit here in the office day in and day out and wear myself completely out. I wouldn't feel like it but I would just force myself, and I'd saddle my horse and take my dog and ride in the woods among my cattle. This Big Thicket is the greatest area, as great as there is on the face of the earth! The leaves have fallen on these hammocks for thousands and thousands of years, and that ground is a natural loam that will grow anything on earth, I guess. It's a botanical paradise. We have every kind of flower growing in Hardin county that you've got anywhere in the world, I reckon. We just have everything. I especially like the wild honeysuckle. It's just as pretty as anything you can find in anybody's yard, and when they first bloom every year, I bring my wife a bouquet when I'm riding in the woods. What I started out to tell you, I can ride thirty or forty minutes and directly I catch myself whistling and singing to myself. I may ride two or three hours and come back home and never feel more rested or relaxed in my life, just wonderful. It's association with nature. The paintings of the greatest artists will never compare with the product of our Supreme Artist, who made things naturally for us.

1887–1972, interviewed 1969–1971.

Introducing Brunce Jordan

Brunce was a logger who always used mules or oxen. "They can do better in mud and water," he said, "and a ox is better than a mule. They don't bog down so bad." This was important to Brunce who, for years, logged in the rain-soaked country of Hardin County. "When I think of this country as it was from here over at Batson and around, I think of mud," he said.

When one thinks of a logger he is not apt to visualize a wiry little man of 115 pounds, but Brunce Jordan never weighed much more. As a result of a logging contest he won years ago, Brunce was affectionately called "King of the Loggers." He knows the job and goes about it deliberately, without wasting effort. I spent a day in the woods with Brunce and Speedy McGee, his helper for twenty-five years or more, and they could work together effectively for hours at a time without saying a word. Even his mules had a working understanding of the job that reduced communication to a minimum.

Brunce still used his original wagon. "In a way it's the same old wagon but there ain't nothin' about it that was there when I bought it. Every part has been replaced, some of it lots of times. And me, I've slowed down these last few years, but I aim to keep on goin' till I'm a hundred, I hope."

Logging was Brunce's vocation, but just being in the woods provided much of his recreation. He was careful to preserve the odd, the unusual, or the beautiful things he encountered, like the largest peach tree he ever saw, or the flowering shrubs, or the tree that grew in the shape of a turnbuckle. He enjoyed showing these things to people who shared his interests.

He and his wife are gracious folk who welcomed us to their table laden with homegrown food; and on a pop call at midmorning, one must at least have coffee.

BRUNCE JORDAN

I was born August 17, 1891, at Honey Island. My mother's people originated from Georgia away back yonder, and the best I remember, my daddy, Dan Rayford Jordan, told me his people was from Alabama. My granddaddy come to this country before the Confederate War, I guess because he would o' had to go to the army. He lived out here right on the edge of this Big Thicket. His name was Sherrod Sutton, on my mother's side.

I commenced drivin' a ox team with my daddy when I was fifteen years old, and I've been at it ever since. Most of my work has been right here in the Big Thicket, loggin' for myself, under contract. Worked for Lance Rosier twelve years, maybe longer, and twenty-four years for the Sun Oil Company. They sell the timber, then I get it out.

I guess it's just what you're raised up in, but I like to be in the woods, done a little bit of everything in the woods. I just like it. I quit loggin' once, sold my mules and wagon, and I never was as miserable in my life. Finally I just got sick, after six or eight months, just got to where I couldn't hardly get out of the house, so I bought my team back, and my wagon, and went back to loggin', and I've felt good ever since, and ain't sick at all. I tell you, I don't believe I'd live a year if I just quit.

I like to be in the woods whether I'm workin' or not; you find lots of interesting things. Now that tree I was tellin' you about, that's kinda interestin' to me because I never seen nothin' like that, just growed in the shape of a turnbuckle. When I see somethin' interesting or unusual in the woods I let it stay. There's a wild peach tree up there, must be sixteen inches through, but I just wouldn't cut it out. It's the biggest peach tree I ever seen.

This country can get wet—used to be much worse than it is now. I got a job workin' for a fella here in the oil field, must o' been about 1919, because the war had ended, and I got a job drivin' a team for him. He took a job over yonder at Batson, movin' a drillin' rig. He had some good mules, too, and by Gad you can believe it or not, but right down where that graded road

Brunce Jordan

is now, the water would run away over the axle of those old-timey wagons, mud and water be three feet deep, and lots of places deeper than that, and we just couldn't get that rig out of there. Couldn't pull that load with all the mules you'd hitch to it.

Well, old man Buchanan said, "Why don't you get my mud boats and go down there?" He had two of 'em. Well, we tuk them things and drug 'em off down there, and that's the way we moved that drillin' rig out of there; put that machinery on them mud boats and drug 'em out to the end of the road and then loaded 'em on a wagon. A mud boat is flat, with both ends turned up, like a slide, about six feet wide and maybe twenty feet long. The runner was a ten-by-ten sill and curved at both ends and floored lengthwise on the top and on the bottom. You'd put your stuff on top and it'd skid over the mud without boggin' down.

Well, we just went on and worked in the mud and water like a mule or ox, and you couldn't put your finger on any of us where there wasn't mud. We'd have to change clothes before we'd go to the boardin' house, just waller in that mud like a bunch of hogs. And that water would stay there, no way for it to get away from there, only that Little Pine Island Bayou over there, but it was nine miles wide nearly all the time. There wouldn't be a spot of dry ground nowhere.

During the boom days at Hull, it took eight mules to pull a wagon with eight joints of pipe on it. I've left here with a little old boiler on my wagon and take me three days to go that five miles to Batson.

Ox wouldn't bog up in the mud as bad as a mule. You can take three or four yoke of ox and you can just go where you can't hardly walk, yourself, and they'll bog up, but they'll just keep a-pullin', gruntin', and groanin', and they'll go on. They don't never get down. But you couldn't lead a mule through it. I drove a ox team over here just across that creek; me an' ole Rodney Salters took two five-yoke teams right over there across that creek when you couldn't get a mule out of the lot. The oxen'd be bogged down so deep their bellies would be touchin' the ground but they just keep goin'. When they are pullin' in the mud like that they bend their front legs straight back from the knee, so they're almost flat on the ground. And then, they've got them cloven hoofs that spread in the mud and keep 'em from boggin' like a mule. Ox not built like a mule. Ox pushes and a mule pulls. Knot on the back of his neck pushes on the yoke. The yoke is strong but light, made out of white bay—grows in the baygalls or magnolia hammocks.

When I first started I used three or four yoke of oxen and a eight-wheeled wagon—four wheels on each side, one right behind the other—skid the logs through the mud to the wagon. Had a pair of tongs we could hook around the end of a log and pull 'em out. You go out and hook on to one of them logs with a five-yoke ox team, take off through them woods and it'd dig out a trench as it went. Then you'd go right back to the same place and get you another 'n and that trench be full of water by then, and the log would float. You can work mules in pretty boggy ground, but mules will lay down when they go to boggin'; they go to layin' down, but a ox ain't gonna lay down.

I worked on a loggin' tram at Oakhurst one time and sometimes the whole track would bog down with ya. We've come out of that old Nelson Creek bottom with fifty or sixty carloads of logs when the track would be plumb out of sight in the mud. There was so much weight the rails couldn't separate.

About twenty years ago I had pneumonia, and people come up there in front of my house and have to be pulled away. And the doctor would come up this little old graded road and wade that mud to the house. In the early days a doctor would ride a horse or drive a buggy, and in later years he got a car, but he kept his buggy, and when it got wet he'd use it, because this country used to just stand in water. In the summertime it'd get dry, but up to thirty, thirty-five years ago, this place would just be standin' in water in the spring.

Lance Rosier is the one who got me started loggin', that is, for myself, not for somebody else. There was a man up here that had a pair of mules and he wanted to sell 'em for two hundred dollars and I didn't have the money. So Lance come up here and said, "I bought the timber and I'll get the money for the mules; if you'll buy the mules, we'll go to loggin'," and that's the way I bought them. He signed my note and I give the man two hundred dollars for 'em, and went to loggin' for myself.

That old wagon there ain't got a thing on it that it had when I first bought it. Everything about it has been replaced—some of it several times—but I never bought but one wagon. They got better equipment in the woods now, but I always have more work than I can do. You've got to give them mules some credit, too. They cost less to run than a tractor and they put out just as many logs. With mules you can get into wet ground, and when you have to cross a creek you don't need a strong bridge like you would for a tractor—just throw some poles across the creek and go on. Besides, some companies, like Sun Oil, won't let tractors on the timber land.

My lead mules are regular-sized animals, named George and Shorty. They also pull the logs up the skid poles onto the wagon with a loadin' chain. My work mules are Tom and Toby. They are all black, but Toby is also black of heart. Toby is the meanest, onriest, laziest, contrariest hybrid that God ever let the devil manufacture at the mule mill in hell. The only way I can half make him mind is to ride 'im.

When I was workin' for Grayburg we had to be on the job at seven o'clock. We worked 'till six—ten hours. Now I go to work

when I get ready, and when I get tired, I come home. When I
worked for Grayburg we used rehaul skidders. Used to be all we
had. You'd take a cable back five or six hundred feet out in the
woods and tie it high up in a tree, with a drum to pull the logs in
and a drum to pull the tongs back out there; they'd just go back
out through the air; and they tore up everything where they went,
and they was outlawed. Then they got to using a horse, and a
boy would ride 'im, always a boy. That boy run the horse back
out there in the woods, carryin' them tongs, and a hooker would
hook 'em on the logs, and then the drum puller would pull 'em
in. That's what I was doin', pullin' drum.

Mud boats was the best rig for gettin' logs out of the mud. It
would keep the log from diggin' in the mud. Then the next thing
that come along was the slip-tongue cart. It's just two wheels,
fourteen foot high, put on a axle, and the tongue is twenty-eight
feet long, and this axle is rigged up so the tongue can slide, and
you can get the log up high enough to get over a stump.

In 1925 I was workin' for Grayburg Lumber Company on a
skidder. One night both skidders burned up and Grayburg
bought twelve head of mules from Kansas and three Martin
carts, slip-tongue carts, from Lufkin and quit the skidder business.

*Brunce Jordan
logging*

Old Shany Richardson wanted me to drive one of them carts
and offered to give me a dollar a day more than I was gettin', so I
did. There was a one-legged fella—had a wooden leg—come in
there named Smut Conners, and they hired him. The work
superintendent said, "I'm gonna' give the best Stetson hat in this
store to the one who can haul the most timber in a day." They
had a big store there at Harmester, on the San Jacinto River,
where the camp was. It was a ten-hour day. We took the logs
about 300 feet, just had to get to the tracks. So me and that old
one-legged man went at it, drivin' them carts with them old wild
mules, him on one side of the tracks and me on the other. We
was gettin' big logs, 24 to 48 feet long, and one was all you could
carry. We fought it all day long, and he was a good cart man, too,
hard to beat. But he had to stop to grease his cart and I got the
jump on him. I hauled 47,800 feet, and old Smut got 46,000
feet—right at me.

Me and another fella was loggin' northeast of here one time
and there was a fox got to eatin' our lunches. He got to where he
come right up close to us. So one day I took a steel trap up there,
and set it, and hung my lunch up over it. I walked off about two
hundred feet out there and sat down, thought I'd watch 'im. He
was down on the other side in a open place, watchin' me fix the
trap. Just as soon as I set down there, he come flippin' along and
got in that trap, and when I went up there he was jumpin' and
raisin' sand. But when I got up close, why, he just sneaked down
like a possum. I stood there with him until the old man come with
the wagon, and I said, "Reckon we could put that thing in a
sack?" He said, "Looks to me like you could put him anywhere
now." So I just got a sack off the wagon—had a sack to ride
on—and we went there and picked the thing up by the tail and
put 'im in the sack and let 'im out of the trap. He didn't move. I
tied the sack up and laid 'im down there, and as long as you was
rattlin' around there, he wouldn't move, no sir, narry a bit in the
world; but if you go off and get quiet then he'd go to jumpin',
tryin' to leave there.

Lance had bought a fine collar for his dog and he let me have
it to put on that fox, and when I put it on 'im he was layin' down
there, sneaked down, just like he was dead. I put a chain on 'im
and tied 'im to a tree, and every kid in the whole country come to
look at 'im. Well, that durned fox broke the swivel on the chain at
the end of the collar and got loose with the collar on 'im. It was
three miles or better to where we caught that fox. In about ten
days I was down there and that fox come runnin' down the road,
still had that collar on. And he's over there now, I reckon, with
that collar on, and that was two years ago. And he'd come back
down there and eat our lunch again. Off and on he ate our lunch
for two months or more. We'd put it in different places. We'd be
workin' here today and over there tomorrow; we'd put it here one

time, there the next, but he'd follow you. He'd see us comin' out there and he'd come up there and trot around outside the camp just like a dog. A fox will eat anything but a apple or a tomater, and I'll tell you what that durned fox done: I bought this favorite chewing tobacco, and J. L., my son-in-law, did, too, and one day he carried his lunch out there and had a full cut of that tobacco. He put it in his lunch sack and hung it up in a bush. When we went to eat dinner, his lunch was gone and his chewin' tobacco too. I guess he just had lunch and then took a chew of tobacco and maybe stored it away for hard times. We never found the sack, tobacco, or nothin'.

Buddy Stevens come in there workin', him and a nigger, on another piece of land joinin' us, and he said, "There's a durned fox over yonder where we're at, eats our lunch every day, got a collar on 'im, pretty little bright, shiny collar on 'im." "Yes," I said, "and if I could get hold of that feller agin', I'd put a bell on him next time." That thing got to where it was plumb gentle, come right up close to ya. He'd hear them wagons comin' through there and pretty soon after we stopped, you look out there, and directly you'd see him trottin' 'round. I guess that fox is still up there now, with that collar on, still eatin' anybody's lunch that comes through the woods.

Born 1891, interviewed 1969–1976.

Introducing Sam Houston Cain

From the time he was sixteen years old, Sam Houston Cain has been a preacher or a judge—sometimes both—and if he did not convert the sinners at church, he often met them later at the courthouse. He handled both jobs with confidence and self-assurance. He is a positive person and even now—at ninety-five—speaks with conviction and enthusiasm of his days, past and present, in a firm, resonant voice.

"Preacher Cain" is a little man, but he does not know it. One feels, and he knows, that he is able to meet most any situation that comes along. Still, he is a modest, humble, God-fearing, Baptist preacher. On April 21, 1974, he was made pastor emeritus by the Trinity River Baptist Association, "In grateful recognition of his long and faithful service in this association." His long and faithful service extends over three quarters of a century. Though he is not a regular pastor, he still "fills in" fairly often.

"Preacher Cain" hunts squirrels with a twenty-two pistol and keeps snakes and armadillos thinned out around his house. He is an expert marksman, a skill he learned from his mother. He rides his horse to round up his small herd of cattle and otherwise handles the chores on the farm where his wife was born, and where they now live.

SAM HOUSTON CAIN

My father was a cavalryman in the war between the states. I was six years old when he died. Where we lived was called the Grand Cane community. The community then was bounded by the Trinity River on the west and Hardin County line on the east, Menard Creek on the north and Liberty Prairie on the south. The Grand Cane Post Office was organized May 22, 1845, discontinued October 25, 1869, and changed to Ironwood, March 22, 1900. Shortly after the turn of the century it was discontinued and the post office at Clark was organized. General Sam Houston built a log house there and lived in it from 1843 to 1845 when he moved to Huntsville, Texas, where he lived till he died, and where he is buried.

Mail was brought by river steamboat, called the Betty Powell, owned by Captain Thomas Peacock, leaving Galveston three times a week, making connection at Liberty with Sawyer's line four-horse coaches, through Crockett by Grand Cane, Smithfield, Livingston, Moscow, Sumpter, Calita, Piney Point, and Shady Grove. There was several boat landings also on the river, especially at every plantation. Vernon Lee, brother-in-law of Sam Houston, was the first postmaster, about five miles north of Moss Hill, next to Bledsoe Branch.

Grand Cane was named because of the cane that grew up fifteen feet high, and higher. That cane, called switch cane, it grew all in the woods, but close to the river, that's where it grew so tall. In the spring and fall overflows, people had to go in there and drive their cattle out onto high lands. The cane was so thick you couldn't get through it unless you followed trails made through it by the cattle. It was thick and grew up tall on those sand dunes along the river. People can't realize how it was at one time. Fire finally got into it, just went like an army. When the heat gets into it, it just pops like a gun and bursts open—just makes a roar when the fire gets into the smaller cane. The fire, that's what finally went with it, but it's coming back.

I began living with my grandmother when I was eight, ten years

Sam Houston Cain

old. She died when I was about fourteen. My mother was a widow and she owned fifty acres of land. We had a big log house and a dirt chimney. I'd read a chapter or two in the Bible every night by the chimney before I'd go to bed. I loved the Bible.

Bears were bad to eat pigs. My grandmother would go into the woods, and she was familiar with all those things, and she would show me where the bears would be, and they'd get under a tree and rake up all the acorns on the ground, and you'd just find piles of acorn hulls, and if they'd find a grapevine with grapes, they'd pull the vine down, and sit down on their hunkers right there, and eat them. They'd catch a fat hog, and eat its neck the first thing, bite him at the back of the neck, and his head would drop down and they'd just eat him alive. Bears go into the cornfield, get them an armful of roastin' ears, maybe take it over the fence, sit down and eat it. They could eat half a bushel of corn.

My grandmother killed a bear just above the house there one night. Her second husband, he come in there, I think, from Georgia, and he hadn't been used to bears and things like that. One night they was sitting by the fire and she said she heard a hog squealing about a hundred yards in front of the house. My grandmother's given name was Sereney, and he said, "My goodness, Sereney, what is that?" She said, "It's a bear, caught a hog; we'll have to go kill it." He said, "No, no, let's close the doors." She killed the bear. They had what they called a slide, horse hitched to it, took the bear to the house. I think it weighed four hundred pounds.

My ancestors had their own fields. My mother's own grand-father, he owned slaves and he had a mill. The slaves lived in a one-room cabin down below the house, made of split logs. They didn't leave when they was freed. I guess he treated them nice.

My mother used to have a muzzle loader Colt, just like they had in the army, leather holster, used buckshot. When she would go off somewhere my brother and me would sneak the pistol out and hunt with it, shoot squirrels, bobcats, birds and things. I had a pistol nearly all my life. That's the only sport I ever had, mostly in the woods, hunting turkeys, things like that. When mother shot a pistol she would come down to the target, but I'd raise the pistol up, just raise it right up to the target and shoot, seemed to come natural. One of my favorite sports when I was a young fella was to hunt wild turkey and deer.

We raised some cotton, corn, sugar cane, and sweet potatoes. We made syrup every year. We had hogs, and we had milk and butter, used to live good. We never had much money, and we had to go to Livingston or Liberty to buy anything, and it would take about two days to go there and back. When we picked the cotton, we'd put a couple of bales in the wagon, and we'd start out, camp somewhere on the road all night. One time my brother said, "You put a fire under the coffee and I'll feed the horses." He set the grub box on the ground. I looked around and he was calling "sooooooeeeee," and there were hogs all around there; they'd got used to people camping there. They got into our grub box and ate up nearly everything we had. I remember my brother set there that night with his ax in his hand and tried to throw it into them hogs. They'd stand around and watch us, but he never did hit one.

There used to be another place where we camped. There was a church house up there called Providence; it was a favorite place. You go down under a hill, and a wonderful spring gushed out under there. We always heard there was a ghost there that would come in the church at a certain time. So my father and some others went in there and hid behind the pulpit, had a wide sort of a shelf there. But anyway that was primeval wilderness in those days. Well, there was a woman who had lost her mind or something, and she had a habit of going to that church, praying in the night, kneeling down. She lived alone. My father and these men watched and some of them got ahold of her and she was asleep. They had quite a time with her. Liked to have scared her to death.

We used to shoot buffalo fish. We had a muzzle-loading gun and we'd put the powder in there and drop the arrow in the gun, tie a fishing line on one end of the arrow, and we'd shoot the buffalo with it. They just come up pawing the water. Sometimes we'd shoot them with a bolt in there. We'd put about a thimbleful of powder in there and pack it, what you call a wad on it, had ramrods. The arrow was about two feet long. We just cut out switch cane and sharpen a nail, put the fish line to it and have twenty feet of line. Sometimes shoot one, maybe weigh four or five pounds.

I was thirty years old when I was ordained, June 6, 1911, and I was baptized in Little Cypress Creek—some call it Cherry Creek—near Concord. I baptized M. P. Daniel, Price and Bill Daniels' father, during the time I was at Liberty and Hardin, 1916, 1917. Old Concord church was where I was ordained. That's where Sam Houston was a charter member. The original church was made of split logs and had a dirt floor. Had split log pews with pegs on one end, with the other end braced by sticking it through the crack in the wall of the house. Sometimes at night they would use a firepan, some rich pine in a firepan for a light; sometimes used candles. Next they built a box house and had a pole to hold up the center, being so wide, being a box house, see, had a post in the center.

I've organized five churches throughout this district, more than any preacher. I organized the church in Romayor around 1912, pastor there, and I reorganized Concord; then I organized a church at Grayburg, held a revival there; I organized Mt. Calvary here, and a church called Long Island, but it finally died.

In 1912 I was elected justice of the peace, and was justice for four years in precinct two in Liberty County. When I was justice of the peace that didn't interfere with my pastoring. I was called to the first church at Liberty. From 1912 to 1916 I was justice of the peace, and I was appointed road overseer. I was the last road overseer. I helped put over a two-million-dollar bond issue and started the first road building in this country, and my name was on all the bonds. Up till then there was dirt roads everywhere. Everybody over twenty-one had to give five days a year on the road work. I'd watch them, of course, and if they was busy in their crops, I wouldn't call them out. I'd give a fella a chance to go when he didn't have nothin' else to do. They would fix mud holes, things like that.

I wasn't making much money, times pretty tight then, so I took a correspondence course in law. So I was elected county judge and served twenty-five months.

One time I was going to Cleveland to supply for Brother Ellis, Baptist church over there. The doctor up there called me and said, "Would you mind going in the saloon there, fellow by the name of Jarvit, and tell him to send me a quart of whiskey? I have a man that's had his fingers cut off and I want a quart of whiskey to give him. You go in there and tell him Dr. Mathis wants it." I said, "Yes, I'll get it." I carried my pistol nearly all the time, used to be some pretty rough gangs up there. So I went to Cleveland, and in the meantime there was a man come in up there to get married. He had never seen me, and he was asking this man Reeves, deputy sheriff, a good friend of mine, how he would know me. He said, "Well, he'll be a nervous little man; he'll be the first one off the train; he'll have his grip in his hand, and in his grip he'll have a six-shooter, and a quart of whiskey, and his Bible." He said, "Not the man I'm looking for; I'm looking for a preacher." Reeves said, "He's a preacher and a durned good one, too." When I got there, Reeves walked up to the door and said, "Here, Judge, let me have your satchel." I didn't know anything about all this. We went over to a little office there, rolltop desk, rolled it back, Reeves set my bag down; he took my Bible and laid it down, and took my pistol out and laid it down, and then took the quart of whiskey and set it down. Then he says, "Pay me off, pay me off." Reeves had heard the doctor tell me to bring the whiskey, and he had made a bet with this fellow.

The last revival I held, one evening a little Nazarene preacher, his name was Kidd, his hair was kind of gray, but he was young and just full of life, and I called on him to pray, and he went to prayin' and he jumped down on his knees, on his all fours, and he just went at it like a lawn mower. He prayed, looked to me like, five minutes. I loved the little feller. A chiropractor and I was stayin' in the same home, serious kinda fella. I said, "Brother

Nichols, have you got a homemade sock?" He said, "No, I haven't but if it is a fair question, Reverend, what do you want with it?" He was a Methodist and they love to call the preacher Reverend. Well, I said, "I'm going to get a doorknob or a piece of brick and put it in it, and if that little Nazarene preacher is there tonight, I'm goin' to time him—when he goes over five minutes, you tap him. You'll know where to do it, being a chiropractor; you knock him out."

We have seventy-five acres of land and rent about three hundred more. I ride daily, take care of my cattle, take my twenty-two pistol along and maybe get a squirrel. Sheriff gave me a police whistle that I call my cows with.

One of the things I guess helps me along, I don't worry about anything. My mission in life is to try to help others. The reason I don't look my age, I guess, is I don't have any bad habits, and I've got just one boss, God, and I don't worry and I don't look back.

1881–1976, interviewed 1964–1974.

Lance Rosier

Introducing Lance Rosier

Lance Rosier was a hunter who never killed anything. He hunted plants—orchids, ferns, mushrooms, mosses, and hundreds of others. His interest in plants began as a boy, first with flowers, and gradually expanded until he knew the flora of the Thicket as no other person. This self-educated naturalist could tell you the Latin names or common names with equal familiarity, but, more important, he knew the relationship of plants to soil types, to each other, and to their whole environment.

Lance reduced living to its simplest terms. He was not rich in worldly goods, but he never wanted more than he had. He never married and for many years lived with his Aunt Mat and her husband in Saratoga, a few miles from where he was born. During the years we knew him he lived alone in his house near the post office, where this unpretentious little man received mail from all over the nation concerning plants of the Thicket.

Writing was laborious for Lance, and the Garden Clubs of America installed an expensive recorder in the living room of his house for recording his botanical observations. I doubt if it helped much because, when I once asked about it, he said, "My heavens, I can't sit by myself and talk to that thing." It is too bad he could not.

Lance Rosier was unexcelled as a guide for he knew the land, the plants, and the animals. His memory was infallible, his patience was endless, and he was unstinting with his time. Lynn and I were photographing the wildflowers of the Thicket, and he knew precisely where they could be found and when they would be blooming. This was indeed a help for, as Lance once remarked, "Plants don't run, but they sure can hide." Once on an overcast day we walked two miles straight through the woods with Lance to photograph a small orchid he said would be blooming. We didn't waste ten steps. He stopped at a point that had no distinguishing feature, no landmark, and when we did not find it readily I was a little discouraged but not surprised. "It should be here,"

Lance said, "I saw it two years ago. Oh, here it is!"

For days on end he took us to rookeries, ponds, lakes, bogs, hammocks, swamps— places we never would have known without him. On one occasion we came late in the afternoon to a swamp southwest of Saratoga and stayed until dark. There was an air of unreality about it. Shafts of sunlight filtered through here and there, highlighting the dark water that stood a foot deep over several acres. Vines forty feet high hung from the trees, and Spanish moss draped the limbs to the tree tops in places. A cypress log, weathered by a hundred years, lay half-exposed in the water, and patches of floating duck moss gave the illusion of islands and odd-shaped peninsulas. The sharp reflections in the water added to the fairyland appearance that surrounded us—mysterious, shadowy, like a dimly lighted hall of mirrors.

The sounds of the swamp came in waves, deathly still or wildly boisterous. We marveled that every frog in the swamp can be sounding off at the same time and the whole chorus stop as suddenly as one can turn off a light switch. When they resume, it isn't so instantaneous but is still in the nature of a concert.

Once he took us to a rookery. "Put on clothes you can throw away," he said. It was one of the few times a recorder would have been better than the camera, for I have never been in a place where the sounds were stranger or more impressive.

We left the car at the end of a dirt road and walked slowly through deep woods that sloped toward a large, shallow lake, almost covered with button willows. As we quietly inched our way almost to the edge of the water, we just stopped and listened for a long time. Every bush was covered with nesting birds, and the tall trees surrounding the water were laden with herons, egrets, and others. It gave the general appearance of an enormous white bowl dropped from the sky into a green forest.

Some bird sounded the alarm, and suddenly the sky was filled with a medley of raucous sounds and flapping wings, leaving only a few fledglings that couldn't fly.

As we waded out, waist deep, to photograph some nests, Lance said, "Watch out for alligator holes." I thought he was kidding, but on our way out Lance himself fell in one. He splashed around getting out but slipped back in again before regaining his footing. "Did it scare you?" I asked. "No," he said, "but I didn't know how long he would be willing for me to play around in his front room." He told us that the alligators get some of the young birds, and the eggs, too, by hitting the buttonbushes with their tails and knocking them into the water.

We can't adequately express our appreciation of Lance because his place was our second home during the ten years that we spent so much time in the Thicket. We anchored our trailer there in his yard, which was the hub of our exploration by day and our conversation by night. We met dozens of other Big Thicket people through Lance because he had so many friends, and he was always certain in his own mind that all his friends would like each other. He was usually right.

LANCE ROSIER

I was born in a house down here south of town, and have lived all my life right here in Saratoga. My grand-father, Tom Jordan, settled here during the Civil War.

There was all kinds of food in the Thicket, all kinds of animals and fish for meat: worlds of wild hogs, wild cattle, deer, bear, squirrel, turkeys; and there was all kinds of berries: blackberries, dewberries, wild straw-berries; and there was mayhaws and wild plums. They'd raise sugar cane for syrup and make sugar from it, too. The land was new and rich and they could grow anything. The dandelion starts coming up around Christmas, and it's very good; eat the leaves just like spinach and cook it the same way. They ate poke salad, peppergrass, and sourdock for greens. There was lots of mush-rooms, but people didn't know how to use them. There was hickory nuts, walnuts, pecans, beechnuts, wild grapes, five or six kinds of grapes for jelly, and they made wine out of grapes, some did.

Many different species of flowers bloom in the Thicket. Some of the most unusual, I guess, are the orchids, more than twenty different kinds. Four of the five insect-eating plants grow here. We have the white and pink Indian pipe, and they aren't sup-posed to be in Texas. I suppose they are the rarest. Then we have a little plant that gets up about twelve or fifteen inches high, with pink blossoms on top and a bunch of white blossoms under the ground, on the roots of it, and they develop just as if they were on top. The flowers on the top of the ground are either all male or all female, and they are always pink. Flowers underground are both female and male. It's called "Polygala polygama."

A lot of this country was so thick that the Indians couldn't get through it, and Sam Houston's army had to go around it. Down here where the old oil field was, it was nothing but a big old marsh with a thick growth of giant palmetto and pine trees. The palmetto was so high you could hide a horse and rider in it. Then there was open country where the virgin pine stood and shaded out all the undergrowth. A lot of the country is about as it was, but where the pine have been cut off it has grown up in thicket. The

Swamp

densest part of the Thicket used to be along the sloughs and
baygalls. A baygall is a wet, muddy place that's real thick with growth. It's usually a deep swamp where there is a lot of mud and water all the time. It is called baygall because the bay tree and the gallberry bushes grow thick there. The gallberry is one of the haws and grows up about ten feet high and then bends over and you just have to hack your way through with a machete, or get down and crawl under them, because they just link together. Sometimes they'll cover four or five miles. You take Panther Den, between here and Kaiser Burnout—it's about five miles long and a mile wide—it's called Panther Den because it was always so thick that nobody could get in there, and the panthers stayed there. A lot of flowers grow around the baygalls; one of our prettiest orchids grows there.

As far back as 1927 individuals and groups have been trying to get a large block of the Thicket set aside and preserved in its natural state. Because of this and the Parks and Corey Biological Survey, people, especially in Texas, have wanted to see what's in the Big Thicket. Hundreds of scientists have come to study the plants and animals, and university professors have brought their classes.

I have always been interested in nature of every kind, and by tramping through the Thicket since I was a boy, I learned to know many of the plants and animals; but not until 1936, when Parks and Corey made the biological survey of the Thicket, and I served as a guide for them, did I become interested in learning the Latin names for the plant life. You have to work year in and year out to learn on your own. I don't know what a lot of the Latin words mean, but most of them I do. The way I learned, I'd just wait until I'd get to talk to somebody who knew, and ask, and I'd always remember. I kept notes, and when I couldn't identify something, I'd send it to one of the professors who had been here from some university, and they'd tell me. This way you don't forget.

Since I guided Parks and Corey, I've guided hundreds of people through the Thicket. The last time I kept track of the people I had showed was in 1957, and there was 568 in one season— that's spring and summer.

In 1940 the State Academy of Science had a meeting here in Saratoga, came on Friday and went back Sunday evening. I was asked to go with Dr. S. R. Warner and the botany group, to guide them. By this time I had learned a good deal about the plant life and was able to help them identify many of the plants. After they left, Dr. Beard wrote me a letter of appreciation and asked me to join the State Academy of Science. Well, at first I couldn't believe he meant it, as only two hundred people belonged to it at that time, and I was more than surprised that I was invited to become a member.

Pitcher plant

Dr. Francis Scofield, head of a paint and lacquer company in Washington, was interested in seeing if perilla, or chi, could be produced economically in the Thicket. It is a source of oil for paint and varnish. The director of the Chamber of Commerce of Beaumont put him in contact with me, and I planted and harvested some seeds he sent me. We found that it grew and produced much more than it did in Manchuria or Mexico, but the labor for harvesting it made it impossible for us to compete with these countries. The paint-and-varnish people import more than three million dollars worth of these seed a year.

During the World War I did a lot of work with Dr. W. M. Potts, head of the science department at A&M College, on the tallow tree. The oil out of these seed is 70 percent protein. That's just as much as a peanut. You can't tell the difference in the oil from it and the soybean. But this didn't prove profitable. The Thicket grows almost anything better than any place else, but labor and marketing often make it unprofitable.

Aunt Dose, second daughter of D. F. Jordan, my grandfather's brother, used to live right up here, and she told me this story: Her father was wounded in the army, during the Civil War, and came home. When he got home he couldn't find any of their hogs. He saddled up and told his wife he was going to find his hogs and to look for him when she saw him. So he put some food in his saddlebags and some corn in a tow sack, and tied the corn behind his saddle and rode off. He was gone three or four days and when he came back he said, "We're going to move; I've found a place that is a regular heaven." He had found his hogs and they were fat, and they all had tar on their sides. He hunted until he found the black mud where they had wallowed, and he went to the court house at Old Hardin and claimed that land. He thought it might be valuable. Even in pre–Civil War days the settlers used the water from mineral springs for their health and used the tar, as they called it, to grease their wagon wheels.

They were living at Dallardville, close to Indian Village. They came down the Liberty road, and then chopped out a road most of the way to Saratoga. When they got to Big Sandy they took everything they could across on a raft and tied logs to the wagon, and the horses swam across.

In order to hold his claim, at first he built a small, one-room log cabin on a hammock just a little east of here. Well, there wasn't room for all of them to sleep inside, and their mother put some quilts out in back of the house, and Aunt Dose and her sister had to sleep there. They had killed some hogs that first day and threw the trash and bones out close. Way in the night Aunt Dose said something woke them up chewing on the bones and cracking them and fighting and quarreling with each other. She raised up and looked and there was three panthers right there. They got scared and ran in the house and their mother said, "Well, Josie, you girls might as well go right on back out there, because you've got to get used to it." She said, "We went back, but we didn't sleep anymore that night."

In 1865 a man by the name of Watts, from New York, heard about the tar in the Thicket and arranged with Fletcher Cotton to put down a well, but it was driven, not bored. They built a derrick of pine poles way up high with a pulley in the top and then a rope fixed with a heavy weight. The rope went through the pulley and was fixed on to a singletree behind a mule. The mule pulled the weight to the top where an automatic trip released it, and the weight hit the pipe with a thud. Each piece of pipe was ten feet long and was literally driven in the ground one hundred feet deep. Aunt Dose said that when they got down about fifty feet, they struck gas, and when the iron came down and hit the casing, it caused a spark and set the well on fire. Her daddy came to the house to get a quilt and he wet it and put it over the well to put out the fire and it burned the quilt up. A few days later the same thing happened, and their mama refused to let them have another quilt. They got down around ninety feet and struck oil. It didn't ever amount to very much, because they didn't know what to do with it. Mr. Watts went to New York and brought back a whole lot of bottles and they bottled it, and he sold it as healing tar. The old pipe they drove in the ground is still there.

Aunt Dose said when she was a girl they had two Negro slaves, and they would farm, make a crop, then when they'd get the crops laid by, her dad would take the Negroes and team and go to Dallas to buy food and supplies for the next year. They would get back about the middle of October, in time to gather the crop before winter. They would buy flour by the barrel, had to buy enough to last them a year. If they ran out of salt, four or five families would get together, make a couple of weeks of it, and go over here close to Batson at the old Fish Lake. There was a salt lick there. The animals all know where the salt licks are. The ground is perfectly white. They'd carry their niggers along with them and a wash pot or two. They'd dig this salt up out of the ground and cook it up in the wash pots.

There was all kinds of game besides what we ate. There was bobcats, panthers, wolves, fox, coons, possums, lots of things. Most of these animals are still in the Thicket. Two weeks ago when the forestry man was in here to measure that cypress tree, two bears ran across the road right the other side of Votaw, right in front of him. We often hear panther and occasionally see one.

Sour Lake has sour water. There used to be an old nigger there they called Dr. Mud and he would doctor with this mud. People would get down and wallow in it. Women would make a mud pack and put it on their faces at night, tie a rag around it and sleep with it on there.

For a while there was a health resort here at Saratoga. We have five or six different kinds of water springing out of the earth. People would come here for treatment of rheumatism or arthritis. It was all rheumatism then. There was bathrooms all around the old lake.

Before the oil boom in 1903 just about a dozen people lived in Saratoga. This part of town, where the post office is now, wasn't here then. I've always lived with my Aunt Mat, Mrs. Evans, my mother's sister. Where the old oil field was, she rented a five-room house, took out all the partitions except her room, and turned it into a kitchen and dining room. She got a lot of tents and cots and put them up in the front for people to sleep. People managed every way, especially during the early days of the boom. She ran this place until she was able to save two thousand dollars. Then she built a hotel where my house is now, just behind the post office. They was going to put a train into Saratoga, but they got it about a mile away and stopped, so she ran hacks and buggies to meet the train and bring passengers on up here to the hotel. It became known as the Vines Hotel because it was covered with English ivy.

The lumber for the hotel had to be hauled on wagons from four miles on the other side of Kountze. It was built out of longleaf, heart pine. The outside wall was made out of planks that extended the full distance from the ground to the roof and it was 2-1/2 stories high. That's the kind of timber that was here in those days. It cost a thousand dollars to build it and a thousand dollars to furnish it. She had fourteen rooms and could seat thirty in the dining room. She served family style and it was two bits a meal. Room and board was three dollars a week. The train came in at eleven o'clock and left at two. When the salesmen came in on the train—they called them drummers—they had such a short time to see anybody, she let them eat first so they could catch the train at two. Then the roughnecks and everybody else would eat. She had to clean the rooms up two times a day, once for the ones that slept in the daytime, and then for the ones who slept at night.

People managed just any way they could. Some of the houses was built out of pasteboard boxes, and those who couldn't buy tents even camped out under the pine trees. They weren't here to stay, just to make money, come for just a while and then leave.

About every other building was a saloon, and somebody got killed nearly every day. I heard my aunt say a lot of times, "Well, if somebody is going to get killed, I wish I could see it." She was going to buy some groceries for dinner one day and she passed in front of the saloon. As she did, a man ran out right in front of her and somebody in the saloon shot him—and he fell right in front of her! She just stepped over him and went on. She said she didn't **ever** want to see anybody else killed. They didn't have much law. The people here, when someone did wrong like that, they more or less took it in their own hands to do what was right.

Batson was tougher than Saratoga. They had six rangers over there. They didn't have a jail to hold people, and whenever anybody did something that was real bad, they'd chain him to a tree out in the street and leave him there until they got a chance to send him over to the jail in Kountze. They'd stay there several days sometimes, right out in the middle of the street, traffic passing by them.

They had to carry the oil away from here in wagons with tanks on them and haul it to Beaumont till the Santa Fe built a railroad here. Took a week to haul a boiler five miles from here to Batson, five miles of mud. The oil boom didn't last long. There is one well down there that was drilled in 1908 that's still pumping fifteen barrels a day; been in operation continuously since then. Later on they took the railroad up, took the tracks.

My uncle, Buddy Cotton, was the first postmaster, and there was just about half a dozen people lived here. The mail came three days a week, and they brought it on horseback, Monday, Wednesday, and Friday. When the oil boom came they had to go get the mail every day in a wagon or surrey, and there was ten thousand people got their mail here in Saratoga. He said lots of times when the mail would come in, people would be lined up in three rows as far as from here to the oil field waiting to get their mail.

Uncle Buddy Cotton had a little farm where this part of town is now. Most of these older houses was built from 1904 to 1909, in what used to be Uncle Buddy's field. The champion tallow tree was planted in 1909 just down the street here. Mr. Charles G. Hooks from Houston planted it when he built his house there.

[The following story by Lance shows that his interest was not confined to plants.]

Little Richard

Little Richard was a crow who thought he was a dog. About eight years ago Harold Nicholas found a crow's nest in the top of a pine sapling and it had two baby crows in it. He and Joe Martin, who was with the Texas Forest Service, brought me one of them. It was the first of April and the little fellow didn't have any clothes on, and he would get real cold at night. I would bring him out in the yard in the daytime and put him in the chicken coop, but at night I'd keep him in my room in a box of old rags. I always read late at night and I'd put a cloth over the box he slept in where he wouldn't be bothered with the light; otherwise, he'd talk all night. Every morning if he wanted to come downstairs when I did he would pull the cover off the box and come on with me. If he didn't, why he'd just sleep on and I'd go back and get him later.

You had to force-feed him. I'd catch crawfish and minnows and things and I'd have to put them down his throat and mash them on in with my finger. When he got bigger, I couldn't give him enough to eat. When he learned to eat by himself, he would eat all day long. He was always flying around the neighborhood mooching something to eat. When he got some feathers on him, he was just as black as anything you ever saw and Joe Martin called him Little Richard, and that was what he was known as all his life.

I didn't have any dogs but all the neighbors did and that's all he was used to, a bunch of dogs all around him. So he'd go over and stay with these dogs across the street at Mr. Crouch's house. He barked just like a dog, and he stayed with them. Mr. Roscoe Crouch had a grocery store and every evening he would bring home a sack of scrap meat for his dogs. Well, Little Richard would go over and sit on the gate, about the time he thought Mr. Crouch would be coming home, and he would holler, "Hey, hey, hey." If Mr. Crouch was late coming, Little Richard would fly down and sit on the porch in front of the store and holler, "Hey." When Mr. Crouch would start home, Little Richard would ride home on his head, then jump off and sit on the gate. As soon as Mr. Crouch would get in the yard, he'd give Little Richard a piece of meat, but he wouldn't eat it then. He'd bring it home and stick it under a plank; that was his deposit box. Then he would go back and beg for another piece, then come back and eat. If it was more than he wanted, he would pick up the piece of meat and carry it back over there and give it to the dogs. He'd lay it down in front of them and say, "Here, here." He'd keep on until the dogs would pick it up and eat it. He stayed with the dogs all around here, and if a strange dog came around the house, he would fight him and run him off.

Little Richard would sit on the arm of your chair and talk to you for a long time, and whenever you were talking to him, he would listen to what you'd say, and he learned to say a lot of words. And if someone came in that he didn't know, why he'd always come down and see all about him. Mr. Sig Bird came here one time and when he came in, Little Richard flopped down and got on his shoulder, and said, "Hello, there." Well, Mr. Bird looked around and couldn't see anything but the crow and finally he decided that the crow was talking to him.

He got to following me to the woods. Everywhere I went, he'd go part of the way on my shoulder, and then after a while, he'd fly way ahead and sit in a tree and wait until I'd come up to where he was, and then he'd go on a little farther ahead. Then finally he got to where he'd leave home in the morning, and I'd never know where he was. Joe Martin went out to Ebbie Cotton's one day, about two miles from here, and he come back and said that Little Richard stayed out there all day long with his dogs, and he went hog hunting with Mr. Cotton. Every morning when they'd start out, why Little Richard would go out with them. And when the dogs would get to where there was a bunch of hogs, why Little Richard would get down on the ground and bark just like a dog. If a hog started after one of the dogs, why he'd get on his back and pull a mouthful of hairs out. And he'd just run the old hog crazy, because he couldn't do nothing about it. For about six or eight months he stayed with those dogs every day.

You couldn't keep him from stealing. He would just steal anything bright that you had—spoons or knives or forks or jewelry, anything he could get away with. You dare not leave a spoon or knife or fork outside the screen door or he'd get it and carry it off. He always had a certain spot where he hid everything he got.

A crow wanted to live with him and he wouldn't have nothing to do with it, because Little Richard thought he was a dog. He didn't know he was a crow. He ate with the dogs and stayed with the dogs all day long and barked like a dog, and hunted with the dogs. He **was** a dog, that's all there was to it.

I didn't split his tongue, but he could talk, and he would just listen to you as patient as could be. He'd sit there and talk crow talk to you just as long as you would sit there. He never did crow like a crow—just barked like a dog. You couldn't tell him from one of these hound dogs around here to save your life.

Whenever he'd come home in the evening, if I was anywhere around, why he'd come and sit down with me and talk a while. He roosted in a mimosa tree just off the porch, and every morning, just as it was getting daylight, why he'd fly off and go back to Mr. Cotton's and stay with the dogs all day. Every night he'd come back and get between two limbs on this mimosa tree, and as long as I was out on the porch, he'd sit there—after he'd go to roost—sit there and talk to me. It was just about as high as the eaves of the house.

He was always outside, because my aunt wouldn't let him come inside—he would steal everything in the house. He was coming home from Mr. Cotton's one day and he lit in Mr. Payne's yard to play with his dogs. His little girl got scared of him and he shot him.

1886–1970, interviewed 1960–1970.

THE JAYHAWKERS

The Big thicket was a good place to hide, and Sam Houston had planned to hide his army there had he lost the battle of San Jacinto. Much later, people who didn't want to fight in the Civil War hid there and became known as the jayhawkers. Bud Overstreet, ninety-five years old and alert as a deer, commented as follows:

"My daddy was Dan Overstreet and my mother was Sarah Collins. Grandpa Warren Collins was one of those who wouldn't fight during the Civil War, was at the Kaiser Burnout. There was lots of them that lay out. Old man Stace Collins, and Newt Collins, they was brothers; and Lige Cain and old man Jim Williford. They was part of the jayhawkers. I know old man Cain and Jim Williford, and I've seen Stace and Newt Collins.

"I've heard grandpa say it was a rich man's war and a poor man's fight. That's the reason they wouldn't fight; they didn't own nothin'. In my opinion it was the best thing in the world they freed the niggers. If they hadn't, all these sawmills where we made a livin' at, we'd been workin' as slaves for them, because the poor white people was just like slaves, too, no better off than the colored man."

A similar point of view was expressed by Randolph Fillingim. "A jayhawker was a follower of Sam Houston who objected to fightin' the Civil War. They were just sensible people. They knew what would happen if the slaves were not freed. It wouldn't be long till the men who had money to start a business of any kind would buy slaves for his labor and poor whites would be left out. These men right up here in the Kaiser Burnout, they were just takin' Sam Houston's word for it, followin' him, and tried to stick by President Lincoln and the Union when the South pulled out. Did you know Sam Houston was a jayhawker? Old man Jim Taylor saw him, an old Confederate veteran who stayed at our house quite a bit down in the Thicket, and he said he saw Houston when he toured the state talkin' to people with tears in his eyes asking them not to withdraw from the Union."

A fuller account was given by Lance Rosier, who lived within miles of their hideout. His story follows.

"The people here was very poor and some of them didn't want to fight for the Negroes. You see the wealthy people here was the only ones who had Negro slaves. So when the war started they said, 'Well, I'll just go out here in the woods and stay.' There's a big, dense area about five miles north of Bragg, so they went out there and started camping.

"These people was called jayhawkers. They had everything to eat without worrying about anything—plenty of game and fish. Their people would have corn ground and carry it out to a big forked oak tree right on the edge of a pond and put it in the fork of that tree. To keep it from getting wet, they had a doeskin they put over it. The pond to this day is known as Doeskin Pond on the map. It's right this side of Kasier Burnout. They didn't have any tobacco or any coffee, but they had everything else. They had even dug them a couple of wells out there. There would be a dozen or two trees right around in sight that were full of bees. They'd cut down a tree and rob it, get all kinds of honey. Where Honey Island is now there was two big pear trees and they taken some plank and built a table between those two trees. They'd put all the honey and deer and stuff that they wanted carried off on this table. Their people would come and get this produce, carry it to Beaumont and sell it, and buy their tobacco or whatever they had to have. They'd take it out to Doeskin Pond and put it up in the tree, or leave it on the table at Honey Island. There was so much honey carried out of there that it became known as Honey Island.

"The government would send soldiers in here and try to get them out, but they never could get them because they kept guards stationed around and when they'd see them coming, they'd leave their hideout. They would have someone assigned each day to go hunting and bring meat and stuff back into the camp, and there was guards assigned each day to watch. The soldiers would search everywhere for them and never could find them. They never would go in or out the same way. They didn't have a trail. They never would break a limb off. They wouldn't leave any sign where they went into their hideout. Their camp was in the middle of this dense area and they never could find them.

"There are several different tales about it. One is that the government gave Captain Kaiser a big sum of money to come down here and get the jayhawkers out; another story goes, he got the money and went out there and set fire to the woods and burned everybody up; another one goes that he gave them the money to get out and leave. I rather think he might have warned them, but I don't think he gave them any money, and they didn't get burned because a lot of people here in Saratoga had kinfolks

James Hamilton "Bud" Overstreet

Bud Overstreet, born February 2, 1879, worked in the woods from the time he was ten years old, doing just about everything that a man was called on to do. He was a friend and contemporary of Sam Houston Cain and Addie Moye. Brown Wiggins said, "When Bud was a young man you could put a 1 x 2 on the shoulders of two tall men, and he could jump it. He was very athletic and strong." The Overstreets came to the Big Thicket from Alabama before the Civil War. Jim Overstreet, the first to come, was a commissioner, and the Overstreets continue to be leaders in Hardin County. Born 1879, interviewed 1975.

who was jayhawkers. You take all the Collinses—this whole place is full of them—well, their ancestors was jayhawkers. If any of them had got burned in the fire someone would have known about it. Some think that Captain Kaiser came from Galveston to Anahuac and up the Trinity River to Drew's Landing, up close to Livingston. Some think he came up the Neches River, and marched across from there. I think he came to Drew's Landing because it is only ten miles from there to Kaiser Burnout. Anyway, Captain Kaiser came down there and all the men was gone and he did set fire and burned the thicket, and that area is still known as Kaiser Burnout. You could do that in the summertime when it was dry. You could just drag a burning pineknot along and set fire everywhere you went, when it's dry.

"They caught a few jayhawkers at one time and carried them to Woodville and put them in jail on the courthouse square, and put guards all around there to guard them. Somebody, in order to free the jayhawkers, brought a lot of whiskey down there and the guards all got drunk. Then someone got a fiddle and started playing, and Mr. Warren Collins, he began a jig and was entertaining everybody, and all the time he was dancing, everyone was leaving, one at a time. So when the party was over there was no jayhawkers left and the guards was too drunk to find them."

Warren Collins was Cecil Overstreet's great grandfather, and Cecil adds this personal touch: "Grandpa was in the jail, which was made out of one-by-twelve planks—board and batten construction—and he took his pocketknife and cut one of the twelve-inch planks at the floor. When the guards got to carousing around there, grandpa started jigging, like all those Irishmen could, and he put on a show till the prisoners all escaped. In the commotion that followed, Grandpa Collins crawled out too, and crawled under the house; and after everything settled down he just crawled out and walked back to the Thicket.

"Grandpa had a little personal difference with Captain Bullock, so after the war he went up to Woodville where the captain was living and they settled it with their fists. He'd fight anybody with his fists and seemed to enjoy it. He didn't believe in war but he had more fistfights than any professional prizefighter to my knowledge. He didn't believe in slavery but he didn't think the North ought to force the South to abandon it."

Introducing Fount Simmons

Fount Simmons was a legend during his own lifetime. His name was mentioned casually and incidentally by different persons until it was familiar to us, but until we had the following interviews with Brown Wiggins and Mrs. McKim we knew very little about him. At twelve years of age he was paralyzed in his legs, which were useless below the knees. Somehow, though, he never used crutches, but crawled. He lived in the heart of the Thicket, and it is interesting that, in an environment that made heavy demands physically, he met every situation without recognizing any limitations on his ability. Except for polio, Fount enjoyed good health until a few days before his death in 1949. He was eighty-six years old.

There was no question of proving himself, for Fount accepted himself as one without limitations, and therefore others did, too. Twice he was elected tax assessor of Hardin County, serving four years in that capacity. As he grew older he always found ways to make a living that were compatible with his age.

Although he hunted alone most of the time, as he did it for a livelihood, he was equally at home with a group on an organized hunt. His granddaddy's saddle, over a hundred years old, and the only one Fount ever used, is now in the possession of his eighty-six–year–old niece, Mrs. Mamie Vickers McKim, of Kountze. With minor repairs it could be used today.

FOUNT SIMMONS

As Told by Brown Wiggins

In his early days he was paralyzed. He had what we call infantile paralysis, I'm sure, but I don't think they knew what it was then. His father was dead and his mother and two or three of the boys, all nearly grown, was on a farm over in Polk County. They had big pin oaks in there with those water oaks, growing in those shallow ponds, and that's where the squirrels stayed. Fount got him a big goat and trained him good, and got a good-sized wagon, and that goat would pull him all over that open pond and he'd kill a mess of squirrels.

When he got grown he went to huntin' in the Thicket on his horse. I don't know how he trained them to do what they did, but I saw how they acted. He had a high porch on the back of the house and that's where he had his saddle layin'. He'd crawl out there—he wore knee pads, like a cotton picker—and call that horse and he'd sidle right up to that porch. He'd put the saddle on 'im, ride to the gate, the horse turn around sideways, and he'd reach down and get the latch, go out, then turn around and latch it back. He rode everywhere, up town and in the woods. If that horse had ever fell we never would of found him, 'cause it was wilderness.

They made those big, long, yellow riding slickers, and he'd carry that with him in the woods, and I've camped with him. One night it rained all night long and he crawled and got up on a little knoll, lay down on a old blanket he had, put that big slicker over 'im, and slept all night, just like a nigger, it a-rainin'.

When he killed a deer, he'd put a rope on him, throw the rope over a limb and ride out and fasten it around another tree so he'd have the deer about a foot off the ground. Then he'd get down and skin it and cut it up, put him in a big piece of duckin', put it over his saddle and go into the nearest town and sell it. When the Santa Fe Railroad was being built from Beaumont to Summerfield they had a big work camp at Votaw, and Fount contracted to supply them with deer meat, and he always had it there. He was a good shot and had lots of patience. He'd dress the hides and sell them for a dollar a pound. Those men that had teams on those loggin' fronts, they'd buy it for whip poppers. Nearly all of 'em tailed their whips with deer hide.

He had a medium-sized horse and when he'd come to your house, or anywhere else—he never got off till he had to—he'd set on his horse and talk to ya two hours. If he ever got off, his horse would stay right where he got off of him till he called him. He was awful stout in his arms 'cause he handled hisself with his arms altogether. He'd catch the horn of that saddle and catch the horse's mane, and pull hisself up there till he got his knee over that saddle. He could stand on his knees and reach the horn of the saddle. He would o' been a tall man. I've seen him get on that horse time and again, and he'd get up there right quick. When he'd get off, he'd just hang to the horn of that saddle, throw his leg over, and he'd be right up agin' that horse's legs, and he wouldn't move; but he was a good hand to train one.

He went to school some, but he studied quite a lot at home. He could write as pretty a hand as I ever saw. He'd order those little blank cards; he'd write you a hundred cards, your name and address on it, and he had one of those old Spencerian pens that you could shade it with, and he'd just make a pretty job. He'd charge for it.

I was runnin' a steam loader there at old Milvid for West Lumber Company and Fount carried water for the men. He had those kegs tied together and his horse covered with them. They'd hold about three gallons of water, and I saw him riding by fifteen times a day. Sometimes he'd be close to a farmer's house, sometimes he'd have to ride a pretty good distance, but he kept the men in water, so he kept that job three or four years. Later, he moved back down to Votaw and lived there till he died.

As Told by Mrs. McKim

Fount Simmons was my mother's brother. He never married. He was crippled from the time he was twelve years old.

Fount come in one day, said he felt awful bad and he lay down on the porch. He had a high fever and it lasted three days, and they just bathed him with cool spring water and put Madeira vine poultices on his head and chest. You don't ever hear about that now. Madeira is like an ivy vine, thick leaves and green, and you beat them up and put them in a cloth and they're just like ice; and my grandma always used them for fever, and my mother used it on us. The third day he couldn't move his feet and Uncle Fount never did walk from that time on. He got to where he could crawl, and the children would pull him in a little wagon they made with wooden wheels. They carried him to school in it. He had a good education, but he got it himself mostly, by reading.

He was interested in everything and was a very likable person. I don't think I ever saw him angered at anyone.

My grandmother made leggings out of brown ducking so his trousers wouldn't get soiled crawling. He wore shoes that just had two laces and the toes were pointed and made out of copper. His feet were short because they didn't grow, and his legs were dwindled away, but he crawled everywhere and never did use crutches. He wore gloves most of the time he was crawlin'. He was a large man and well-developed except for his legs.

Uncle Fount rode a horse since he was fourteen years old, and I've got his old saddle upstairs now, the only one he ever used. My grandfather bought that saddle when he was a young man. He told Uncle Fount to get a gentle horse, and use this saddle. Uncle Fount had his horse so well trained that he never had to tie it. That horse would stay where he left it till he came back. When one horse would get old, he'd get another one and train it.

In those days the deer in the Big Thicket were plentiful, and all the deer he ever killed, he killed from the horse. He was a good shot, and it was estimated he had killed over three thousand. During the time they were so plentiful, you could sell the meat, and he would dress the deer and squirrels in the woods, and go to the different stores and sell that meat; it sold cheap, just like sellin' beef.

Uncle Fount said that when he was dressing those deer in the woods, he would tie them up just as fast as he could 'cause he knew a panther would be coming. The woods was full of panthers then, and he lived right in the heart of the Big Thicket. The panther would smell that blood and follow him almost to his field fence.

When the older children all left home he and grandmother lived together. He served two terms here as tax assessor.

Uncle Fount could do almost anything. He started half-soling shoes, just on his own, and he had a good business. Then people got to bringing their deer hides to him to cure. He soaked them in lime water overnight to loosen that hair, and he had a long board with slots in it and he would pull the hide back and forth until the hair would come off. Then he would beat up eggs and soak it in a egg solution—eggs about ten cents a dozen then. People would buy those hides, and they were dressed the prettiest you ever saw. The little fawn hides, lot of them was so white you'd think it was white suede, it looked so pretty.

Then Uncle Fount started making baskets. He would go into the woods and cut small hickory trees, as many as he could drag, and tie them to his saddle, get up on his horse and drag them in home. Sometimes he hired someone to bring him white oak logs. Then he would fasten them someway and pull the bark off and cut them into thin pieces that he could weave into baskets. He made all kinds of baskets. He made little ones with handles, and picnic baskets, and great big ones. We had horses and cows then, and he made one to measure corn in. He made those baskets for years and sold every one he could make.

Our fence needed painting, and he painted it. He could pull himself on his knees and kind of brace himself and stand up on his knees to reach. He could do nearly anything.

Introducing A. Randolph Fillingim

Few people know the Big Thicket as well as Randolph ("Dolph") Fillingim. He knows its geography and its creatures from his own experiences as a boy who hunted, fished, and trapped from the Brown settlement on Black Creek for miles in all directions. As a boy he and his brother trapped fur-bearing animals and sold the hides to help make a living. He killed hundreds of squirrels, which he skinned and then walked fifteen miles to sell for ten cents apiece in Sour Lake. Times were hard and money was scarce.

We spent a rewarding day with Dolph visiting his daddy's old homestead, and we saw the giant poplars that grew from small plants his brother brought from Mississippi in a suitcase. He took us to the places where he ran his traps, and he showed us where his tent was pitched the night a panther nuzzled the canvas as he held his gun in readiness and the creek that flooded and kept him from getting home for an extra day or two. What a boyhood he must have had, living in the depths of the Big Thicket in what was regarded as the best bear country to be found!

Dolph Fillingim has an inquiring mind that probes beyond the obvious. He is a close observer with a good memory, and he is a student at heart. He has a persistent curiosity. He is careful not to exaggerate and to separate fact and opinion when he relates his experiences, even on points of minor importance. He speaks deliberately in a soft but firm voice.

A few years ago he drew a map, freehand, that is widely regarded as an accurate delineation of the historical Big Thicket and its waterways.

Two of his brothers were Pentecostal preachers, and one of them, J. W., is now pastor at Moss Hill. The other, Robert, began preaching at eighteen, but, Dolph says, he preached so hard his throat went bad on him after fifteen years, and he had to quit. Randolph himself is a quiet man of deep religious faith. He doesn't talk about it but one senses it in conversations, even when he's telling of bobcats, wolves, or rattlesnakes. Habitually, he sees the best in people and is charitable in his assessment of people or events.

A. RANDOLPH FILLINGIM

My daddy was William Archer Fillingim and he came to the Thicket in 1903. We were natives of Mississippi, but daddy moved to Alabama in about 1901.

Uncle Warren Brown, who married my father's sister, he came to Texas in 1885 and settled about five miles southeast of Kountze, in the piney woods, about one mile north of the Big Thicket, on the old Samuel Andrews homestead. Uncle Warren, in 1903, went to Alabama and helped my father and mother and seven children come to Texas. After working for Uncle Warren for a year or more, daddy moved into the Big Thicket, the real Hardin County Big Thicket.

South of Kountze seven miles, we chiseled out—I say chiseled out, because it was a pain to put that land in cultivation—a little field, with virgin timber on it and no market; we had to cut and burn it. The Big Thicket wasn't touched except for a few acres each family whittled out for growing corn for the horses and hogs. It was so thick and so much big timber on it, it was just impossible to have a big farm. Now we had about eight acres and there was four of us boys to do that, clear it and put it in cultivation.

Alvin Jones was our closest neighbor. When we first knew Jones he was about seventy. He lived in a house built by his father, Joseph Jones, in the fifties. It was about three miles south of Hardin, and was occupied by four generations of Joneses, lasting for about a hundred years before being torn down. The framework of their house, and the pillars that supported the front of the building, was built of yellow pine heart, hewn with an ax. Lumber was from pine logs that were cut on the Jones' homestead and hauled by wagon to the sawmill, over on Village Creek, called Old Plank. It was on the front porch of the old Jones' house that I learned about what happened in or near the Big Thicket before my time by listening to Mr. Jones and my father talking.

When the slavery question began to get hot in Georgia,

*A. Randolph
Fillingim*

Joseph Jones sold his plantation but kept his slaves and moved to Texas. After he got settled down he took his slaves into the Big Thicket to a hammock that was dry enough to cultivate and cleared about fifty acres. It was about two miles from the field to the house. He planned to hide his slaves at the field if the war did come. The old field is now in the Hardin County Game Preserve and is still known as the Jones Thicket Field.

During the Civil War, during the blockade, there were lots of things they couldn't get, and the Jones family ran out of salt. They took big kettles, syrup-making kettles they brought from Georgia, to the salt springs at Sour Lake. They boiled and evaporated the salt water until they had enough salt for curing the meat and for cooking. The Joneses were a hard-working people who made their own way. One of their many virtues was honesty.

There were also sour springs and sulphur water there and somebody got the idea that the sour water and sulphur water were good to bring back your health, and they built a health resort at Sour Lake before the Civil War. Sam Houston came to this hotel to regain his health and stayed for quite a while.

Alvin Jones was a cripple. His ankles and knees could not bend. He moved about on crutches and when he sat he had to sit on a high stool made for him. Alvin Jones never married. He was taken care of by a widowed sister and hired help. This sister was Mrs. Sarah McMillan, who married Dr. McMillan soon after the Civil War. He died a short time later.

It was Alvin Jones who told us about the Pigeon Roost Prairie which was near the Jones homestead. He said so many pigeons stopped to roost in the pines in this area that they broke the limbs off the trees and the trees died, so there was prairie there. There wasn't a living tree for 150 acres, and it was called Pigeon Roost Prairie. That was virgin pine timber they killed. The pigeons were almost as big as a chicken, not the homing pigeon; they were two or three times larger, about the size of a pheasant. Not thousands of pigeons but millions of pigeons! I tried to learn all I could about this pigeon migration. I was interested in it. It was something to think about. There would be so many they would darken the sun for three days, all going north.

There was another pioneer family named Bly that settled on the south edge of the Thicket, seven miles from the Jones' place. He had three thousand acres, must have been a soldier in the Texas Revolution. It was only about seven miles from one homestead to the other, but Mr. Jones said, telling my daddy, "I don't know what happened to the Blys. They left and went somewhere. I heard they killed enough bear meat to last them two or three months, and cured it, before they left the homestead." So a few years ago, in Sour Lake, I met the husband of Nellie Bly, granddaughter of the original pioneer. He told me that his wife's grandfather sold that three thousand acres of land for twenty-five dollars and a new wagon. They had heard of the rich cotton country in the west and they wanted to go out there.

The Flowers and the Collins lived up on the north edge of the Thicket. The old Collins place is still called the Old Poplar Place—probably brought some poplar trees in from the east and planted them. We did that on Black Creek. My brother went back to Mississippi on a visit after we'd been in the Thicket about five years. When he came back he brought ten poplar trees in a suitcase and planted them on our old home place down on Black Creek. They're still there.

My brother and I trapped a lot for small game, and sold the hides. We had traps set for five miles and run 'em every day. When we trapped for raccoons we trapped in the water, but if we were trapping for bobcats, we'd set the traps on a log where he would walk to keep out of the water, to keep his feet dry. Bobcats are like all cats, they don't like to get their feet wet. A bobcat wouldn't pay any attention to the water if a dog was after him, and he'll go to the thickest places in the baygalls, where rattan vines, possum haws, and Indian arrowwoods grow. If they can get in a place like that they can stalk around and throw a dog off his scent and stay in a small area, say three or four hundred yards, for a good while. A cat will run in small circles, and dodge, go a little way and turn again. The whole Big Thicket is good cat country, a hammock and a baygall, hammock and baygall, all the way through.

My first trap line, when I was fourteen years old, was down on a hammock near Black Creek. I set a few traps, and, boylike, I killed a robin and baited one of the traps with it. Another trap I baited with a chicken hawk, hung it up over the trap. Next morning I had two bobcats. We never had cat dogs, and never hunted cats. Their hides weren't worth much then. Fred Willard was a good trapper and made more money than any man on Black Creek. He had a string of traps for miles.

We never hunted for bear but we'd kill one if we had a chance. My dad killed his first bear on the north fork of Black Creek. Gene, my brother, had gone squirrel hunting and found one of our hogs dead. A bear had killed it and eaten part of it. A bear isn't like a panther; he never covers up what he kills, just eats what he wants and leaves the rest till he gets hungry again, and comes back. Gene hurried home and told father about finding the hog dead and dad went back with him and found it.

They went home and ate dinner, and when they went back dad carried an old gun that was made not long after the Civil War. It was a single-barrel, twelve-gauge gun with about a twenty-four-inch barrel. My father called it Old Zulu. My brother Gene molded a big lead ball that just fit the barrel. My dad looked around and found where the bear had been crossing the creek on a log. The creek had about four or five feet of water in it. At evening, about sundown, they set two shot guns at the hog and dad took Old Zulu to where the bear had been crossing the creek and set it there, pointing just high enough above the log to hit a bear if it was discharged. Then they stretched a vine above the log so the bear would discharge the gun when he pushed against the vine as he crossed the creek on the log. They started home just before dark, but before they got through the field in front of our house, we heard one of the guns shoot. My father said the first thing he thought of was what if a hunter had started to cross the creek on the log. Dad and Gene hurried back to see what had happened. They knew which gun it was that shot because the short barrel made a different sound, so they went to Old Zulu first. The big lead ball had knocked the bear off the log into the creek, badly crippled. My father watched while Gene ran and got the other gun, and shot the bear in the top of the head. They tied a big vine to the bear to prevent him from floating down the creek, and got some of our neighbors to help pull him out of the creek and skin him. He weighed four hundred pounds.

In the early days people didn't want to admit they lived in the Big Thicket. There was bad blood moved into the Thicket, and we were looked down on by dyed-in-the-wool Christian people; we were second rated, the Black Creek community was. Pine Ridge folks were the ones that looked down on us more than anybody else. They didn't beat the devil around the bush in trying to show the Black Creek people how they felt either. Our young men would go to Pine Ridge and try to find girl friends down there that wasn't kin to them. So my brother fell in love with a Pine Ridge girl, and he went home and wrote her a letter. About a week later he got an answer to his letter and she said, "Thanks for the letter, but I think if I wanted to live with the dogs, papa has a bunch of them here." The reason she said that, there was a family in the Black Creek settlement that had quite a few dogs and they allowed the dogs to come in the house and in the kitchen and under the table while they ate their meals. This girl had heard about that, and she didn't want to live with people that let their dogs in the house to scratch fleas under the table while they ate dinner.

However, we wanted something better. The way some of our ancestors had done, we knew it wasn't no good, and so we had a desire for something better. The Little Rock community went up. I have two brothers that are licensed, ordained ministers of the gospel, and scores of others who were raised there have done well and are highly respected.

We didn't have a full-time minister. The Pine Ridge settlement, five miles northeast of Sour Lake, now their minister for years and years was old Uncle Billy Teal. He lived in Saratoga and there was a trail cut through the Thicket to Pine Ridge, and every Saturday after he ate dinner, he'd take his horse and buggy and drive that fourteen miles and preach Saturday night and Sunday morning. They'd get in all the preaching they could because he'd have to start back Sunday afternoon. I wish I knew how many years he pastored that church.

Rev. James Jordan, a pioneer minister, organized that church at Pine Ridge and that community didn't take to drinking or dancing or anything like that. Later on they would let the young people have a Josie party, but that's all. It's practically the same steps, the same figures that they dance by a violin and a guitar, except they would sing instead of having musical instruments. They sang the "Little Brown Jug," "Little Brown Hen," just like a square dance, without the instrumental music.

There were not enough people to have a school until I was twelve years old, only about five families. The mother and father of the bank robber Red Goleman stayed at our house before they had any children, and her husband went off to a logging job somewhere, and Mrs. Goleman told my father and mother, "If you will get these children some first-grade books, while I'm here I'll teach them." So they did. That was Henry and Agnes Goleman.

Later on, Professor Longwell came into the Thicket and made his way to my father's house and asked if the community wanted to hire him to teach their children. We had never heard of him, but my father's brother in Mississippi told him we might want to hire him to teach. We didn't have any school and we didn't even have a house to have school in. But they chipped in and hired the old man for twenty-five dollars a month and board and room. He lived first with my father and then D. W. Brown, just here and there, and they got permission from Tom and Mirtie Laird to use their little board house to have school in. That was the first school in the Little Rock community.

Later on, they organized a church and a school and called it Little Rock. The county surveyor, Carter Hart, had already marked the east fork of Black Creek as Little Rocky on his map, so they named the place Little Rock after Little Rocky Creek. The community built the schoolhouse and the county hired the teacher, and that was our first public school.

I remember the first marriage in Little Rock, long before we had the school. Robert Allen Brown was a Baptist preacher in the Little Rock community and his wife was kin to young Tom Laird, a preacher up in Angelina County, near Zavalla. So he came down and preached in the Brown settlement and met Mirtie Brown, daughter of Emma and Warren Brown, and they decided to get married.

Uncle Warren Brown was one of the original settlers in the community. He liked people and he liked crowds, so he invited everybody for miles around to come to his house. He was going to have a big wedding dinner, and his daughter, Mirtie, was going to marry Tom Laird, the preacher. So people came from all around. But on the morning of the wedding day it started raining, and it rained and it rained, and it wouldn't stop. The groom had talked to a Baptist preacher in Kountze about coming out in his buggy to perform the wedding ceremony as Robert Allen Brown hadn't moved into our community at that time. Well, it rained so much the minister couldn't get there. So we all waited there all day.

We didn't have any covered wagons, and it rained, and rained, till the women and children just couldn't take off to go home; so the women and children stayed over at Uncle Warren's house, and the big boys and young men went back through the rain to the different homes and took care of the livestock, fed up everything. The next morning it stopped raining, but Black Creek was bank full, and there wasn't a bridge anywhere on it. Two days after the wedding was to take place they decided that two of the men would ride horseback to Sour Lake and get another minister. Everybody just stayed and waited for the preacher. They wouldn't give up. They were going to see a wedding, one way or another.

The preacher came out from Sour Lake in his buggy to the creek, about 150 yards from the Brown home, and he rode one of the horses across the creek and performed the ceremony. So Mirtie and Rev. Tom Laird finally got hitched. They stayed there with Uncle Warren while they built a split-board house about 600 yards from the Brown home. They put a fireplace in it, with a mudcat chimney, and Mirtie and Tom lived there till the first child was born, Albert Laird. He was the first baby born in the Little Rock community. He still lives in the Thicket.

High water caught me and my brother across Black Creek another time and we couldn't get home. One of the most miserable nights that I ever spent was trying to sleep in a crib full of peanut vines with the peanuts and dirt on the roots. I got down there in them vines, and that dirt gettin' in my ears and down my shirt collar, and tryin' to sleep, and it a-blowin' a blizzard cold enough to freeze the horns off a billy goat, was one of the worst nights I ever spent. Black Creek had got up, overflowed where we couldn't cross, and we were goin' home from our trappin' camp up on the west fork. The Rev. Bob Brown had a field and an old crib on our side of the creek. We got to the creek and couldn't cross. We came back and Bob Brown had harvested his peanuts and piled them in the crib, so we tried to sleep in those peanut vines. There was several of us met up there. Old man Bob Brown and his son Arthur had been hog hunting and they got to the creek about the same time we did, and Fred Bullard had been at a trapping camp with his wife and two children in a wagon, so when they couldn't cross the creek all eight of us went back to Bob Brown's crib and spent the night.

This country could get wet! The first thing that comes to my mind when I think about Sour Lake is mud. If you got off the boards they used for sidewalks, you'd bog halfway to your knees. It was just a tremendous mud-lolly. One time a tractor was coming down the street pulling a load, during the oil boom, and it started bogging, and went down farther and farther, until finally the top of the tractor was even with the ground, right at the main intersection. The owners built a little barricade out of two-by-four's around the top of it, so nobody would run over it, and left it there from May until July. When the ground got dried out some, they went in there and dug it out, and it ran all right.

The people, of course, they wanted a better living, so some of them started making whiskey after they found out they could dispose of it and make money, 'cause most all of the people in our settlement either made it, or sold it, or drank it, except my father and my brother and me. My father persuaded us not to have anything to do with it. Our family didn't make it, and didn't sell it, but our neighbors did and we treated them just like we did before. We didn't fall out with them. We didn't try to hurt them in any way. They were still our friends, our neighbors, and they trusted us.

A quart of whiskey would sell for ten dollars a quart, forty dollars a gallon. Our neighbors told us they could take a hundred pounds of corn chops and fifty pounds of sugar and put it in about a 50-gallon water barrel and ferment it, and distill it, and get 2-1/2 gallons of good corn whiskey. Well, that would be a hundred dollars for one sack of corn chops and fifty pounds of sugar, and just a little trouble; so it was one of the most tempting things anybody ever had to overcome if they needed money to take care of their family.

Three of our neighbors made whiskey—a man and his son and another man. They had the reputation of making the most and the best whiskey, so they made pretty good money out of it. At first he would pass by our house, and we could see the sugar and corn chops in his little mule wagon. The first thing we noticed, he bought a new wagon, and a few months later we heard something come buzzing down the old country road—just a wagon trail is all it was—and it was a shiny Model T Ford, a brand new one.

I was courting a girl in Saratoga and he knew it; so one day he came by our house and said, "How would you like to go see that girl? I'm going over there and I'll bring you back tonight." Well, I went with him, and when we got to the edge of town there were four men waiting by the side of the road. These men came to the car and he raised the back seat and there was twenty-eight quarts of corn whiskey. We went on to town and he let me out, but he came back about midnight and said he had sold the twenty-eight quarts and was going back for some more. But it was Saturday night and I decided to stay in Saratoga and go home the next day.

Later on, two hog hunters from another settlement came through and found the still. They could smell the mash and the whiskey still a-runnin', and our neighbors knew they would report them because they were against whiskey making. So that night they moved everything. They moved the mash barrels and the still to an old stave-maker camp on Black Creek, about a mile away. The next day the law came, and the man's twelve-year-old boy happened to be down in the woods where the still had been, and the law picked him up, made it pretty rough for the boy, and made him tell where they had moved the still. He was a kind of timid boy anyway, easily frightened, so it wasn't long till he started crying and told them where it was. So the law walked right in on them and arrested them.

They got the stills and started to pour the mash out on the ground. Well, news travels pretty fast by the grapevine, so by the time they got everything rounded up and under control, there was half a dozen men there from the settlement. They wanted to pour the sour mash out on the ground—it still had a quantity of alcohol in it—and one of the settlers said, "If you do that it will kill two dozen hogs." He knew by experience that when a hog ate that sour mash and got drunk, almost everyone of them will die. He said, "If you'll just leave it in the barrels, there's an old aban-doned well down there about fifty yards; we'll take the mash down there and pour it in that old well." The law said, "Okay." So after they all left they went and got another still and brought it that night and run the mash off and made seven gallons of whiskey before they poured it in the well. I know that's a true story.

They picked up another young man not far away, so al-together they got three that day. One of them got a year in the penitentiary, and one left and went to West Texas; and the one that made the most whiskey and the best whiskey of anyone in the Thicket, he was on bond, waiting for his trial in February. He had got him another still and had fifteen barrels of mash about a half mile from his home. Well, he took the flu and it came a misty, drizzly, cold day in February and this whiskey had to be run so he stayed out in the rain that night with the flu and fever, and about five days later he died of pneumonia.

Hogs was the money crop for most of us. One year we cured and smoked a awful lot of meat and had two thousand pounds of ham, after we had sold a good deal. In the spring my father would send me—I was about fourteen—in the wagon to Sour Lake to sell the surplus meat. All I had to do was go in there and find a place to tie up my horse, and people would flock there to buy them hams. It might seem strange that I'd remember such a

detail, but I remember quite well that I got seventeen cents a
pound for it.

The only place people settled to amount to anything was
around Saratoga and from there on up toward Votaw. Now that
was better drained than from Saratoga east, toward Beaumont.
The old road to Sour Lake went from Kountze, Old Hardin,
around to Old Nona and circled around the east end of the
Thicket, about five miles southwest of Ariola, and doubled back
to Piney Woods Cove, and then on to Sour Lake. It didn't attempt
to go through the Thicket.

Fires crept down through the piney woods every fall. It came
on down until it reached the baygalls that run from Ariola, up
Boggy Creek, and on up around the Jones' place, and all the way
up close to Honey Island. The string of baygalls on the north side
of the Thicket stopped the grass fires and the pine-needle fires
and kept them from killin' the hardwoods.

There were a lot of shallow ponds in this country and my
father had a big part in naming one of them. My brother, M. Q.
Fillingim, lived near us and asked a few of our neighbors, and
there were only a few, to help him split some railings to fence a
field. We killed a bunch of squirrels and my mother stewed them
with dumplings in a big tin pan. Dinner time came; yes, it was
dinner time, twelve o'clock noon. When people start calling the
picture of the Lord's Supper "The Lord's Dinner," then I might
call dinner "lunch."

Anyway, dad took the pan of squirrel and dumplings and rode
through the woods till he come to a big pond. The water was
about twelve inches deep. The horse began to bog and he
pitched and scrambled till he went down, and dad dropped the
pan when he got off the horse. The pan stayed right side up, but
some of the water got in the dumplings. Dad took it on out to
where the men were splitting rails, and told them what happened.
The men said a little baygall water wouldn't hurt anybody and
they wanted those squirrels and dumplings. The people in Little
Rock settlement still call it Dumpling Pond.

[Then Dolph Fillingim continued with this story of Red Goleman.]

Red Goleman

Jefferson Goleman in the early days was a horse trader, and
horse traders traveled; they never settled down. He carried horses
from East Texas into Louisiana and back down the old Spanish
Trail through Orange and Beaumont and on up in East Texas as
far as Woodville. He drove them. Just one man could tie up a few
of the leaders and hit the road and the others would follow. He'd

camp, maybe for a week, at any farmer's place, and anyone that needed a horse, or had one to sell, would go see him. He never knew just how legitimate, or just how lawful the stock was that he was buying, so that kept him on the move. That was Uncle Jeff Goleman's trade in the early days.

Later on when they started cutting timber and putting up sawmills and logging camps, he switched to timber work. Well, he had married before he came to Hardin County and had two children, Henry and a girl. Henry married Agnes Collins, and they would come through our settlement and stop over for a month or two while Henry was working; and when the job was over, he'd move out. He really never settled down until he got to be an old man. He was the father of "Red" Goleman, Thomas Jefferson Goleman. He never was a permanent settler in the Little Rock or Black Creek community.

The first time I saw Red, he was about six months old. They came by and stayed at our house several days. Then I'd see him off and on until he was about twelve years old. Then they moved to Beaumont and lived there up till the Depression. By then Red was old enough to get out on his own and he followed oil-field work, usually boom towns.

It got to where he wanted the reputation of being the best fighter in every boom town that he went to. Just like a doctor or a lawyer hanging out his sign, Red Goleman hung out his sign that he could whip any man in town. He didn't make no bones about it. He wasn't a large man, about five feet ten, and weighed about 175 pounds.

My brother-in-law, Edgar Davis, was there at Boling, Texas, during the oil-field boom and, of course, Red went out there. In the evening Red would tell anybody around town that he could whip anybody in Boling, and it wasn't long until somebody took him up. They'd have certain places to meet so everybody could see the fight. So they fought and this other man whipped Red, so my brother-in-law told me. After it was over Red said, "Well, meet me back here tomorrow evening and we'll try it over." So they got together next day and went at it again, and Red whipped him, and I guess he would have asked him back again if he hadn't.

Red wasn't a mean man. He was good natured, always smiling, but he probably had a high temper, judging from his flaming red hair. That was where he got the nickname "Red."

Later they began drilling oil wells down at Corpus Christi, and Red went to work down there. He drank and run with a rough crowd, but as far as being an outlaw, or thief, he wasn't. He was just an ordinary, good-natured man. Well, this is the way I got it from men who were there, relatives and others, and out of the newspaper, too. Red got in a fight with a man quite a few years older than he was, somewhere up the Nueces River. He was a tough, rowdy old man, and during the fight the old man died, probably on account of his heart or something like that. The old man just dropped dead. Red went to the sheriff and told him, "I killed old John while ago up on the river." They said, "You're joking," and they wouldn't believe it until he took them up there and showed them.

Well they put him under bond of three thousand dollars, which is light. The charge could have been manslaughter where he could have gotten a suspended sentence or something like that; it wasn't serious. But he had to have a lawyer and he knew that he would have to pay this lawyer, and he didn't have any money, so the thought came to him, I guess, that he would just rob somebody, because he had to have the money to pay his lawyer to handle the case. So that's when he came to Hull and planned to rob the Hull State Bank. I don't know how he got by with it, but he absolutely did. He put on women's clothes and went to the Hull State Bank and stood around there learning the routine and details of how things went on. One man, after it was all over, said, "I wondered about that woman; I saw her standing out in front of the bank, and she raised one foot like a man will, and propped it back against the wall. A woman won't do that, but a man will." Well, that was Red Goleman. He learned that the best time to rob the bank was between twelve and one o'clock because about half the employees would go to lunch. So he got another fellow, Smith, from Liberty, to go with him, and a few days after he scouted the place out, he held them up between twelve and one o'clock. He put the employees in the vault and got away with twelve thousand dollars.

They got in their car and went west towards the Trinity River. They left the car and swam across and went on out of the bottom to the first road running north and south, and flagged a ride into Dayton. Red had friends there and that night they made their way on to Houston. We heard that the bank at Hull had been robbed, but we didn't have any idea who did it. Red's half-uncle lived on the old Jones' homestead, and I went by the old place and Red Goleman was on the front porch with his arm bandaged with white gauze from his shoulder to his wrist, about six inches through the bandages. I never saw so much bandage, and the word got out that Red had broke his arm on a drilling accident.

He stayed there one or two days, but somehow he found out that they were hot on his trail. So he got up early the next morning and walked into the Thicket and found a jug someone left in the woods. He took that jug and crammed it full of the money that was hid under his bandage. He said later that he buried ten thousand dollars in that jug and went on down farther into the thicket and hid the balance, and stayed in the Thicket close to some of his relatives. He hid out a week or two while the law was looking for him. Finally he decided to give up, and he went to one of his relatives, Dan Brown, and told him, he says, "Dan, I'm ready to give up. I want you to take me to the law." He said, "Okay, if you want to go in, I'll take you." So Dan carried him over to his father's house and they turned him over to the law. They kept him in jail, and people that went to see him said that they give him so much truth serum until he didn't have good sense, so he stayed there but he never did tell. Somehow, before he went down into the Thicket he slipped out to his grandfather Goleman's house at Loeb and buried six hundred dollars under a culvert, sixteen hundred dollars in the yard of a rooming house in Houston, and the rest was wrapped around his arm under that bandage.

While he was in jail he told them, "I'll get you the money, all that I have"; so they carried him to Loeb and they dug up the fruit jar with six hundred dollars in it, and then he carried them to Houston, and they got the sixteen hundred dollars over there. So that made twenty-two hundred dollars, but he still wouldn't tell them where the rest of it was. They kept holding him, so after a couple of months he said, "All right, I filled a jug full of money and I buried it down in the Thicket by a forked pine." Now that is something unusual to find a forked pine tree, but he said, "It's down there, and if you'll take me down there, I'll see if I can find it. I was just passing through, the morning I went down there, and I buried it, and it will be pretty hard to find, but I believe I can find that forked pine." So a Texas Ranger and a local deputy carried him down there in the Thicket. I remember, I lived down there at that time.

About eleven o'clock they came out of the Thicket and passed by my house going to my neighbor's house to get a drink of water, and I remember quite well as they passed by my house, he saw me and said, "Hi, how you doin'?" I said, "It's too hot to talk." I wondered a lot of times afterwards what the law thought about what I said, but really, the weather was what I was thinkin' about. I had nothin' against Red; he had nothin' against me; there was no hard feelings any way between us, and I wouldn't have turned him in; I wouldn't have caused him any trouble whatever, because I had known his family for years.

Well, they didn't find the money, and my idea was that he wanted this as an excuse to get down in the Thicket, thinking they might take the handcuffs off, but they didn't. I imagine he gave them a pitiful time draggin' them through that Thicket. Finally they dropped his bond to three thousand dollars. Some of his people from Baytown came over to visit him and he told them where he had buried a bunch of this money, and he told them to dig it up and take three thousand dollars and deposit it for his bond. So they did and they turned him loose.

Pretty soon afterward he went to where he had the money buried and he claimed he was five hundred dollars short so he went to Baytown to see these people that paid his bond. They had two sons, and he told them, he says, "Let's go down in the Thicket and shoot some squirrels." So this man, his aunt's husband, and his aunt's two sons, went squirrel huntin' with him down on Black Creek. When they got down there Red got the drop on them and he tied the old man up, and he put the two boys, about sixteen or eighteen years old, in the trunk of the car and locked it. He told this man, "I'm short five hundred dollars and you are going to get it." He drove on down to a relative's house with the old man tied up in the front seat of the car and the boys in the trunk. He went in to talk to this man and while he was in there the boys managed to take the back cushion out and work their way up into the front of the car. They grabbed their daddy without even untying him and they hit out through the Thicket and finally made their way to a house and told them what had happened. So they got what guns they had and got out and waited for Red to come, but he didn't show up.

When he come out of his relative's house and went out to the car and saw the old man was gone out of the front seat, he hollered back to this fellow; he said, "Well, he's gone, but his wife knows just as much about it as anybody, so I'll go to Baytown and kidnap her. I'll get my five hundred dollars." So he hit out on the Sour Lake–Kountze road. They had been working on the road and Red missed a short right turn and wrecked the car, and that's when he found out that he didn't have the boys. He went around and looked in the trunk, and nobody was there.

I heard later that he was crippled up pretty badly in the wreck, but he managed to get to some friends in Sour Lake, and they took care of him till he got able to travel, then he went back in the Thicket. Now this was about the last of October or November. He stayed in the Thicket with the law looking for him, and Secret Service men and law of all descriptions came in there to try to find him to get the five thousand dollars reward. People who lived down there, they would come by and ask questions, pretend this, that, and the other, you know, as an excuse, trying to get information about where Red was. Well, he was somewhere around there in the Thicket and somebody knew where he was. Anyhow, the law hunted him. I remember a hobo came to my house late in the afternoon and he played like he was blind. My dog walked up to him and he reached down and said, "Baby, baby," making out like he thought that dog was a little child, you see. So when he left my house he said, "I'm going a mile and a half down the road, and sleep under the bridge tonight." He knew where the bridge was, knew all about it. The hobo was Secret Service. There were dozens of them came here and tried to get information on Red. Well, he couldn't go back, he had to stay hid, because he would be charged with kidnapping, and they would arrest him and file new charges against him. So he stayed out in the woods from November until April, and during this time I didn't know anything about him. I never saw him except the day the law came by the house with him, but somebody was helping him, I don't know who. It wasn't any of his immediate family. Well, they didn't find him, and along in January he moved from that part of the Thicket up towards Votaw. I remember we had snow in January, between the fifteenth and twentieth, about four inches, and I lived in the Black Creek settlement.

I heard later that just before this snow, Red's brother came to him and they skipped out and slipped down to Beaumont. There was a taxi driver down there that Red said he had been wanting to get for a long time because he had mistreated his sister. So his brother, Darius, went down in Beaumont and told this taxi driver that he wanted to go to a certain place out in the edge of Beaumont. It was the driver Red wanted. When he got out there, Red was waiting for him and one of them shot the taxi driver. Since it's all over, I doubt he wanted to kill him, but anyhow they shot him, and they took the taxi and left the man laying there, and they drove it back up to the Big Thicket, west of Saratoga several miles out on a pipeline as far as they could, and this snowstorm came on about the twentieth of January, so he and his brother slept in that taxi during that snowstorm. The law found the taxi on that old pipeline, and the evidence showed that he and his brother had stayed there for a good long time—the cigarette butts and everything. The taxi driver lived, that's why I doubt that Red really wanted to kill him.

Anyhow he came back and stayed in the Thicket, traveling from one end to the other until along about April. He'd had so many fights, and was in so many brawls, he had a horribly large nose. It had been flattened out almost completely, and he would be easily identified anywhere by his flat nose. So after he was killed, my mother went to the funeral. I had the flu and didn't go. The paper stated that there was at least two thousand people at Goleman's funeral. They buried him at Old Hardin. Well, I'm getting ahead of my story. Red left the Thicket for days at a time, because my wife said, "Dolph, nobody would have knowed Red Goleman; he had the prettiest, nicest, little straight, slim nose that you ever saw. Nobody would have recognized him." He went out and somehow had his nose shaped up. I got it by the grapevine, pretty reliable story, that he had been out several times.

Well, Smith, his partner, was tried along about April in Liberty, and Red's mother and father went to the trial and Red knew they were going and told them, "You talk to the district judge or district attorney and find out what is the least sentence they can let me off with if I surrender." Well, his mother talked to the judge and they told her that on account of the things he had done, that twenty-five years was the very least he could give him. So whether he had decided to take a chance on that twenty-five years or not we don't know and won't ever know. But his mother came back and was spending the night at the old Jones' home-stead. Red was to meet them out there that night when they got back from the trial. But that day a man rode up on him back in the Thicket and talked to him, probably fed him, and he told this man, "I've got a feeling that I'm going to be sick, a bad spell of sickness or something bad is going to happen to me." So it came up a thunderstorm and he got wet and he came on out just before dark to this old homestead and hid in the crib to talk to his mother. The law found out he was there, and just as soon as it got dark they surrounded the old corn crib where he was hiding. There was about five; there was Sheriff Miles Jordan of Kountze, the sheriff from Beaumont, and a couple of Texas Rangers, and others that surrounded this corn crib. They know whether they gave him a chance to surrender, but nobody else ever knew; but anyhow, they begun to pump lead through the walls of this old crib until he fell at the door. They said that to avoid the bullets he had got up on something close to the top of the crib, but anyhow they gave him a fatal wound and he fell at the door. The sheriff from Beaumont, I forget which sheriff it was, he shined a flashlight through the crack in the door—the door wouldn't close tight—and shot him twice more before he opened the door.

So that ended Red Goleman's career. He wasn't mean; he was probably a little high-tempered, but you know how things go like that, one circumstance leads to another; they get deeper and deeper until circumstances can destroy a person. He was only thirty-two when he was killed.

Born 1897, interviewed 1970–1975.

Corbitt Brackin

Corbitt Brackin is a member of one of several families that raised sheep. So did his daddy, Bud Brackin, renowned bear hunter. There were many hazards to sheep raising, but wolves were the worst. They would cut the throats and lick the blood of several sheep in one night's killing. Dogs sometimes killed sheep, too. But, despite the hazards to sheep raising, wool used to be shipped by the carload. Born 1897, interviewed 1975.

Introducing Carter Hart

Carter was a bear hunter, and, to him, it was the greatest sport on earth. He didn't hunt bear for meat, though he ate what he killed, or because they killed wild hogs, which people depended on for food. "Some of the biggest bear hunters didn't have hogs," he said. "It was sport, pure and simple, but the hardest work on earth."

Carter did much of his hunting with the Hooks brothers, Bud and Ben, eminent bear hunters who had a hunting camp in the Big Thicket south of Kountze. Incidentally, the first bear he ever killed was with Bud Hooks, and the last one was with Ben. A lasting picture of Carter, a friend said, was of him out in the backyard cooking for his dogs—meat scraps and cornmeal. He'd use an old iron pot and cook enough to feed his pack for two or three days.

For all his love of the hunt, I believe he would rather lose his top dog than to exaggerate in telling of it. Judge Hightower, noted judge and noted hunter, once remarked that Carter could talk longer than any man he ever saw without telling a lie, and he paid him a notable compliment by leaving him his favorite gun when he died. Carter once remarked that the biggest bear he ever saw weighed 640 pounds, but he did not say that he killed it till I asked.

Carter liked nothing better than a week or two at Ben Hook's Big Thicket bear camp in the company of a few friends looking for bear. Carl Richardson and Killraine were two people that everyone wanted on these hunts. Carl was not a noted hunter, but his presence insured the success of any hunt. He was sought far in advance by any group planning a hunt, whether for bear,

deer, or whatever. As one friend said, "He just had a little way of making something funny out of ordinary conversation, always kept us laughing. He was a good storyteller, too, usually kept a straight face even when he said something real funny."

Killraine was known all over the Thicket, but it was years before we met anyone who knew what his real name was, and we never did learn how he came to be called "Killraine"; but he was a black man, universally respected as a hunter, a humorous storyteller, and a cook. He would often be asked to cook for a hunt a year in advance. Corbitt Brackin described a feast he put on the table at the close of a hunt, consisting of bear, deer, turkey, possum, duck, quail, and wild hog—any kind of meat a man might want. Anything not eaten at camp was divided up and taken home. Killraine's real name was Johnny Williams.

Carter Hart, though, was much more than a bear hunter. He was a large, friendly, somewhat reserved man, over six feet tall, who gave the impression that he enjoyed every minute of his life. He was an early surveyor, and he named many of the landmarks that serve as reference points today. He was as precise in his speech as he was with his surveying. He spoke directly and got right to the point. He was uncommonly shrewd in sizing up people and saw humor all about him. I never heard him utter a negative thought or an uncharitable remark. Even after he lost his wife, Ethel, and the amputation of his leg confined him to a wheelchair in a nursing home, he would somehow lift the spirit of friends who came to see him.

CARTER HART

I've lived in the Thicket all my life. My daddy came from Tennessee; moved from there to Union Parish, Louisiana, and then here. My mother was the daughter of Jeff Hart before she married my father, Eli Hart, in August 1881. My mother's people came here in 1838, I believe. My great-grandfather, William Henry Hart, was raised in Alabama. He went over into South Carolina and married a woman named Sarah Harrington. Then they moved to Florida. They had eleven children, raised seven of them, six girls and a boy. My grandfather was the only boy in the family. They said he was spoiled rotten, absolutely rotten—mean as the devil, play tricks on the niggers, whites, everybody. My great-grandfather moved back to Alabama, and on to Mississippi, bringing his married children and their families with him. I don't know how long they stayed there, but Jeff married there, married Epsy Bazer. William Henry come on over to Louisiana, up near Pineville, in DeSoto Parish, and some of my uncles and aunts were married there—Jeff Hart's children. But old William come on over here and established a settlement in Hardin County, about 1840, six miles northeast of Kountze. He built his house out of fourteen-by-fourteen timber that his slaves hewed out. It's still there, built of heart pine.

They'd sometimes come in eight or ten wagons. I know when my great-grandfather moved here he didn't have enough wagons of his own and his son, Jeff, come with some oxen and a wagon and helped move him. Aunt Adeline Teal, I heard her say that's the only time she ever saw Jeffie cry. That was her brother. When he got in the wagon to start back, he cried, leaving his daddy and mother here.

They used oxen for pulling the wagons. I never heard of any mules pulling wagons until after my grandfather was dead and Uncle John, one of his boys, was driving that wagon. Uncle John was a smart aleck, raised up there just like all boys at that time, and I can tell you this and tell it just like it happened, because Uncle John told me.

He come along and overtaken a fellow walking, had a stick

over his shoulder and a bag with his belongings in it. Uncle John said, "Ain't you getting tired of walking?" He had never seen the man before, and he answered, "Yes, I am." Uncle John said, "Give me five dollars and I'll learn you to pace." The man just reached up and pulled him off the wagon and gave him a whipping. When he turned him loose, Uncle John run to the wagon and got an ax, but when he started back he met a pistol. This fellow had a pistol pointed at him. He said, "Drop that ax, boy." Uncle John said, "I dropped it." He said the fellow gave him his ax and sent him on down the road.

A few days after that he was in Woodville, walking down the street, and this fellow saw him and called him. He said, "Come here, I want to buy you a drink." And he took him in the saloon and bought him a drink. He said, "Young man, I'm not mad at you, except I just hope you learned a lesson, that you won't say that to the next man you see on the road that's tired."

After a few years Jeff moved over here and settled where West Nona is, the R. J. Hart Survey. He was my grandfather, the only boy in his family. He didn't live there long, went up here in Tyler County and dammed up two lakes and put in a water mill. Twin Lakes was where he settled and run a mill there. Warren Bevil come over there from Jasper County and bought Jeff Hart out, everything: his mills, his ponds, his home, and everything else. That was Leak Bevil's granddaddy. My grandfather took his people and moved down the creek a piece and put in another dam and another mill. That was on Cypress Creek.

My grandfather and great-grandfather bought land from the state. You could buy it for a few pennies an acre and get forty years to pay for it. They nearly all would pay it out a long time before that time was up, because they'd trade or sell. Jeff Hart run that mill till it washed away, flooded. The mill and dam and everything went with it. It was the biggest rain that had ever happened.

My great-grandfather, William Henry Hart, owned all that territory around Saratoga, and he cut a road in there, and moved his sons-in-law in there: old man Dick Teal, old man Gwynes, two Cottons—Fletcher and Florida Cotton, and Tom Jordan, who married one of the Cotton widows. He divided all this property before the Civil War, before the Negroes were free. I've got a copy of his division, and he gave every one of them fifteen hundred dollars in money or property. He had appraisers to put the value on the niggers, the land and other stuff. My grandfather got old Hester and two children. He raised them niggers, and I was a great big boy when old Bob died. They all had niggers. The Mitchells and the Arlines and the Bosteds, Mayos, Williams, all settled on the edge of the Thicket and all had niggers. Old Arline and Hawthorn and them had lots of niggers, and they had big farms around the edge of the Thicket.

They had a church house and if a traveling preacher came

through, they asked him to stay and preach. If they didn't have a
preacher, great-grandfather, William Jefferson Hart, would read
and explain the Scriptures. At the back there was a little place
built up and that was where the slaves sat. The benches were
around the wall. The rest of the church had an aisle down the
middle with square pieces supporting the benches at the aisle,
and braced in the logs at the wall.

After the niggers were freed, my grandfather went up there to
Woodville and bought eighty acres on the northeast side of town
and built a house for every one of his niggers: Old Dicey and
Hester and Bob and Frank, and all of them. He had a mill about
six miles from there. He fixed every one of them a place to live
and gave them a piece of land and deeded it to them. Old Bob
and Dicey and some of them never left, just stayed there where
he raised them. But after the mill washed away, they went to their
homes up there. Old Dicey and Frank used to come down here
to see Aunt Martha Bevil. She was the oldest of my grandfather's
children. She married John Bevil.

I was born October 5, 1883, at Village Mills. We moved to
Saratoga and stayed about four years, but moved back to Village
Mills in 1889, and lived there from then on. I was the oldest of
eight children, five boys and three girls.

When I was a boy we had to make our fun, had horse races
and foot races and fish fries and things like that. Rice brothers up
there at Hyatt would give a dinner, maybe a fish fry, and people
from Warren and Village Mills and Plank and other places would
come. One year, I remember, Village Mills had a pond out there,
had lots of fish in it. They drained that pond and scooped up the
fish, killed them right then and cooked them. They ran the train
out there to this pond, it was on the tram logging road, and
carried people out there. Of course womenfolks had bread and
cakes and pies and things like that, but the main thing was the
fish, and they cooked them right there. Village was in the center
of six or eight mills. There was a little rivalry between every mill,
friendly, of course. Each one of them tried to have some
amusement, what the country afforded.

But I want to tell you about the first football game that was ever
played in Hardin County, right there at Village. I was about fourteen or fifteen years old. I'm just afraid people won't believe,
won't realize what all took place. I want to tell you the circumstances, everything that led up to this game.

R. G. Moon was woods superintendent. He had charge of all
the tram roads, and the log engines and the teams and the
cooks, and the niggers and the whites and everything else from
the mill out. When they left the mill, they were on Moon's territory
and under his control. Sometimes it was several miles, sometimes just a few, to the front where they worked. F. F. Welker had
charge of the mill hands.

W. G. Woodard was the school teacher. We just had a teacher

about three months in the year. Somehow or other, Woodard got a football down there for him and his older boys to play with. They would just throw it around; there wasn't enough of 'em to play a game. It was the only football I ever saw till I was twenty years old.

I don't know how they did it, but they got the niggers interested in that football. Moon and Welker got up a little jealousy or something between the loggers and the mill hands, and they got those niggers to using that football, playing with it, and matched a game between them. Some of the niggers from each group helped Welker and Moon select their men. They got eleven on both sides. They didn't have no substitutes. They just went out there and played till they fell out, and nobody took his place. He was just out.

The only open place big enough to play was at the slab pit where they burned the slab. It was open all around there, nothing but charcoal and dirt, nothing clean, but a big open space, and that is where they practiced and that is where they played. The mill hands would practice one day and the loggers the next, and they'd practice on Sunday afternoons, too. They must have practiced two months or more.

I think every one of them was married. Their families come. Everybody in the country for twenty miles around come there to see that game. You see these were big sawmills, mills that cut from 75,000 to 100,000 feet a day. They had one at Nona and two little mills at Kountze; one at Olive, three miles from Kountze, and one two miles from there, Old Trian. And four miles up was Old Plank and then Village Mills, then Hyatt, and then Warren. It would average about three miles from one sawmill to the next. No two of them was connected financially. But the word got out about this game and everybody come that could get there; come on trams, horseback, wagon, or afoot. The mills closed down for twenty miles around, and that was just unheard of.

Woodard knew something about some of the rules and did the judging. They had a goal and center spot, and one nigger run from each side and kicked that ball. It had to be kicked off the ground, and then after it was once kicked, why they did anything they could; take it away from each other, try to take it to each goal just like they do now, but they didn't have no ten-yard lines, nothing like that. They just had two posts down there, and they had to get that ball across that line between those posts. I don't think they had any rules. Woodard had a book of rules, but I don't think they ever looked at it.

Well, they started those niggers to wrestling with that ball. I don't know what time they started, but in the forenoon sometime, and I don't know how long it took them, but after a while they made a touchdown, you call it. What interested me more than anything else was the sight of them niggers a-wrestlin' each other, and it was hot weather, and them sweating. They soon got to tearing their shirts off, and they didn't have on nothing but pants after the first hour or two. They never quit playing. They started in the morning, and they must have played four hours before they just decided they'd quit. Lots of the fellers had just give out. They had no padding, nothing but nigger skin from the waist up. Lord o' mercy, I'd love to get you to realize, if you can, just how all those hot, sweaty niggers wrestled that ball! They went at it enthusiastically, even right up to the last, wrestling when there wasn't but two or three left on each side. The others were give out and some of them give out for good, for that day. They wrestled there for I don't know how long, but after a while they declared the game in favor of Welker's mill niggers. They claimed the reason Welker's niggers won was they were smaller and more active and could get around them logging niggers. You know they were big old husky six footers, two hundred pounds or more, and not fat either. Welker's niggers were small.

Well, now that was a sight and I don't know how to describe it to you so that you would realize how much fun everybody had, encouraging these niggers fighting and wrestling with each other. Nobody was angry; it was just a friendly affair. That was the first football game ever played in Hardin County. I have said all my life, and still claim, that that was the most wonderful damn game that ever was. There just never has been another one like it that I ever heard of.

I have spent eighty-seven years in the Thicket—as surveyor, timber cruiser, logger, and I hunted every chance I had. I shot my dad's old single-shot muzzle-loader from the time I was eight, but didn't go with the hunters until I was fourteen or fifteen; had my own gun then. In the summertime, when they were fat, we hunted deer, and in the wintertime, when they were fat, we hunted bear, black bear. I hunted everything there was, except turkey. I never went turkey hunting in my life. I didn't hunt any-thing, never did, where I didn't use a dog. I like to hear a dog bark, bark plenty, that is, if there's purpose to his bark. A dog will bark on a trail, on a running trail, and he don't know or care where his master is. He's a-smellin', and I think there's a certain amount of pleasure and excitement he gets out of smelling that makes him bark. Some of them will bark a dozen times, where another will bark twice. I like a dog with plenty of mouth.

I had a pretty big pack of cat dogs until six years ago. A hound is best for hunting cats, and they're best for fox hunting too. I just got rid of my dogs four or five years ago. Used to have twenty dogs. Had to cook for them every day. Couldn't buy dog food like you can now. I would cook meal and cracklin's in the wash pot, and scraps from the market; have a big stew there, enough to last two days unless I had a large pack.

We tried every kind of dog we ever heard of for bear huntin'.

Some would run the bear and some would run from the bear. I've turned dogs loose after the start dog jumped a bear, and they'd go back the way they come from, and we'd never see 'em again. After a dog finds out a bear has teeth, if he goes back, he's a bear dog. The best dogs we ever found for bear was the cur. Ben Hooks had two good ones, Ramsey and Alec. The best dog I ever had was Jack. He'd fight close, fight in front. He would go to the bear's head, and he wouldn't bark anywhere else. You keep your dogs coupled up until the lead dog strikes the trail. A bear will stop and fight, and sometimes he'll run just as hard as he can go. A dog has to be pretty good to keep up with one, especially in the summertime when they're not so fat. A big fat bear can't run much.

Bear hunting is the hardest work a man ever did on earth. You had to walk all day in mud, water, and you were in the sloughs, canebrakes, baygalls, and palmetto swamps a lot. Lots of times I've left early in the morning and come in after dark, and not have a bite to eat all day. I never took anything to eat. I don't know why. None of us ever did. We would ride if we could, but lots of times a horse would bog down, right out on level ground, bog down anywhere. Whenever a horse bogged down, some of them was all right, but it scared some of them to death, and they'd go to fightin' and jumpin' and pawin', and you'd have to get off and get off quick.

The best bear country ever known was right between Kountze and Sour Lake, on up nearly to the Tyler County line. It was thick and plenty of food, no roads, nothing to bother them. I had a camp down there, two rooms, and we'd go and hunt for two or three weeks sometimes. Ben Hooks had a camp down at old Captain Parker place, and he had another one six or seven miles, at the edge of the Thicket. People would build a small place so they could go and stay with comfort and hunt.

One winter, about 1907 or 1908, we killed sixteen bears: me, Ben and Bud Hooks, John Salter, Ben Lilly, McConico, and several others. We always kept the meat; put it up just like hog, salt it down, hang it up and smoke it. You can bake bear meat just like you can a hog. A young bear is good eating, but you take one of those old bear, four hundred pounds, it's old black meat, and you've got to cook it till Christmas to get it where you can chew it. I killed a bear one time that had five and a quarter inches of pure fat from the middle of her back to her rump, looked just like hog lard. We didn't waste it, put it up one way or the other. It would keep a long time, longer than we ever let it. But me and the Hooks boys, we hunted for sport, sport altogether.

One day we killed three bears, and the last one we killed, Ben said, "We'll just have to gut this bear and hang it up." We did, and when we started to gut it, Ben said, "Looky here, this old thing is a-suckin'; she has a bag here." Well, there wasn't nothing we could do about it. We hung it up, and Ben says, "If a man could go back to where that little bitch was barkin', he could find them cubs. She's got some cubs there." I said, "I can find them." He said, "I bet you can't." I said, "I know I can. I can't this evenin', I haven't got time." It was gettin' late then and we went on to camp, and Ben had to be in Houston next mornin' in court.

Next day I took a couple of niggers and a wagon and went back down there and picked up the meat we had hangin'. I went in as far as I could with the wagon and took me a sack and went back down there to the place where the little old dog was a-barkin', and found two cubs about the size of a grown coon. There was a little pin oak tree there on the knoll, and it was beat out at the edge just as clean as that floor all around there, and they were right up at that tree like they were trying to get their noses under it. I had a nigger with me, Lige Arline, and I caught one and said, "Lige, you catch that one." He did and it bit him. You catch them back of the neck. I brought them home and gave Bud one and I raised the other. Mine followed me all over town, and the boys would tease him, you know, and they got him to where he would bite. Bud had two down there in a log pen he built for them. I carried him down there and gave him to Bud. He was about a year old and weighed about one hundred pounds. They aren't hard to tame and you can just feed 'em scraps like you would a puppy.

Biggest bear we ever killed weighed 650 pounds. I killed it in 1906 or 1907. It was the day Teddy Roosevelt was supposed to go hunting with us. You know he had a date with us to go hunting here and sent his outfit. Cecil Lyons and Joe Rice in Houston made all the arrangements, to get old Teddy down here. They were Republicans and they made a date with Teddy to come down here and go with us bear hunting. He was president then. You could get the exact date by finding out when Robert Hooks was born. Robert was born just a day or two before Teddy was coming down here. We went a-huntin' and killed a little old two-year-old out of a pine tree. I never saw but two bear in a pine tree in my life. We left our horses nearly three miles back. It was so boggy you couldn't ride; horse would bog down every ten feet. I mean bog down! Bog down till his belly was layin' on the ground! We went back there and got our horses and come down there to get the little old bear, and put him on Ben's horse. He was a little old fightin' horse, mean, and we had to blindfold him and back him up under this bear so he didn't know what it was. We put it on him and tied it, had it tied on there good, Tom Jordan style. He could tie one on there and a horse couldn't get it off.

Tom Jordan would put the bear across the saddle, his tail on one side and head on the other. Then he'd put a rope around the middle of the bear and tie him to the pommel, good. Then he'd tie the rope 'round the bear's flank and to the front girt, go to the other side and tie his head to the front girt. Then he'd tie the rope 'round the bear and bring it under the horse; it's just an extra brace to save the girt, keep the girt from breaking and losing the whole thing. It will stay there.

About the time we started out we saw that some of the dogs wasn't there, and just then we heard 'em comin'. Ben said "I'll go down there and see what it is, and if I holler you turn these dogs loose," and before the dogs got to us, he hollered. I turned the other dogs loose and they went to it. I asked Ben what he was going to do with this bear and horse. He said, "I don't care what you do with them." It was his horse and bear.

I went to a big black gum tree that had limbs twenty feet out, I guess, and tied the horse to a limb so he could move around a little. He was kickin' and fightin' all the time with this bear on him. I wasn't wastin' no time, and when I started to leave, I got about twenty feet from him, and the horse started to pitchin' and kickin' and bogged down, and turned over backwards with the bear on him. Well, I didn't know what was going to happen, so I waited, and the little old horse scrambled around there and got up, and when he got up the bear was right there just like it belonged. I never looked back no more.

You see this was in the afternoon then. Ben and the dogs went right towards Black Creek, and I went in that direction. After while I met them comin' back, the bear and the dogs, and I got in with them, and of course kept tryin' to get where I could get a shot. They was just walkin' and a-fightin' and once in a while they'd stop. I followed them along that way till I was just about give out; try to run, but couldn't in that country, sort of hoppin' along. I saw an opening where a big tree had fallen. Heavy vines had growed up on one end six or eight feet above the log, and I jumped on the log and went crawlin' down toward them, and that bear come up there on the log I was on, come meetin' me. When he come up there about twelve feet of me, that was about as close as I wanted him, and I shot him right in the sticky place, and he just rared up on his hind feet and pawed the air. I shot him twice more, and he jumped right over toward me, and fell on the right-hand side of the log, right against my knee. He weighed 650 pounds. We brought it out on horses next day. The sticky place is the jugular vein, just in front of the forelegs—just like you would stick a hog.

We got back to Bud's little horse just about dark. He was standin' with all four of his feet right together on a little hard place, and everything around there would just shake, except that little place about fifteen inches long. He had all four of his feet on that, standin' there. I just untied him and led him out, the bear still on him.

Roosevelt didn't come. Something happened and he couldn't

come. We unloaded all his stuff at Bragg, then had to ship it back to Houston later. There was two wagons, a lot of horse feed, grub, camping outfits, three tents and, I believe, six horses.

I never saw but one bear bed, where she hibernated. She built it on a knoll out there in the thicket, and it was pretty open woods all around. It was the only one I ever saw like that. The trail was awfully cold. The old dog, he was a Redbone hound, registered, and it took him, I know, two hours to work that trail a mile. When he chopped it, the bear run off up the country, and we followed it, turned the pack loose, and it turned and run back toward Bud and he killed it. It was an old she and there were three little ones in the bed. She had made her bed there on what we call a gallberry knoll, and she had pulled the gallberry bushes in, and it looked like she had tore up tree tops, limbs and vines, so it didn't rain on her, and she was warm. That was in April. They hibernate about three months.

Most of the good bear hunting was over around 1910. The last one I killed was in 1911, I believe, although I was with Ben Hooks on a deer hunt in 1918 when we happened to strike a bear and he killed it, and that was his last. It just happens that I went on my first bear hunt with Bud Hooks, and my last one with Ben. On my first hunt I killed the bear about three miles south of Saratoga, at Uncle Tom Jordan's place, but Ben got the last one. We were deer hunting at a camp on Lost Gulley and that old nigger, Killraine, had a pack of dogs coming down the creek, hoping to jump a deer, and his dogs run over a bear. He was a young one and ran right close to Ben, and he shot him. That was his last bear. When the bear got scarce we didn't quit hunting. We'd hear of one over here, one over there, go hunt it and kill it. They're all gone. It was the greatest sport on earth!

1883–1973, interviewed 1969–1971.

Introducing the Slavonian Stave Makers

We first heard of the Slavonian stave makers when Dolph Fillingim told of taking refuge in one of their abandoned camps one night during a storm that prevented his crossing a swollen stream to get home. It seemed odd that Yugoslavians had found their way into this remote wilderness, and our curiosity grew as we continued to hear occasional references to them. Extensive inquiry led us to three of the original Slavonians who came to America to cut staves and remained. One is Pete Mihelich, who now lives with his daughter and son-in-law, Mr. and Mrs. L. S. Shrader, near Cleveland, Texas. He was in the stave business for many years.

The two stave makers whose stories follow are Pete Racki and Anton Knause. Pete Racki, who is well known and still lives in the area, has an immaculate homestead just north of Rye. He has been in the lumber business there for years.

Anton Knause, eighty-seven years old, lives with Mr. and Mrs. Paul E. Lombardino, his daughter and son-in-law, near Beaumont. When I called at the house in midafternoon, he was alone, and he made his way to the door slowly. "Mr. Knause," I said, "I would like to talk to you about making staves." "Oh, my Gott," he said, "I'm too old for that!" We did, however, have a rewarding visit with him.

Everyone who mentioned the Slavonians said they were good workers and hard drinkers. We were also told, as Mr. Racki surmised, that they put whiskey in their drinking water, but he tells us differently. In any case, they drank a lot of liquor and made a lot of staves.

THE SLAVONIAN STAVE MAKERS

As Told by Peter Racki

The Slavonians came from the state of Croatia before Austria
and Hungary busted up after World War I. It included Austria and
what is now Yugoslavia. The part where the stave makers came
from is Yugoslavia. My daddy's name was Matthew ("Matt"), and
he came from the old country around 1900. Me and my mother
didn't come to America till three or four years after my daddy. He
worked for the other fellow about four years and then lit out on
his own, and at one time he had just a little short of a hundred on
the payroll, Slavonians.

The Slavonians didn't come as groups, just come as individuals. Some of them work a year or two, go home and spend the
summer with the folks, and come back again. It wasn't very hard
to come and go then, just slow travel was all. They left over there
'cause they couldn't make a living. Five acres was a devil of a big
farm, and I've seen five crops on one acre, little patch, just little
old valleys between the mountains. Most of them had a wife and
family in Europe.

They loved their eatin' and drinkin'. There was one thing they
didn't do, which you've probably been told, was carry their liquor
to the stump, tree, where they's workin'. Them little kegs they
had was water kegs, and I've drunk out of 'em a million times,
and they didn't put liquor in their drinking water. When they was
workin' they wouldn't get drunk, unless it was on a weekend.
When they got up in the morning, they had a big slug of whiskey,
come in at dinner they had one, come in at night they had one,
and sometimes, before they went to bed. Every once in a while
they'd pull a drunk; they did a lot of drinking.

Before prohibition one of them had a birthday and he went
down to Beaumont and got him a suitcase full of liquor and
brought it back there. They started celebratin', and he heard
another crew working not far away and he took two quarts and
went over there. I followed him just to see what the devil was
goin' to happen, and when he got in sight of them, he said,
"Look what I got." One old man throwed down his tools and

Pete Mihelich

started; the rest of them followed and went to the camp and proceeded to get drunk.

They made no effort to do much work in summertime. All they wanted to do was make expenses, but when it got September first, now they cracked down, started at four o'clock in the morning, and all day at it, worked hard, terrible hard workers.

They felled their timber early in the morning because it was cooler. There was two to the saw, old crosscut saws. They'd cut enough blocks to last them that day, then one would do the splittin', one would use the froe and rive them out rough, and then the next fellow would hew the bark off of them and chip them up on the heart side; then the last fellow, he'd draw them off with the drawing knife. They used to work with two, but really four was a standard crew.

They were very economical, something to eat and it wasn't fancy food, only staple stuff. Squirrel was about all they ever hunted, few deer, whatever happened to be where they was workin'. They'd hire the stave haulers to bring their groceries for them. One time they come out there with five mule teams and I mean good ones, too, and three of them hauled liquor and two of them hauled groceries. I saw that.

They got a payday about the first of September, and then they got a big payday the first of June. I've seen the time my daddy carried forty-five hundred dollars in cash into the woods, paid them off, and some of them wasn't very well learned. Everything was split even. Time they got through dividing it, we brought back to town that evenin' forty-two hundred dollars. They didn't keep but three hundred dollars in cash; said put it in the bank for me. They looked to dad for that, too. If he'd lost it, it would have been his hard luck.

There was no boss among the crew but they always had a leader. I've seen where they'd put a thousand dollars out there on the table, divide it, five for you, five for you, five for you, five for me, and like that till it played out. If there was any odd amount in it, why they'd throw it in the pot, buy shotgun shells. Everybody paid for them whether he hunted or not, for they all eat what was killed.

We had one guy come to town and dad paid him off by check and told him where to get it cashed, and he went up there and handed his check to the cashier. You remember when money come in sheets? These banks got it in sheets lots of times, like stamps, and the cashier started cutting it off. Well, this old fellow, he picked up his check and come back to dad and said, "I don't want none of that money they're makin' up there." They went all over town to get enough old paper money to pay him.

This country gets so wet we've had staves to wash away after they was on the railroad. We had four carloads of them one time. Had terrible rains! Somebody on the train knew dad, said, "Matt, I

Peter Racki

see you moved your staves." He said, "Why, no, I ain't moved nothin'." Next day he said to me, "You better go see what that fellow's talkin' about." There was five staves left where they was stacked. They didn't go over a quarter of a mile, but they weren't stacked! Snakes and staves was all piled together!

Never found any substitute for oak barrels in the wine industry, charred oak barrels. Scotland's using a lot of them now for whiskey, but the primary business started for wine barrels in France. Now this country used a sawed stave. You take a tree and bust it up in quarters, where a man could handle them. Dad had a mill out here in the Thicket, and he had a saw that would make that stave come out concave, shape of a barrel. Now that was a domestic stave, what they call bourbons. They worked as well, but for a long time Europe wouldn't have a sawed stave, and it is just the last few years that Europe has taken some of them.

There are a few being made all over the country, but it has gone down because the white oak was cut out, the freight rates went out of sight, and we lost the market we used to have for culls, for seconds. There's a bug that gets in white oak trees, not all of them, little bitty bugs that make real small holes in the wood. A stave with these holes in it is a cull, wine would leak through, but they could be used for the heavier liquids like palm olive oil and different kinds of syrup, things like that; but now there's no market, and we have to absorb all that. And before World War I, France shipped wine over here in big barrels and it was bottled here, but now they bottle it over there.

Born 1897, interviewed 1975.

As Told by Anton ("Tony") Knause

I was born in old Austria, January 10, 1889. I come to America October second, 1906, just come here to make a living. I had a brother and I joined vith him ven I come from old country. He vas Joe. My Daddy come here this country 1902 and my brother Joe come 1904. There was five of us brothers, ve all come. Daddy and Joe didn't stay, but the rest, ve all stayed.

Most of stave makers vas married, but they leave her home. They just come, know there's jobs here open. I explain you that. Austria-Hungary nation vas little larger than state of Texas, and state of Texas didn't have more than about two million people ven I come over here, and there vas forty-eight million in Austria. Ven United States gets that many they going to starve to death. Go to the moon? I don't believe anybody ever been up there. You can't convince me on that 'tall. I don't believe it.

Ve made staves back home. I cooked for the stave makers there. I vent first time in the voods ven I vas thirteen years old. I cooked for thirteen men five months. Mostly ve ate cornmeal and beans and sauerkraut. Here, ate eggs and rice and bacon for breakfast. For the other meals ve alvays buy the beef, cook beef or pork. Ve hunt good smart, but not vorkin' day, just on Saturday evenin' and Sunday. Vild hogs, biggest hogs I ever saw vas between Kountze and Sour Lake. Ve kept dogs at the camp, but mighty little. Ve couldn't keep it hardly. Most of the time a hog killed them. You got to have a very special dog for the hog, cur dog.

Ve built the camp. Cut the tree and sawed them up in the blocks and split it, make a big shingle out of it. Ve made it thirty-six inches long, shingle boards. That's vot ve built the camp vith, make roof out of it and sides and all. Summertime ve build a kitchen, cookin' space outside, live in one side and cook in other place. Ve had opening at the top for the smoke to get out. Sleep under a mosquito bar. Ve buy cots in the store, folding cots, and just put one mattress on the top. Ve had a place in the middle and keep fire in there ven it vas cold, about six feet long. You know there vas four corners in the camp house, one man each corner, and middle vas just fireplace for the heat in the vintertime. In the vintertime ve cooked on that, too. Room vas about sixteen feet long and fourteen vide.

The man ve vorked for had a foreman inspected the staves in the voods. Ve vouldn't let them go, no sir, don't trust nobody. Ve get the money for the staves before anyone vas moved. Stumpage got to be paid and labor for makin'. Most of time ve got paid ven ve got through. One time I vorked thirteen months vitout the pay. I believe I got four hundred sixty-four dollars. Thirteen months, that's a long vait. Buy the groceries on credit in the

store. Thirty-six inch staves usually get thirty dollars a thousand pieces, that be three dollars a hundred.

I seen a voman born the kids out there in the camp. Her husband help her, didn't have no doctor at all. Man come here stay two, three years, and then send money back there and she come behind him. They live in the voods vith them. Mighty few had citizenship, I tell you. Most of them vent back home anyvay, but some of them live here all their life and never did have 'em. I took out citizenship papers. I never been back to old country. My parents died 1924. I marry girl from here, Hemphill; she vas a Carter.

Snakes! I've seen so many of them, killed so many of them, all kinds. I killed one had twenty-two rattles. None of us ever got bit. You know vat I saw, man done it, surely he done it just accidentally, valkin' on the logs, across the creek, and that moccasin layin' out there in a coil on the log and ven he open up that mouth, man vas chewin' heavy, you know, had a big old chew tobacco, and he spit right in his mouth, and, you know, that tobacco killed that moccasin. I can show you place vere he done it. He spit that chew in his mouth, he grab it and swallow it, dropped down in the vater, he vas just rolling. I look at him, I vas vith him. Moccasin fightin' heself for his life, he die right there. Tobacco kill him.

I vas used to being in the voods, but some places here you couldn't go through at all vitout a hack knife, make a trail, vines, briers, ti-ti. It vas a svamp, but in summertime, sometimes you can't get a drink of vater novere. In all that country there's no drop of vater. In vintertime standing in vater, foot deep in mud, and ve vorked in that. I vore out two pair rubber boots in thirteen months, but vas on my foot every day in the vater that deep. Put the house on ridge, little ridges look like they blown up vith gas or something, mounds; ve built it right on top of it. It vas boggy through that country. The mosquitoes, oh, they vas bad. In the camp ve always burn vood, smoke. In the night ve slept under mosquito bar. You can't stay vitout 'em. Ve had malaria, plenty. Just go to common doctor like all the rest of them. Quinine, go back to the camp. Help one each other. Not able take care himself, ve feed him.

Born 1889, interviewed 1975–1976.

Anton Knause

Arden Hooks

Introducing Arden Hooks

Arden Hooks is a well-educated man with deep roots in the woods of Hardin County. The Hooks name is almost synonymous with the Big Thicket, and Arden's daddy, Bud Hooks, was one of the most beloved persons who ever lived there.

When I first came to the Thicket I heard the story that Arden attended Harvard a couple of years but it didn't "take," and he came back home, put on his overalls, and hasn't taken them off since. It isn't true. He did go East for studies in electronics, found it interesting, liked it, but for personal reasons decided to give it up; and, though he doesn't wear overalls, he habitually wears khaki trousers, cap, and shirt, which is generally known as his "uniform."

Arden is a philosopher at heart. Stanley Coe, district attorney, says Arden used to sit in the top of the huge cypress trees near the old Hooks home and meditate for hours at a time. Arden agreed but said it was usually to get away from a house full of company, and sometimes he read, or meditated, and sometimes he slept, being careful to find a place in the crotch of the tree so he would not fall out. He does not just see or hear—he ponders. "Just looking at an armadillo makes a man think a long time," he once remarked.

He is the only man I ever knew who chews tobacco but never spits. "When I get to feeling sorry for myself, I just change my tobacco to the other side, and it makes everything all right, seems to help me."

Most people in the Thicket were hunters, and Arden is a hunter too, but he never kills anything. He has no heart for killing, but he is none the less a woodsman, for keen observation and a knowledge of the outdoors are just as important in his sport as in killing a bear or a bobcat. Coursing bees is his hobby, which he calls a science and an art. Although he is recognized as an expert bee man, it is obvious that his main satisfaction comes from just being in the woods. His gentle philosophy filters through as he discusses his favorite recreation.

ARDEN HOOKS

As a boy I was on a farm. It didn't make anyone's living. It was a very inefficient one, but I enjoyed lots of it, soaked it up. Had ambitions along in the early twenties and went up north with the idea of doing research work in electronics. Got a job in the Thompson Laboratory in the suburbs of Boston—G. E. Thompson Laboratory—and just the thing I wanted to do for years, but it went stale on me. And being young and not having any better sense, I quit and came back down here. Another thing, the winters up there started a little too early to suit me and quit a little too late in the spring. I've never regretted leaving up there, but I would have been very successful had I stayed on, in a worldly way. Dollars are a whole lot more powerful than they should be.

My hobby is coursing bees—hunting bee trees. Coursing bees to find their honey has been a human occupation for thousands of years. That was the only form of sweetening we had until some of the plant sweeteners came from the Middle East, about the Middle Ages, I think—sugar beets or sugar cane. I remember one of the American pioneers, Bowie or Boone or Crockett, visited northeast Texas in the early days, and he said, "It is a fair land, plenty of game and honey." And you know the old biblical description of a good land is "a land of milk and honey."

Animals find lots of bee trees. I don't know how, by smell, maybe. I remember my Uncle Ben showed us boys a tree in the woods once, with fresh claw marks on it. He said, "That's where a bear recently climbed to rob that bee tree." We looked up there and the bees were all disturbed, swarming around on the outside. So animals like their sweetening, too. Coons love it. They say a coon will even rob a yellow jacket nest for their honey. It takes lots of guts. They're bound to get stung a good deal.

One or two things I'd like to bring out is the fallacy of this bee-line theory. They'll go around a thick place in order to find an open route to their tree. So when you're watching them leave your bait, you better check out there a piece, fifty or more feet out. Get out there, and of course you need lots of bees on the bait, and look up and you can see little black dots going away, and after you're out sufficiently far from the bait, you can see that they have avoided those bushes or thick trees, or whatever it is, then you can depend on that course being straight. Any bend in their course would be fairly close to the bait, or sometimes to their tree. I found a tree, and I had previously walked the course out, Jerry Anderson and I had, without finding the tree and we kept on walking the course. So I went back later and put another bait out a little farther along on the course and noticed they were on course all right, and I was delighted, and I went out there about seventy-five feet and looked up at them and lo and behold they were making almost a right-angle bend going into their tree. Jerry and I had walked about seventy feet past that tree, following a true course. But they'll take advantage of an opening. I've seen them go to a tree, a close tree particularly, with a thick bunch of shrubbery there on the tree, and part of them will go around it on one side and part on the other. We call that a split course. They all come together at the tree. If they've got a forest to go through, and far to go, they'll get high. If they don't have, they'll pick their way around. A windy day seems to make them fly lower, too. I guess the foliage may protect them from the wind a little bit, I don't know. There aren't many places down here where they could fly a straight course and fly low.

Another thing many people have overlooked—a bee when he first finds that bait is a little bit interested in it, but cautious, but he'll finally get in there and fill up. When he leaves he'll circle, about the first three trips. He'll make from two to six circles, trying to orient himself, and it's a sure sign that he plans to come back, too. There's very little use trying to course them at that stage of the game. You've got to wait until they've made enough trips, until they've picked the shortest course, then it's reasonably straight. After that first bee has made two or three trips, usually others begin to come. He does his little dance, or whatever it is he does at the hive, and lets them know. After that you see an increasing number of bees.

For bait I use sugar and water, no particular proportion, just so it isn't too thick and syrupy. If it's too syrupy, they'll get it on themselves and can't fly off without cleaning themselves up. It kinda goos them up. It's highly liquid—all the sugar you can get in water without making it syrupy. And it's good on a new loca-tion to mix a little honey with it, because the smell will attract them. There's very little smell to sugar. The bees are attracted by smell. That's the way they find it, odor. The surest way to get them, and the quickest, is to take some of that same solution, your sugar water with some honey added for odor, and go around to the small trees and bushes and dip some limbs in it and let them fly back up. That scatters a little bit out in the air. Some coursers have a variation on that. They take a mouthful of honey, chew it up and spit it out on a bush; same thing only another system. A passing bee will smell that and he'll check himself and turn around and start hunting it. They'll find it on the plants first, and then, eventually, as new ones come in, they don't know where it is, one or two of them will smell it first in the bait can, and when they go to that bait can, they'll fill that thing up pretty quick. If you're close to their tree, or if there are a number of bee trees around, they'll eat it up in thirty or forty minutes.

Another interesting thing, they're completely harmless when they're feeding on bait. They won't sting you unless you mash one of them or unless he gets tangled in the hair on your arm. They'll crawl all over you. Makes me think of one time when I went over to the bait and there was a hornet. He crawled on my arm, and I had considerable misgivings, but nothing happened. But all kinds of things are attracted: hornets, yellow jackets, wasps; I've seen those three things. When you toss the bait in the air a certain amount is suspended in the air just like moisture in any form, and when they fly through that particular part of the air, they can't help smelling it. Our ideal bait can is an old-time coffee can, with a big opening and not too high; gives them more room to get out. You put in one or two cups of bait, no certain amount. Wouldn't hurt to fill it, but you must also put some small dry twigs in there for them to light on when they get it; otherwise, they'll get in there and fall around and some of them will drown, and the rest of them will come out all stuck up with the stuff and they can't fly away. Just let the twigs float in there.

The crows got a bad habit. I'd like to know whether it is curiosity or if they're catching bees. If the place is real open, they'll come to a bee bait and knock it off the stand. Alec Work devised a good stand. He's one of my bee-hunting buddies. It's just simply a stick with a little piece of flat wood on top. You take your machete and drill a little hole in the ground and put it in there, tamp it, and you've got this flat piece of wood, probably six inches square, anywhere from two to four feet above the ground, and this way you can see the bees better as they leave the bait. A stump makes an excellent place if it doesn't have any ants in it.

I'll tell you another thing that's a little bit useful—you can time those rascals if you'll get that first bee and notice the time he leaves. I got started timing them with a cigarette—you can boil it down to minutes, though. A modern cigarette burns about eight minutes. And it takes about four minutes for him to unload and tell the others about his find, and his traveling time both ways is just about a hundred yards a minute. In other words, he makes just about two hundred yards a minute, a hundred going and a hundred coming back. If it takes a full cigarette time to make that return trip, you can figure that's about four hundred yards from your bait to the tree. The best way is just to watch that first bee, because he's going to make two or three trips before the rest of them come. Two hundred yards a minute is about what he'll make. You can pretty closely calculate how far that tree is.

Another trick we use in trying to find them—we get some hard ones we can't find—if the course is going a certain direction, we'll get way off to one side, get the course from there, and from where the two courses cross, we're usually within a hundred yards of where the tree is. I remember one we had, northeast of here, that was particularly hard to find, and I pulled that stunt on them. We put a bait where the two courses came together and left, figuring they'd hit the next morning. I came back and sure enough there were lots of bees on it, and they were all going northeast. I felt I had it straightened out, so I started out to follow the course, and over there about thirty or forty feet they were flying up sharply over some shrubbery and then dipping down to go into a tree about a foot above the ground. That shows you how close that triangulation will get you.

Now the most wonderful trick in the book is this: After you've gotten your first course, and you've walked out there about a quarter of a mile and haven't found them, catch a pretty good bunch of bees in your bait can and throw your handkerchief over the can so they can't get away. Take it in one hand and your stand and machete in the other and move up on that course anywhere from two hundred yards to four hundred, and put that stand down again and set your bait on it and take your handkerchief off. Well, they'll scatter like a bunch of quail. Some of them will circle around as they leave, and they're the ones that will come back, and they'll hit that bait again anywhere from five minutes to an hour after you make that move, and you're that much closer to the tree. You can find practically any tree by moving your bait. It's a tremendous advantage.

We noticed another thing in that connection—if you go too far and pass the tree, it may take them two days to find that bait again. They've gotten used to the idea of going a certain direction, I guess, and they don't think it can be on the opposite side. I don't know how to explain it. But when they drop that bait you can figure you've passed their tree. You can have them working from any number of baits—same tree.

Hugh Roberts and I were bee hunting west of town here—Alec Work had found a bee tree in there. After they found our bait, we trapped some of the bees in the bait can and deliberately carried them farther away from their tree. Those bees make a sound and leave a smell in there, and surrounding bees will detect it and come to the bait quicker—bees from another bee tree—so we carried those bees with us, and those things followed us over two miles, so we got so tired of them we just stopped. They might have gone farther. They were great eaters and had a big population, and they'd almost crowd the bees from the new courses away. But as long as they kept coming to the bait, they'd attract bees from surrounding trees by their circling and their noise and the odor they leave in the air. But it's a good way to find bees in a new country.

The native bee seems to be a little black bee, and the so-called Italian bee is a larger bee and yellow, and he's better tempered, too. Those little black ones will sometimes keep you from robbing them, and they're very effective honey makers, more so than the tame ones. You find as much variation in the temper of bees as you do in human beings. I don't rob bees, I just find them. I just turn it over to those who want the honey. I get my fun out of finding them, and they have the honey, and the bees will have a better place to live. The modern hive, you know, it's perfect; it's designed for bees. It's better than any tree they could find.

The plants they work most here in the Thicket are holly, blackberries, rattan, and the Chinese tallow tree. They love them, and huckleberries. I've never seen one feeding on honeysuckle or a big flower of any kind. They like the little flowers. There are two or three little hedge-type plants that they like very much, too. The first thing they start feeding on in the spring is maple blooms, and the second is mayhaw, and from then on it's good bee hunting. They're very active, and they're able to multiply and have more foragers. If it is above sixty degrees, they'll come out promptly, and they're just as good as the best thermometer.

There are some things we don't completely know about. They get nectar and pollen; that's their two main foods. And they get something from the ground. I've seen them watering a long way from the tree, with plenty of water closer by, and the usual thing is for them to water at the nearest place. In fact, when you find a bee's water you consider that you've found a bee tree, because that's the closest water to the tree, and he's traveled it so many times he's got the course straightened out. Where water seeps out of a bank, that's an ideal bee-watering spot. They don't want it standing on the ground, but they want it moist. They can get it through those little capillaries somehow from the ground. They light, and it takes about a minute for them to get water—about the same time as it takes for them to get their food.

Up at Alec's place, that tree was about two hundred yards off and just surrounded by water holes, but they were watering at a little moist spot on the ground. I think they get something out of the ground. I don't know what, some mineral they need, possibly. And just recently, out here I found a hive in my cypress tree, right in the middle of Cypress Creek where they'd have unlimited water, and I found them watering three hundred yards away and going to that tree. They were getting something besides water there. Usually they will get the closest water they can find. I've seen them just drop down out of a tree close to the creek. They always get on something solid; they don't light on the water and drink. They like moist ground to get water from.

One of the best ways to find a bee tree is to take a boat like your canoe and go up any stream big enough to navigate and watch for them watering on the bank. If you see them getting water, that's the reliable cue.

When a bunch of bees hatches out and the hive gets too many bees, then they swarm, part of them leaves. We've had a little unusual experience this year in connection with swarming; they swarmed a little early and we know of two hives that sent out three swarms within a month's time. If you hit your hoes together, or make a bunch of racket, this will cause bees to swarm, to settle on something. If they're in the air, flying over, you can make noise—now Travis Hare said he can make them settle just by starting a power saw and running it a minute. He's a bee man, too. It must be the vibration and it interferes with some other vibration and it makes them want to get together until it's all over and they reorganize. I haven't had as much experience getting them to settle as some of my hunting buddies.

Alec Work, Lester Holmes, L. G. Roberts, Jerry Anderson, James Hargrove, Carol Beacon, Travis Hare—there's a bunch of us. Most of these folks keep the honey. They like it. I like it all right, but it's a little bit too rich. I can't eat too much of it. I've already got my thrill out of it before the honey's on the table. I feel like I did the bees some good and the people some good, too.

It's almost certain that man used honey in prehistoric times. I imagine they got honey before they killed game of any size, because it was easier to get and certainly very plentiful at that time.

One nice thing, if you have more than one man, is for one man to follow the course either by compass or by sun, and just forget about finding the bee tree, just keep on the course; and a man on each flank about a hundred feet to the side. They'll look for the trees and you can keep the course. We use the compass frequently. When the sun is shining, though, I use the sun. I'll take my machete and either face the sun and put the machete at right angles, or face my shadow and put the machete at right angles, then eyeball it into halves and quarters. It's fairly accurate.

I would guess that the average distance from the bait to the bee tree would be three quarters of a mile. We have a tract of land over here west of town, and our cousins own the other half of it. It's a section of land, 640 acres, and I found sixteen trees on that tract in one year, 40 acres per tree, which would make them an average of a quarter of a mile apart. For modern times I imagine that's pretty high density. At one time I don't think that would have been considered high.

We don't like to cut a tree after May. That won't give the bees time to store up enough for winter. Before that time, you get your honey and your bee gets his food too. Not an undue strain on him to go after some more. A lot of this is handed down from father to son, Campbell, and no telling for how many hundred years. It's ingrained in us, just like tilling the soil and clearing land. Just think how long we've done that!

I'll never forget the early days of the sawmills in this country; they'd be logging these virgin pines, come to a big old red-hearted pine with bees in it, maybe seventy-five or eighty feet above the ground. Somebody would holler "Bee tree!" and they'd shut down the works. Those grown men would become boys, and to heck with the job; and they'd cut that tree and all of the whooping and hollering and having fun that took place! Somebody always got stung. They didn't save the bees. They just let them go and they didn't have much regard for the time of year. They'd cut them any time they found them; they got the honey and ate it on the spot. They didn't have a storage problem.

There is a slight indication that a bee prefers height. I think on account of animals robbing them and on account of high water. In this country they like pin oaks and water oaks better than any. When these trees get a little age on them, they begin to get rotten, doty, and develop knotholes and hollows in them. That might be the reason they prefer them. But you'll find them in all kinds of trees. Seldom in solid trees, say a live oak, for instance. Find them in cypress, pine—they used to love the old virgin, longleaf, redheart pine. Hardly ever find them in the pine any-more since those are nearly gone. Some in white oak, cow oak and post oak, occasionally, and sometimes in magnolia and occasionally in hickory, but not often.

Alec and Jerry got one out of the woods the other night—they move after dark so all the workers will be home and in the hive. Alec knew they were bad and he told Jerry they were bad. Jerry said, "Well, I'll trade you such and such a hive for those bees." They made the trade and went out there after them. Through some mistake or other there was a hole in the back of their hive, and those bees started filtering out and stinging them. He thought he had them in the hive. The hive has some slots in there for air circulation, and they put a little board over the main entrance when they got the bees inside.

It's interesting to watch them transfer the bees from the tree to the hive. I intend to do some of it, later on, when I'm ninety-four. They'll tap on that hive and reach over and grab a handful of bees, throw them on the front porch, and usually they'll crawl in it, the entrance, go into that dark place, you know. It's an ideal house for a bee, so they like it when they once get in it. The whole secret seems to be to get the queen in there. If they don't get her in there right away, she'll fly off up there to a tree, and the other bees will find out where she is and cluster around her, like they do in swarms, you know. It will be a pear-shaped cluster anywhere from a quart to two gallons in size.

They've got gloves on usually, but some of them will work them with their bare hands. Alec Work is one of the best I ever saw at that. He'll go in there with his sleeves rolled up, no hat, bareheaded lots of times. They can tell when a bee is mad by the sound they make. I can't. They'll holler out there to me—I'll be hid forty to a hundred feet away in the bushes, "Better run, Arden, they're mad," and about that time I'll hear them slapping. They don't hurt them, because they're wrapped up, usually. Alex is an exception. It all depends on the temperament of that particular set of bees and also on their mood at the moment. If they're smooth-natured bees and nothing happens to make them mad, then they can just handle them like they want to, rake them in, pour them in there. I'm talking about the folks that do the robbing. They're also hunters.

One real serious brush with bee stings and they'll keep away from bees. They seldom get stung badly. I think I'm one that gets stung more than others. They don't hurt me. They're about like these marsh mosquitoes down there, but I just don't enjoy the sensation too much, anyway.

The way I got to hunting bees—I had some honey out in the yard here and noticed the bees on it. And I recalled the old days when my dad and my uncle would hunt them. I said to myself, "I believe I'll course those bees," and I coursed them and they went off down that way and I told L. G. Roberts about it. He has an eye like an eagle, incidentally, and we found those bees down there on the brush, and we got to talking, and he told me about trees he found, and I finally got to putting out bait other places, and it wasn't long before I was head over heels in the game. The main enjoyment I get out of it, well, it's like searching for anything else of value, and it's not a cinch; that also makes it interesting, and it's partly an art. You have to exert your skills and patience. It takes lots of patience and, you know, it's a constructive thing, too. It's good for the bees and good for the people who get the honey. But it's just like searching for gold or Easter eggs or squirrel hunting. By the way, squirrel hunters make the best finders in the world. They are used to looking up in the trees and detecting the slightest move. They seem to have a natural eye for bees.

It's my excuse for getting out in the woods. You have a world of fun there. Why, I've found more new plants while bee hunting, and seen more interesting things in the woods. You have lots of time. In fact, time is hanging on your hands. Requires a lot of patience and waiting. The longest wait is waiting for them to come to the bait, then determining what the true course is, and then as you go through the woods looking for the bee tree, you'll see any number of other interesting things, but you don't feel

rushed at that business at all. It's a game of patience and deliber-
ation. Very often I've cut me a bush and bent it over a certain way,
so I'll know the spot, and then pursue some other interest. And I'll
remember my course, north thirty-two degrees, or whatever it is. I
use surveyor's terms, not the seafaring.

Some more flowers I didn't mention to you are corn silks, corn
tassels, makes some of the best honey we have in this country.
Flower gardens and vegetable gardens, they feed in them till the
world looks level, but corn and rattan and holly honey are supposed to be about the best honey we have in this area. You'll
think you've found either a bee tree or a swarm of bees when
they're feeding on that holly, they're making such a roar in the
tree.

My favorite bee-hunting season is July, because they're making lots of noise at that tree. When you walk out on the course,
lots of times it's so thick you can't see the bottom of a tree, or
someplace where they're going in may be crowded with limbs,
but you can hear them in July. There's no blossoms then that
they are particularly fond of, so they hit the bait good. And they'll
roar at the tree. I don't know whether it's because of the heat's
just coming on—they're not that way in August, which is usually
a hotter month than July—or whether they have more bees out
working. I don't know what it is, but anytime I find a hive in July,
they're always just a-roarin'. I like to hear 'em.

My grandfather William Hooks came here in 1848 or '49 from
Early County, Georgia, and settled on the bank of the Neches
River, opposite Weiss Bluff. I believe he made the last part of his
trip by boat. Weiss Bluff was a port on the river. Weiss was an
interesting old gentleman—Simon Weiss. He was a Polish Jew
who came here in the early days of Texas and went all over the
country from New Orleans to various parts of Texas, and he had
a lot of money. He married a Sturrock in Louisiana. Those folks
were a little bit suspicious of him. They hadn't known him long,
and they made him put up something like thirty thousand acres
of land before they'd let him marry their daughter. But he had a
bunch of descendants, and most of them were very successful in
business. One of them was president of the Humble Oil Company for a while, grandson of Simon's.

Anyway, my grandpap settled near Weiss Bluff on what is
known as Belreaux Slough, and my Uncle Davis declares that the
only meat they had that winter—a dog treed a squirrel, and they
cut the tree down, and the dog caught the squirrel for them. I
don't see how they could hope to live without a gun to kill game.

Pap, my grandfather, was very likable, had everybody's respect. He was short built, but powerfully made and not given to
anything showy. He used to work without anything on but one
garment, a shirt—no hat, no underwear, no trousers, no shoes. I
guess it was a concession to civilization or he wouldn't have worn

the shirt. Old man John Simms would come up that road from Concord with the mail and if it was noon hour, why, he said Pap would be sitting out there under a tree with nothing on but a shirt, maybe readin' the "Galveston News."

Lev Roberts, who was later on sheriff as long as he wanted to be, he married Pap's daughter, Dode, and they had a fuss and parted. Later they made an appointment to meet at Pap's house to see if they could settle the quarrel. My grandmother wanted everything to go smooth so they could get back together, so when she saw Lev comin' she sent Pap some clothes to the field by one of the children, thinking he would take the hint and wear his clothes when he came in. When it came time for him to quit he just came in whistling as cheerful as you please and the clothes draped over his arm. There's been some question about how long the shirt was, but according to old man Simms, it wasn't too long.

I don't know how Pap came to this part of the country, but Uncle Auss, his brother, started out with an ox wagon and one of the oxen died, and he lost his temper and knocked the other one in the head and walked back to Georgia. He came here later. I describe Uncle Auss's bunch, not all of them, as people who made their own rules as they went along. They didn't go by anyone else's rules; they just rigged up a set. I always called them the river-bottom strain.

Gus Hooks, one of Uncle Auss's sons, raised two families. He married one of the Durham sisters and lived with both of them—separate houses and separate families, across the field from each other. After all, polygamy has been in this world more years than it's been out. I always think about Sarah and Hagar. What I noticed first was, Abraham, when he went through Egypt, I believe he wanted his wife to pose as his sister. Well, Sarah had no children and she suggested to Abraham that he see if he could have children with Hagar, a servant, and he did. Then Sarah's version is that Hagar grew haughty, so Sarah hated her very much. Sarah in the meantime had a child, and right now the descendants of Sarah and Hagar are still fighting. The Arabs came from Hagar's side, they're all Semitic.

I've always wondered, suppose our forefathers were coming to this country and lost their ax, the most useful tool they could have, dropped it in the water crossing some deep river. Why, that would be a major catastrophe. Of course, they had already burned their bridges behind them; they had to go on and do what they set out to do, but it certainly took courage. And guns and powder and lead for bullets was scarce for many of them. I remember the Browns, in comparatively recent times, fifty, sixty years ago, the head of the family would give a certain number of cartridges to this son and so many to that one, and he had to have some game for a cartridge. You'd find that one man in every family did nothing but hunt. I think of two instances: Uncle Buck in my dad's family, he'd fool with cows, but he wouldn't work a field, things like that, just hunt; and my dad's cousin, Henry Hooks, he would hunt and go around through the woods drawing beautiful pictures on the beech trees, turkeys and quail and what have you, and he made out someway.

My daddy, Bud Hooks—Henry Allen was his name—he was the youngest member of the family, and the biggest one, physically. He was affable and carefree, just like his father. He didn't worry till later years. He was no manager of his finances. He knew how to make investments and profit from them, but he spent money like water. Unlike his mother's side of the family, the Colliers, he didn't have an ounce of thrift about him. His financial worries hit him in his later years, only worrying I ever saw him do. They used to say that if God was as good as dad, we had it made.

1900–1976, interviewed 1970–1975.

Dr. John Richard
Bevil

Introducing Dr. John Richard Bevil

Dr. Bevil practiced medicine in the Batson–Sour Lake area for three quarters of a century. He is about five feet eleven, medium build, with a ready smile and kindly disposition, a living example of the old-time family doctor. One just couldn't imagine Dr. Bevil inquiring about a family's ability to pay, or withholding, for any reason whatever, a service he could render. He is beloved by all who know him as a good doctor and a good man, and it wouldn't be an exaggeration to say that, at one time, half the babies born in the western half of Hardin County were named after him. There are more "John R.'s" than any other name in the county.

On our last visit he received a phone call, and when he finished, he said, "That call was from a 'baby' I delivered seventy-two years ago. It's his birthday, and he was calling to wish me a good day, too."

One does not talk to Dr. Bevil long without recognizing his high regard for women. It is easily inferred that, in his opinion, women are responsible for man's finer achievements. "Women's Lib is nothing new," he said. "Women have always told man what to do. In the Garden of Eden woman told man what to do, and he did it, and he's been doing it ever since. I observed that when my daddy talked plans over with my mother, they usually turned out right, but when he didn't they often failed."

Dr. Bevil is fond of poetry and can recite it from memory for hours, ranging from Robert Browning to Sara Teasdale. His active mind, varied interests, and vigorous health belie his ninety-six years in a rugged environment. Only recently has he given up riding his horse and caring for his cattle. "My daddy always taught me that work never hurt nobody. I'm ninety-six. I was still driving a car when I was ninety, and I'd go to my farm and build fences and clear up land, ride my horse and brand cattle. It was exercise and relaxation and I enjoyed it. I sold my cattle a couple of years ago, and I can't drive a car because of my eyes, and I've had to slow down some."

The last time we saw him he was planning a trip to Kerrville to get a truckload of peaches. "I've found," he said, "that people like peaches about as much as anything I can give them, and those Kerrville peaches are fine, the best I've found. My son is going to drive the truck and we're going after a load, and I'm going to give them to my friends." The trip to Kerrville and back was 350 miles, but he made the trip and got the peaches—a small thing to do for his friends.

DR. JOHN RICHARD BEVIL

I've lived in this section of the country all my life. My mother was a Hart, daughter of Jeff Hart, granddaughter of William Hart, who organized the government of Hardin County. His sons and sons-in-law were its first officers. They moved to a location on Village Creek, just above Kountze, in 1853. When they crossed Village Creek it very much resembled the river where they had lived in Alabama. In crossing it they found a lot of switch cane, which was very good grazing for cattle in the winter, kept them fat, and horses also. There were a lot of acorns for hogs and there were deer and turkey, and plenty to eat. So William Hart stopped and bought a section of land there. It was bought from a private individual. Gold was used nearly altogether. I remember the time there was very little money in the country, and there was as much gold as there was silver or currency. They built a house there, and the house is there now, the old Gwynes' place. That old oak tree there is over a hundred years of age. They lived there till the Civil War. My mother was playing in the yard, in 1863, when they had the battle of Sabine Pass, and she heard the bugles. My mother said that my grandmother cried.

Zack Gwynes married William Hart's baby daughter. They built a church there that had a main auditorium and a side auditorium, one side for white folks and one side for the niggers. That settlement was called Old Providence. When William Hart came from Alabama, he brought with him Zack Gwynes and Richard Teal and Fletcher Cotton and Dan Overstreet. But Dan Overstreet didn't stay there, and he went on over into Polk County, and half of Polk County are Overstreets. Fletcher Cotton was married to one of the older Hart girls. Dick Teal married another one. Another man married his daughter Sarah. Grandfather Hart had forbid her to have anything to do with him, but she went off with him. He put her on his horse behind him and they went to West Texas, and that family is still out there.

We trace our history, on my father's side, back to the time the Normans overrun Great Britain in about the year 1000. One of the Bevils had charge of the execution of Mary Queen of the

Scots. Elizabeth demanded it, you know. The Bevils had two brothers and they criticized it, so their life wasn't worth much, and they come to Mecklenburg County, Virginia. We follow them on up to Jasper, and I am John Bevil the Fifth, and John Bevil was one of the signers of the Declaration of Independence of Texas, and was one of the legislators.

When Stephen F. Austin got his privilege to come and settle here in Texas, why, he was allowed a league and a labor of land. A single man only got a labor; that's 177 acres. A league is 4,280 acres.

While John Bevil lived at Bevilport, out from Jasper, he was riding into Jasper one morning, and he had a very good horse, bridle, and saddle. And in those days you never passed anybody you met on the road without stopping and talking to them, because there was no other means of communication. There was no telephone, hardly any newspapers. There was a little telegraph, but that was on the railroad. But, anyhow, they got to talking, and the man said, "That's a good horse you got; you want to sell him?" John Bevil said, "No." Well," the stranger said, "I'd like to have that horse, and I'll give you a league and a labor of land for him." He said, "The horse isn't worth that much. That's just too much." "Well," he said, "I've received this league and a labor of land. I'm a married man, and I'm on the road now to go to see my wife and daughter that's three hundred miles from here. That horse will be a great help to me, but that land's not worth anything to me." And they went into Jasper and he deeded to him that league and labor of land for his horse and bridle and saddle.

Daddy wasn't but three months older than my mother and they ran away and married when they were eighteen, and I'm their fourth child. There were two sisters older than me and one brother. This brother died before I was born. I was born up there about seven miles below Woodville and we lived up there. My daddy moved from Twin Lakes to Saratoga when I was about four years of age and built a sawmill there—thought he could make some money out of it and didn't. We saw some pretty hard times.

When I was about twelve years of age my daddy moved to Kountze, and he helped build the courthouse there. He bought half interest in a livery stable and put me to driving a team, and I drove almost day and night till I was eighteen. Drove an old hack. People would come there and stay at Kountze and hire dad to carry them to Nona, Olive, Village Mills, Warren, Woodville, on like that. And people living here, there and yonder, would require daddy to carry them, and he always sent me. Drummers were the ones I carried mostly. The only money there was in this country was at these sawmills.

Most of the mill towns had a saloon. Nona didn't. Olive did.

Plank did. Village Mills didn't have one, but there was one just a mile below. Then you go up to Hyatt. Joe Rice was a good-natured kind of guy, and he had a saloon a mile up, between his mill and the next above him. Quite a number of those old Irish had come over here from Ireland. Most of them was good-natured, and helped build the railroad, helped build these dumps for the tracks, lots of them through this country. Nearly all of them were drunkards. Anyway, they'd work, say three months, and they'd get a big payday, and they'd get drunk and stay drunk just as long as they could get hold of a dollar or bum a dollar. They were truly alcoholics, but good-natured, nearly all of them. But Joe Rice wouldn't have a saloon right at his mill, so his men wouldn't drink too much, you know. One day he got on his horse and went up to the saloon to get him a bottle of beer and see how things was goin', and one of those Irish had got drunk and was out on the porch a-vomitin'. Joe said, "Pat, are you sick?" He said, "Be'jerries, and do you think I'd be doin' this for fun?"

I never had much time for fun, but bear hunting is the most exciting experience I have ever enjoyed. It was a well-organized procedure. It was done mostly with cur dogs, because they're smart and they're good fighters. We'd use a well-trained, experienced dog to trail the bear, and sometimes he'd trail him two or three miles, going slow, you know, for the trail might be cold, and a bear always inhabits the densest part of the Thicket. You can tell from the frequency and sound of his bark how hot the trail is getting, and you don't turn your other dogs loose until the bear is afoot, till the dog finds him. But all that time you're going through country so thick that sometimes you've got to get down and crawl, and you've got to have your hat tied on your head or you won't have it long. And you're expecting to come upon the bear at any time, and if the bear gets you in the Thicket he's likely to kill you. Bear hunting was extremely exciting to me. We'd lead the fighter dogs, because the younger ones would sometimes go off on the trail of a fox, deer, a wolf, or a bobcat. But when the start dog found the bear, we'd turn 'em all loose, and you needed four to six dogs to stop a bear. A dog must bite the bear and get out of the way, because if he ever hits him, he'll kill him. And if the bear ever squeezes him and throws him down, he's dead. The dogs cover the bear, slow him down till the man can get there and shoot him. But a bear is hard to kill. When we lived in Saratoga, a bear caught a hog in the chimney corner of our house, right at the house! They killed lots of hogs.

There was a controversy in Hardin County about whether a panther ever squalled, screamed. Daddy told me this: He was the oldest boy and my grandmother was a very resourceful woman, and one night they heard the cows a-sniffing and lowing and running around in the lot which was near the house. Well, they had no lanterns then, and they cut up long splinters of rich pine to make a light. They had a nigger woman in the house with them. My daddy went out there with this nigger woman to see what was the matter with the cows. The cows were milling around the edge of the fence and the calves were in the center, switching and lowing. About the time he got to the lot this panther let out a squall. He said the nigger woman threw the light down, ran in the house and left him out there. Most everyone had cur dogs, varmint dogs, and most of them were very wise, very good dogs. Those dogs took this trail and run this panther, and our neighbor three miles from there killed that panther next morning.

There were wild cattle and horses in the Thicket. They got scattered when the Mexicans came from Mexico going to Nacogdoches—supposed to have gold there one time. They would lose some, and the Indians would raid them once in a while, and that's where the cattle and horses got wild. That's what some people did during the Civil War, caught wild horses for the Confederate army. Show you how some people conducted themselves—one year there was no mast up in Tyler County where my daddy lived, just none at all. They had lots of hogs, but nothing to feed them on, and they gathered a hundred head of hogs and brought them down here. They left a man to look after them and he got sick. The hogs got fat, but they were stolen, every one.

Jarson Guedry told me this: They were always trying to catch cattle thieves. Well, he saw the buzzards circling one day, and he'd lost several head of cattle—thought something might have killed one—so he went to investigate. Well he found a cow all right, and she was dead. But before he reached the cow, he heard a moanin', like a human in pain. And what he found was a cow that had been disemboweled, and a man sewed up inside of her with his head and feet sticking out. The man was stealing the cow, fixin' to butcher her, when the owner caught him, shot him, just injured him, and sewed him up in the cow. As the hide dried, it got tighter and tigher on him. He was out of his head—and the buzzards were flapping over him.

Life was pretty hard then. Lots of times I've seen men work in the woods with nothing on except shoes and a hat. My daddy used to make staves. He sent them to France, and I hauled them, and he made these big tank staves, be eight or ten, twelve feet long. They split them out and then they took the broad ax and smoothed them, and they could smooth them just as clean as you could with a plane—why them fellows worked out there in the woods and all they wore was a hat and shoes. They'd have so many chips around, they had to wear shoes, and everybody wore a hat, but other than that, why that's all. When they left the woods they put on pants and a shirt. Now I saw that.

We have lots of snakes, especially in the bottoms, always had them. An old doctor here at Liberty, Dr. Lovett, I believe, had some ribbon cane down in the Trinity River bottom, and that cane grew so profuse that the snakes gathered in there, and they couldn't hardly get anybody to cut it because the snakes were so bad, and the doctor imported armadillos here to kill the snakes, and that's how come they started in this section of the country. Now they're all over the country, and I don't know how they get across the rivers unless they walk across on the bottom.

I started practicing medicine in Sour Lake in 1903. As a doctor I done everything—treat them, do all the laboratory work and nurse them. I done everything. That was very beneficial to me. I saw nearly every kind of disease you can imagine. Went through a smallpox epidemic in Sour Lake when I first got started practicing. Used to be a woman nursing up there, and of course I was young looking, and she used to call me kid. That hurt my pride. I looked so young, and an old doctor was supposed to know more than a young one. My youth was a great disadvantage. I remember when my daddy was about forty years of age, his hair was black as tar, eyes were blue, and his mustache was red as fire. He had two redheaded children. I decided when I was about twenty-four to grow a mustache so I'd look older. I grew this mustache, and it was black as tar on one side, and about two-thirds black on the other side, and the rest of them was red.

There was a lot of malaria, but quinine was our mainstay. I used more quinine than anything else. Quinine would abort pneumonia at times. It was a long time before we learned that children had hookworms, but they had plenty of them. First evidence we had of hookworm, the United States government sent a medical crew through, and they got rid of most of it.

There were lots of home remedies. We made a cherry-bark syrup—we'd take a drawknife and take the bark off the wild cherry tree, and mama would take that and put it on the stove and boil it for a while and then put sugar in it, just enough to taste good, thin syruplike, and that's one of the best cough syrups you ever saw. I've never seen that fail to help a cough.

If you stuck a nail in your foot, soak it in kerosene. We always had a five-gallon can of kerosene. Bluing is good for a wasp sting. And you know the saliva from a chew of tobacco is good for a wasp sting. It's the saliva more than the tobacco. The tobacco makes the saliva flow. Saliva is semimucilaginous and, with the alkalinity, takes away the sting to a certain extent. I don't know anything better for a burn than aloe vera. Good for corns, too. And here's a specific for whooping cough. Take a teacup and cut an onion, slice it a quarter of an inch thick and put it in the bottom. Put that much sugar, then another layer of onion, and another layer of sugar, till you get to the top. Let it set half an hour and it forms a syrup. Take a swallow of that every time you cough. That's what mother did for me and it bothered me very little.

I moved to Batson in 1904, and Batson was a rough place

after they found oil. One afternoon a smart-aleck boy was talking to some old drunk, and the drunk slapped him. Boy's name was Breeding and the fellow's name was Sam. Next morning I was standing out there and I saw the boy's brother coming down the street. He saw Sam standing by a horse rack and shot him four or five times and killed him. That afternoon another man was killed there.

I had my office in the drugstore, and there was a saloon on both sides. There was a funny incident just before Christmas. Those walls were thin, made out of one-by-twelve plank, mostly. There was a fellow in the drugstore, a great big German, and we heard a boom, boom, boom, bang, bang, bang—and we all got down between the counters to miss them bullets that came through the walls. There was lots of shooting, and directly this Dutchman said, "Doc, you better go in there. They might need you in there." I said, "I guess the doctor thinks just about as much of his hide as you do of yours." As it happened there wasn't anybody killed. Two fellows were wrestling over a gun, and it would shoot once in a while, but didn't hit anybody.

I saw two men come out of the same restaurant and one of them sat down across the street, and the other one drove his buggy by and shot him right in the back, and he walked about a hundred yards and dropped dead. They were bad days, boom days. I took out a life insurance policy about then—twenty-year pay. Cost me ninety-eight dollars and eighty-six cents, I believe. I paid it out in 1926, and I've been getting a dividend on it ever since, and they're due to pay my beneficiaries three thousand dollars when I die.

We had a man in Batson that was a bird-dog trainer. Him and his brother run Butler Brother's Livery Stable. They got hold of a yellow-pointer pup when he was about three months old, slept around the livery stable. That puppy, they began teaching him to bring them their socks and shoes, and gloves, and their hats. He'd bet you five dollars he could send that dog back to the house and get either one of those things, and he always won. Half a mile from there was a blacksmith shop, and he could put the bridle reins in that dog's mouth and send him to the blacksmith shop to have the horse shod. The dog would take him down there, and the blacksmith would know what he wanted, and the dog would go out there and lie down and go to sleep. When he got done, the blacksmith would put the bridle reins back in the dog's mouth and he'd take the horse back home.

That dog knew me; I hunted with him some. Why we wouldn't think anything about sending him a quarter of a mile to put a bird we'd shot in the buggy. If he knew you, he'd bum you for money. He'd come up and smell in your pocket. You give him a nickel, he'd go to the candy store, put his feet up there and drop his nickel on the counter, and that candy man give him candy, and he'd bring that candy back to you to feed him—wouldn't eat it unless you gave it to him.

We went hunting five miles from Liberty, hunted all day, stopped late in the evening. Butler said, "Vance, I left my hat at the camp. We're going on to Dayton to stay all night. You go and get it and bring it to me." He went back five miles and got that hat and brought it to Dayton. The dog's name was Vance, and Mills Butler owned him. Everybody in town loved that dog. I've seen him sitting on the seat of a buggy with the buggy lines in his mouth and a shotgun in his paws. I had a picture of him.

To show you how smart the dog was, we was goin' huntin' one day and the dog pointed some quails. A boy with us wanted to shoot the quails, but he was unaccustomed to shooting. Mills said, "All right, go ahead and shoot 'em." When the boy went out there the birds flushed and flew between him and the dog. He shot the birds and hit the dog in the face and put out one of his eyes. I said "Mills, do you think this will ruin him?" He said, "No, I don't think so. I told him it was a mistake." Now that's a fact, the Lord being my judge, that's the truth.

Now I'll tell you something that beats that. I saw this, too. Now one of their uncles got hold of a nigger boy about six years of age and gave him to these Butler brothers to take care of. Well, there was no other nigger children around there and this nigger boy would run away, go off and play with the white children, you know. Every once in a while, when that nigger boy would run away, they'd send that dog after him. Now I saw him send him after him and saw him come back with him. The boy's name was Rex. They'd say, "Vance, Rex is gone. Go find him and bring him back." I saw him bring him back, holding him by the arm with his teeth. He'd talk to him just like I'd talk to you. If I hadn't seen it I wouldn't believe it, and you may not believe it either, but that's a fact.

Somebody poisoned him. And, of course, Mills was so mad about it that he offered a fifty dollar reward. But after he thought about it a while, he said he was sure nobody would have poisoned his dog. They might have had poison out for somebody else's dog and he accidentally got it.

In 1886 or 1888 I had an uncle that lived in Bryan and he came to Batson, and he had two Irish setters. They were named Doc and Cap. My uncle Dennis Hart lived in Batson, and met him at Kountze, twenty miles, and got a man to bring a two-horse wagon to carry them back out there to hunt. And when he went to get in the wagon to go back to Batson, why this uncle put these dogs in the wagon and the man said, "No, them dogs not goin' to ride in my wagon." Why," he said, "We'll pay you for it." He said, "That don't make no difference. Them dogs ain't goin' to ride in my wagon." That was not unusual; dogs walked everywhere. "Why," he said, "They're good dogs. I'll pay you for it. They're all right." "No," he said, "they ain't goin' to ride." Finally he let them ride, but he didn't like it, made him mad. This uncle waited until they got down there in the Thicket—about seven miles—dogs lying down there in the back of the wagon asleep. He got up and just sailed his hat out in the woods, just as far as he could, and these dogs were asleep there. The man stopped and said, "Go git your hat." His name was West, and he said, "Go git your hat." My uncle said, "No, go on. Don't worry about my hat." They went on about a quarter of a mile, and this uncle spoke to one of the dogs. He said, "Doc." These dogs jump, you know, just like you shot 'em when they're called. He said, "I lost my hat. It's back yonder. It's out that away; you'll find it." Doc jumped out and in about twenty minutes here he came with that hat. The dog could ride from then on.

They used to kill cattle there in the afternoon, butcher, kill four or five in the afternoon and put them in a screened place. You know, they had no way of cooling it other than that. They'd go out next morning about four o'clock and go to cutting beef, and all the neighborhood would buy beef. They'd send Cap, partner of Doc, to market. At night they'd put a note in a basket, and Cap would get up at four o'clock and take the basket and go to the market to get beef. He'd get the beef and start home with it, and if other dogs would accost him, he'd put the basket down and fight 'em, then take the basket home.

I'll tell you a different kind of story. It's about Major Dark, and it's true, too. I think he got the title of Major for having served in the Texas army under Sam Houston. He lived in Batson. But this story begins like this: The road from Beaumont didn't run up through Kountze at that time because Kountze was not the county seat; Old Hardin was the county seat. It seems that Mrs. Magnus built a house somewhere on the road about halfway between Beaumont and Old Hardin, and it was an inn, place where people who were travelin' would stop overnight. She had a son, and people coming along with good-looking stuff, why they would do away with them. I read that they dug into some old wells out there and found signs of buggies and things like that they had destroyed to get rid of the evidence. But anyhow, this fellow, Magnus, Mrs. Magnus, and her son had accumulated a good deal of money.

At that time, you know, there was no currency. Everything was silver and gold. I remember my daddy doing business with twenty-dollar gold pieces, and my great-grandfather sent his son-in-law to Galveston and bought this league of land up above Kountze for 850 dollars in gold. You know, then there was no banks. Everybody kept their money at home or buried it around.

Well, anyhow it seems that Magnus heard that Major Dark sold his cattle and land on Big Pine Island, north of Sour Lake, for twenty thousand dollars in gold, and moved across the Bayou to the northeast corner of Batson Prairie and made him another home. Well, Major was a very popular man, all right, and Magnus and a man by the name of Willis made up their minds to go up there and kill him and get this money. They got another man by the name of Cheshire to go with them. Well, Cheshire didn't want to go, but after they approached him, they said, "Well now if you don't go, we're goin' to kill you." He finally agreed. Well, they evidently knew about the situation over there where the old Major lived. The Major slept with his head right close to a window, but he was a suspicious and a bright old fellow, and the evening this occurred, he had changed and put his head at the other end. But anyhow they went over there just about dark, Magnus, Willis, and Cheshire, to kill him and get his money. As they went in Cheshire killed the nigger boy that was in the barn. He was a servant boy. And they got to shooting, and they shot through the window there about where old Major Dark's head should have been, and it wasn't there, but they hit his wife in the foot. Shot her in the foot. Well they kept shooting around there, and Major Dark, he had a lot of stamina and was a brilliant man, and he killed Cheshire.

Well, it seems that then Magnus and Willis ran. They lived up in Tyler County, and Major Bullock was one of the officers that went after them, and they finally caught them. They caught Willis in Woodville, and Magnus, they caught him at Jasper. They had them there at Woodville and going to bring them down here to Hardin County where they had committed their crime, but there was very little law around there then. They said they put them on horses, hands together, tied their horses together and followed them on down to Old Hardin. Well, the whole country had been alarmed over it and they met there to do something about it. While the crowd was outside discussing the situation—seems like Willis was an attorney and he was writing a confession—the crowd decided to hang them, and they issued the celebration of it and Willis fainted. But nevertheless they took them out there and put them in a wagon, put ropes around their necks and tied them to a tree and drove the wagon out from under them. That pretty well ended them.

Of course Major Dark was a good citizen, and all of the west part of Hardin County and east part of Liberty County, they thought a great deal of him. I don't think he was a doctor, but he had a good deal of common sense and a good deal of knowledge and he treated a lot of people, and they had the highest regard for him. And when they buried him, they buried this gun he used to kill Cheshire, put it in the grave with him.

You know there's lots of good livin' in this Thicket. When I was a boy, at Sunday meals, grandmother used to have fried chicken and chicken and dumplings, a variety of fresh vegetables from the garden: tomatoes, cucumbers, onions, and usually turnip greens fixed with salt pork. Then they would have pies, and always they would have sweet potato pie and baked sweet potatoes and sometimes she would have cake and other things; but she always had two kinds of chicken. After dinner they put a tablecloth over the food. You could come back in and eat again at about four o'clock, and then the adults would have coffee, and maybe dessert, potato pie and yellow cake with chocolate frosting—be several kinds of cake—and biscuits and cornbread and all kinds of preserves and maybe pickled peaches.

They kept lard in those crocks. They had a smokehouse and smoked the sausage and bacon. When you make sausage you also cut out ham, backbone, hogs' heads; made cracklin' from what's left from cuttin' up the hogs, and lard; and then they put the lard in a big crock. Then when the sausage has been cured and smoked, put it down when the lard is hot. Then that lard is ready anytime, and the sausages are, too. Then they had a big brine barrel that you put the backbones in.

I'm a great believer in the Bible. Man thinks he's smart, but at no time, in no place, in no manner, has he improved on anything that God done. God made it so young people would bear and raise children because old people are not capable. They're too lenient. That's what's the matter with the nation now, the children haven't had any correction. They're growing up like stock instead of being raised up like they ought to be raised. That's exactly what's the matter with the nation. You can say what you please, but it's true.

I found an interesting thing from reading medieval history which they claim gives the history of mankind from about 400 to 1492, when America was discovered. You can see in reading it that regardless of how humble a man's origin, how meek his manner, how diligent he is in doing good, or how high his ideals, or how persistent he is to do good to mankind, you give him honor and power, and he will become a tyrant.

Born 1880, interviewed 1972–1975.

Introducing Jude Hart

If Jude Hart were dropped barehanded in the middle of the Big Thicket wilderness, I would expect him to have food on the table for dinner and a shelter to sleep in that night. His whole life has been a lesson in survival, and he has mastered it as fully as any man I know. In a general sense, this was true of every family that settled in the Thicket, but no one knew the resources of his environment more intimately, more completely, than Jude.

His father was the son of one of the original Harts that settled in Hardin County, west of Kountze. Jude was the oldest of four boys. When he was a small boy the family moved into one of the wildest parts of the Big Thicket and settled on Big Pine Island Bayou, northeast of Batson. His father died when they were young, and his mother and the four children made a living the best way they could. He never attended school a day in his life.

Jude is a tall, lean, quiet, soft-spoken man, easygoing and friendly. He can talk or listen equally well. When he talks he is utterly relaxed and watches you as he talks. When he is finished, you somehow feel that, although you have learned a great deal from him, he has learned a great deal about you, too.

It is impossible to think of Jude Hart without thinking of wild hogs, for he has hunted them, handled them, worked them, and depended more on them than on any other animal for his livelihood. He knows them like he knows his cur dogs, which, he says, are equal partners with a man in the woods. "They don't work **for** you, they work **with** you," he said.

"A hawg don't bite," he said. "When he's fightin' and hits a dog or a horse or a man, he just opens his mouth a little bit and throws his head sideways and up, and that's the way he cuts. When he gets as high as he can go, he jerks his head and cuts another slash comin' down. A hawg is a dangerous animal."

Bill Brett agrees: "A razorback boar from two, three years on up, outside the grizzly, brown, or Kodiak bear, is the most dangerous animal on the North or South American continent. Now I mean panther, jaguar, whatever. I don't believe there's anything more dangerous. Two years ago Clarence McNeely's brother, up on Village Creek, had one hit him, knocked him down, and they took seventeen stitches in his leg and nine or ten stitches in his arm."

Jude himself wears a scar from a tusk of a boar that cut him recently. He was on his horse, working a bunch of hogs in the same area and in the same manner that he did half a century ago. Life has changed very little for Jude.

A good blowing horn is a valuable possession, and each person has his own preference for size and sound. Jude uses the left horn of a longhorn steer. "I use it because I hold my horn in my left hand so I can keep my right hand free. The hollow is not more than two to two-and-a-fourth inches across, and their horn is fairly straight. They're easy to blow and the sound carries a long way."

The last time we visited Jude it was late in the afternoon, and we sat on the porch and talked with him and his wife until twilight. We noticed thirty-five or forty Rhode Island Red chickens come across the yard and fly up in a sweetgum tree at the side of the house, one or two at a time. I remembered Addie Moye's story about his folks bringing a few chickens when they came to Texas and the care and attention given them on oxcarts, rafts, and ferries, only to have them eaten by varmints before they got a pen built at the Big Thicket homestead. I asked Jude about it and he said, "They wouldn't last one night in that tree without a cur dog around. They're better than a pen."

JUDE HART

Ever since I was five years old, I used to ride behind my daddy a hawg huntin', and from then on I just kept a-ridin', and we had lots o' hawgs. People in this country made their livin' off'n hawgs. It was their money crop. We'd get three to five cents a pound for 'em, way back yonder —wild hawgs. It actually cost us a day's ridin', goin' and gatherin' 'em, markin' 'em. Then in later years got to havin' cholera, and we'd have to vaccinate 'em, which would cost about ten cents a head. But if we had a big mast, we'd make lots of money out of our hawgs.

Wild hawgs don't go in big bunches. You get over twenty or twenty-five and they'll make two bunches, and nine times out of ten about half of 'em just leave this whole country, go twenty or thirty miles. We had a bunch cross the river at Romayor, that'd be twenty miles. People all had their hawgs marked. We went by the mark on the ears, and they all knew marks. Back them days old people was honest; they'd go check that record and find the mark. They'd ride down here and tell us, or my daddy would tell them about a certain mark bein' in this country. If we knew anybody had lost a bunch of hawgs, we'd let him know and we'd pen 'em and they'd come get 'em. Of course we know marks just like you know writin' and figures. Far as I can see a hawg, I can tell you the mark on it.

Before the stock law come on, hawgs kept a-gettin' wilder, woods gettin' thicker and thieves got worse. Lord o'mercy, people come in here just like them cattle rustlers, and they'd get a truckload of your hawgs, and they got to be worth somethin', twenty and twenty-five cents a pound, on the hoof. In the summertime a hawg's no good to eat off the range. We won't eat one. Now in the wintertime, when the mast falls, they get fat, and that kind o' meat is good.

What I always enjoyed—we had good dogs, I've got 'em now, five cur dogs—we take our dogs and go to the woods. We've got 'em trained; they'll stay behind till I get up yonder five miles in them woods, and I hiss at 'em to get ahead and they'll leave me. *Jude Hart*

Well, when I hear 'em a-bayin', I know they're bayin' hawgs. You can hear them hawgs a-rallyin' and a-fightin' the dogs. I've got two dogs here now that bark at nothin' but a hawg. If it's a wild hawg, I can tell you whether it's a bad hawg or not from how the dogs is a-bayin'. You know, they got a kind o' quiverin', scary voice. If it's young hawgs and sows 'n pigs, they'll be fightin'. You know your dog will get ahead of 'em, and hawgs will keep a-runnin' at your dogs and you just keep a-drivin', shovin' up behind, and I've penned as high as seventy-five head at a time, right by myself, two good dogs. You naturally get a kick out o' that, you enjoy it. You cut your meat hawgs out and keep 'em, big old barrows. Then you cut out and mark the others and turn 'em loose. You mark your pigs so you'll know they're your'n, turn 'em out and they'll go back to your range.

In the early fall they eat overcup acorns and then post oak, then they go to the red oak, then the white oak, then they'll eat pin oaks last. In the spring they'll come back on these big old oak acorns, eat them a little bit after they begin to sour. Overcup is your first acorns that falls, then post oak falls. Everything likes post oak—deer, cattle, goats, hawgs, crows, squirrels. Pin oak acorns won't fall till 'round the last of November. White oak begin to fall last of October. Post oak will fall earlier; some of 'em crowd off last of September. Squirrels go to eatin' overcup the last of August. We've got a streaked oak that don't fall till long in February to April. Haven't got much of that. It's mostly back in what we call Long Island. Used to be lots of 'em back there. But your hawgs will travel your mast. If we miss our hawgs here on post oak, we know they moved over on white oak. We know where the white oak country is. We got this red haw and black haw; they eat it. The berries fall along in May and June, and the hawgs eat 'em then. But that's bad meat; it's got a whang to it. You got to have acorns.

A hawg is the nastiest thing goin'. I know of them comin' out here and rootin' in these ditches, and I know they've eat dead cows 'cause I've seen 'em. He'll eat a dead horse or a dead cow, yes sir. I don't know of 'em eatin' a man, but I do know of 'em rootin' up two men over here above Kountze. Carter Hart, a cousin of mine, and Leak Bevil went out and helped find 'em. An old outlaw, M. Sapp, had killed and buried 'em out there. That's the way they found 'em—hawg hunters, dogs bayed these hawgs, you know, hawgs commenced rallyin'. They went there and they seen them hawgs a-rootin' somethin' unnecessary on a kind of a knoll, and they seen a shoe and a man's hat there, smelt this awful odor. They thought it was a dead cow, generally see whose cow it was, what kinda brand, but they found out it was a man, and they went in and reported it.

I've heard my mother talk about him, M. Sapp, tough fella. His father was a doctor and respected. Older half-brothers of mine

said they was a-workin' with M. Sapp, here in the woods, and he
cut his finger off, and they jumped down to take him to the
doctor, and he slapped 'em away and taken a red handkerchief
and tied around that finger, just kept a-workin'. Always had coal
oil in the woods, to file saws, such as that, and he just poured
coal oil on it. Now Carter Hart knew him, and he was deputy there
when they put him in jail. Carter had worked with 'im, and Carter
knew he was a outlaw.

He was workin' on Santa Fe railroad out in southwest Texas
and he found a old rich widow woman. She was called Aunt Ellen
and she was old. He had a personality and was a nice lookin'
fella. I've seen 'im. He stayed dressed up, clean, neat, all the time.
But he got in with her and married her—he knew she was rich,
and she was old. They come here on the Trinity River bottom
and went a-fishin', and he hired two fellas to go in there with 'im,
and kill her. One made out he was cleanin' a pump shotgun,
settin' around the camp, and let it go off, shot her twice in the
stomach—fellas by the name of Dick Watts and Haverd—but
anyhow he got all that money. And they was hangin' 'round in
saloons with 'im, and he paid 'em off, give 'em five hundred
dollars to do that, but they blowed that in and they kept wantin'
more money, more money; that's what Carter Hart said. He seen
'em drink 'round there in saloons with 'im. Dick Watts cried all
the time and talked about shootin' her, so M. Sapp and his
brother Lude just taken him out there in the woods and killed 'im
and buried 'im, the one that mooched 'im so much. Carter and
them seen 'im leavin' with 'im out there in a car. He had money
to buy a car. You know money in them days was tight. He had her
money. So this other 'n, he kept talkin', moochin', so they taken
him, killed him and buried him, and they sent M. Sapp to the
penitentiary for life, right here at Rosharon.

So he got in with the guards down there, and he even got to
carryin' the mail. He was stayin' out at this prison, Rosharon, but
he'd go seven miles from prison camp to Rosharon and meet
the train and get the mail. You know he got to be a trusty, right
quick, and he was carryin' the mail, but he got in with some big
furniture company out of Houston and got to be a agent to sell
furniture, you know. He was smart, like I tell you, and had plenty
time 'round that little town, and he'd sell anybody a big bunch of
furniture, gettin' it on time, and he never would send no payments in. He'd just pocket the money. So this furniture man
come out of Houston, brought the law with 'im and went there
and asked at the post office, did they know a fella by the name of
M. Sapp. Said, "Yeah, he's the mail carrier. He'll be here at eleven
o'clock." So he come in and this fella introduced hisself. He said
to him, "You're behind on your payments." Charlie Lord told me
it was about forty-four, forty-five hundred dollars. "Oh," he said,
"I know it." They said, "What ya goin' to do about it?" He said, "I

ain't goin' to do a damn thing. I ain't goin' to pay you people nothin'." Said, "Well, we goin' to arrest ya and try ya and send ya to the penitentiary." Sapp said, "Well, do that! I just like to know how much deeper you can put me in the penitentiary; I'm in for ninety-nine years. You people better wake up."

So in the meantime he was makin' whiskey, bootleg. He was in with a trusty out there. So he stayed there about two or three months. The prison was near the Brazos River, and he stripped like he was goin' swimmin', and then turned the boat over like he had drowned, and they missed him. He had a brother named Tom Sapp, and they learned later he used his brother's name and went to Tennessee, carryin' his brother's name, and was chief of police down there. Tom Sapp was dead and years later his wife put in a claim for a pension, a war pension, I believe. They wrote back, said "You can't draw your husband's pension 'cause he's livin'; you got a livin' husband." She wrote back and said, "No, he's been dead for years." And they got behind it and found that M. Sapp was in Tennessee, chief of police. They went and got 'im and he come back and served a year in the penitentiary. They paroled him out of the penitentiary, and he come right back to Kountze and hired out as a kind of watchman there. I talked to him.

But I was tellin' you about wild hawgs. On a hawg drive you'd leave early, naturally, in the wintertime, and it'd be cool. The largest drive I ever made was from the Trinity river bottom to Beaumont. Usually you have a wagon come behind. Fat hawgs would burn out and you catch 'em and put 'em in the wagon. Be two-fifty, three hundred pounds, and they couldn't travel as good as them lean hawgs. You'd make about twenty, twenty-five miles a day with 'em. That's as good as you could do. You just had to manhandle 'em to get 'em in the wagon—be three or four big old men and boys. They'd catch 'em and hawg-tie 'em and throw 'em in the wagon. The drive to Beaumont was about forty-five miles—seldom have more than three dogs—never use more than one after you get 'em started. After you drove 'em five hours you could just use one dog, and he'd just bark ever' now and then. Not over four people go on these drives. Have overnight at Sour Lake. Usually pen 'em. Be some stock pens along there, pen your horses, too. If you knew somebody, stay all night with 'em. If not you slept on your saddle, if it wasn't a bad night. If you didn't have a pen, just let your dogs bay 'em all night. The hawgs'll bed down; they won't leave there. The longer dogs bark at hawgs and bay 'em, the tamer they'll get. Just like you go in the woods and we find a bunch of wild hawgs, well, wintertime we just get down and build up a fire and we let 'em bay 'em, work 'em, never move 'em for at least two hours, but the dogs ain't let 'em leave. Then when you get ready to move 'em, ya ease up. A good dog always works on the opposite side of ya. If ya move to the right, he'll move to the left, and ya move 'em anywhere you're goin' without sayin' a word.

Lots o' times you'd lasso a hawg, just like a cow. I had a brother, seemed like he couldn't miss. Seemed like he could rope one in the thicket better than he could in a cow lot. I've been down in the thicket, me and him tryin' to catch one. If one of them old boars would run at ya, you better catch 'im or kick 'im off; don't run from 'im whatever ya do. You can't outrun a hawg, man can't. And they'll catch your dog lots of times, cut 'im, ya know. We carry needles to sew our dogs up. You see a wild hawg runnin' at ya, if you're on to it, go towards him. If you'll kick 'im twice't, most of the time just once't, right on the nose, he'll stop. When you kick 'im on the nose, he'll cut at ya; but you kick 'im. Lots o' times a dog get a little nervy, and those old boars'll catch 'im. We got some over there now, their guts was cut out last year. You just catch 'em and pack them to camp and sew 'em up.

This scar on my leg here—that's the only time I was ever cut. Just got too nervy, four or five weeks ago. I was on my horse, and the dogs was makin' it so hot on that hawg—I was wantin' to rope 'im, ya know, and change 'im, make a barrow out of 'im. He was a big old long-toothed boar, but I was on my horse, and he was runnin' the other way, and them dogs caught 'im. I had three dogs and they whipped him out in the openin', and I run to lasso 'im. Well, I missed 'im and he turned back. Well, I knew he was goin' to cut my horse—they usually ruint your horse if they hit 'im, get 'im in the leg. When he cuts your horse, your horse will jump, and ya better be ready to ride 'im. So I clinched 'im, and throwed my foot down, and instead of him a-gettin' my horse, he got me. He no more than hit me till my dogs got him, and I jumped down on top of 'im and tied 'im up.

I'm not scared of a hawg as long as I can brace myself and kick him off, but I slipped down one time, the only time I was ever scared. He was a wild boar, and he'd swam the creek and the dogs had him out in the open, surrounding him. An old boar, when he gets ready to cut, is just like a barber sharpenin' his razor when he gets ready to shave ya. They sharpen their teeth, and they'll go to snappin' 'em. You can see that old dust flyin' off his tusks. I've seen it many a time. My horse had swam the creek so many times, he was about burnt out, so I tied 'im and walked a foot log and taken a gun. I was goin' ta kill 'im. Well, he went to sharpenin' them teeth, and he made a run at me. When I went to kick 'im I slipped down, but them dogs was right on 'im, or he'd got me. A hound wouldn't o' done that, or a feist or a bulldog. They'd run the other way, but not a cur.

In the late fall we usually set up camp, hawg camp, up there close to what we call Duck Pond. We still got two camps up yonder below Bear Thicket. Lots of wild hawgs in there. That was headquarters for 'em, you know. Just like outlaw people go to

Chicago. But hawgs, these outlaw hawgs, they'd all go to Bear Thicket, which was the worst thicket in this whole country. When you went to Bear Thicket, you went to stay all day. It taken two of ya, one of ya ahead with a big old long hack knife, the other 'n leadin' the horse, and we'd camp just as close as we could to that thicket.

A camp wasn't nothin' much. Used to take a tent and sleep on the ground. We'd go in there many and many a time, maybe take one blanket, two blankets, be freezin'. We'd build us up a big fire before night, big log heap. Well, about night we'd rake them coals out and that ground would be warm. We'd throw our tent down on that ground and cover up with that blanket. We'd build us a big fire on both sides of us and sleep just like you would in a hotel. At least we thought so—didn't know no better then.

Lots o' times, when we's goin' to camp several days, we'd go in the woods and rive our boards out, split 'em out, put 'em up; maybe we'd wall up one side, and put us a mud chimney up there. It would take four or five hours. Chimney would dry out, you could build a fire in it as soon as you got it built. Wouldn't wall the south side. Did you know Spanish moss makes a good bed, the best? You boil it and cover it with tickin'. If you don't boil it, it's still alive and would make you itch. If we's goin' to camp long we put a bunch in a old tub and boil it, put it out there and dry it three or four hours, pile it there and make you a good bed.

We'd get up 'fore daylight. These wild hawgs feed at night; they don't feed in the daytime. A wild hawg will come right out there and feed under that tree, and if you had leaves four inches thick, which they will be in the wintertime, they'll never turn a leaf over to where you'll know it. If you ain't very particular, you can't tell they've been there. You got to know what you're looking fer. You'll find leaves covered with dew, and maybe a dry leaf next to it, one that's been turned over, and that's the only way you can find where a wild hawg's fed. But before daylight he'll leave and go to his bed. He don't make no racket.

I've been settin' down, still-huntin', and wild hawgs come right up to me. I could see 'em, but never hear 'em. If they ever suspicion anything, smelt ya, they'll throw that head up and groan one time, "arummmmm," and he's gone. I been a still-huntin' and wild hawgs come up that way, wouldn't have my dogs; they'd be at camp, and I'd go get 'em, be gone hour and a half, and put the dogs on 'em, and them hawgs would be a mile and a half from their bed. If the little ones is real small they stay in the bed, if they're still a-nursin'. If they're weaned, they all come, feed at night, and you can drive a hawg at night. You can handle 'em where you can't in the daytime.

If we found a bunch of hawgs anywhere in reason of our camp, three, four miles, we'd take our dogs and go in there just at night. Sun goes down they come out and go to feedin', we'd bay 'em, try to catch a moonlight night. You can put your dog on 'em and pen the wildest hawgs in the country. They'll run at 'em about twice't, and then your dog will get ahead and take 'em straight to the pen. Sometimes you couldn't get through, have to get down off your horse and work your way 'round, but them dogs would go right on with 'em. If you wanted to see the show it was all right, but they'd do the job anyhow.

We had one dog that would catch a hawg by the tail, the only one I ever saw catch a hawg that way. Old Frank, I've seen him catch a-many a-one, and them hawgs would just open their mouth and set down, and never move, and never squeal. He'd catch a hawg right at the root of the tail.

The hawg's main enemy was bear and wildcat. I've seen several wildcats around a hawg bed, dead, that the hawgs killed. He'd jump in there on 'em, catch 'im a pig, and they'd just cut 'im up. They wouldn't eat 'im. I've never knowed one of 'em to eat a bobcat, but they kill 'em. Usually when they feed, always at night, they'd leave a big old barrow to care for the baby pigs, and the mammy would go and feed. I've bayed the old mammy two or three miles from their bed. You'd know they had sucklin' pigs 'cause you could see their bag was big. You take your dog off 'em, they'd go see about their pigs. Old cats and panther follow 'em 'round, sneaky. We've heard 'em holler at night right in our hawg bed, seen the tracks trailin' our hawgs. They'd trail along there, and as long as the hawgs didn't smell 'em, they'd jump in there and get 'em a pig. If a hog gets the wind on ya, he can smell a long ways. Hawgs raised nearly half their pigs. We always figured if we got a third of the pigs, it was a pretty good crop.

The bear, he'll get the big hawg. A bear will just slip up on him or go to the bed. Lots of times when they're ganged up in a bed like that, those old boars will put up a fight with a bear. Down here one time a fella found a big old boar with long tushes, and a bear tied up in a fight. The bear actually killed the old boar but the bear died, too. They both died within fifty yards of each other. You can tell when a bear catches a hawg. He catches him in the neck, right back of his head, and he'll eat all that off. He'll start eatin' there. We've penned lots of hawgs with chunks tore out of their neck, have a half-moon there, healed over. A bear can't outrun a hawg in the Thicket. They have to catch 'em in the bed. Hawg's scareder of a bear than anything; they'll bust out if they can get away, won't gang up and fight. They'll gang up on wolves if there ain't a big pack. We've got more danged wolves now than we have squirrels. Bear is smart, ya know. He smell that hawg— he's got a good nose—he'd go 'round them hawgs layin' there asleep, and slip on in there, take the wind blowin' towards 'im, he jump in there and catch a big hawg. Usually the rest of 'em will run.

I remember one time daddy had some old gentle hawgs

sleepin' under the house, bad yard fence, they'd come at night in wintertime. Had a old chimney, fireplace. It was warm, and those hawgs come there and bed, and you couldn't sleep for them squealin' and, you know, what we call pullin' cover all night. Well, daddy and some others killed a bear and they brought that head, and he said, "I'll get rid of 'em." He taken that bear head and throwed it under there, and they liked to turned the house over. Two years later he heard of them hawgs the other side of Honey Island. One of them old guys over there, one of those Suttons, found them in there. So he wrote him a letter and told him he got his hawgs. He went up there and got 'em, him and my brother drove 'em back.

There's a old man 'round here—I won't call any name—he's a thief, and he'll steal hawgs. But some folk will steal his hawgs, too, but he just laughs about it, because he'll go get 'em out of the pen at night. He'll take this dog of his, and when he opens the pen, he'll get down and pull the dog's ears, and put that dog ahead of him and he'll never bark. His old red dog was worth a lot to him when he wanted to steal hawgs, 'cause he'd never make a racket. He would hear about someone pennin' a bunch of hawgs, and he'd go there that night and open their gate, get them hawgs, and that dog, he'd never bark.

He made that whiskey, too. I remember five stills. They always told us if we come upon a fire in the woods to get back, don't ride on. In later years I got to samplin' a little of it and got to huntin' 'em, and they trusted me, ya know. They didn't at first. They'd have a guard out. They usually ask what you boys doin' here, and get on away from here. We'd get away, too. I guess they's afraid I'd tell, and they got to givin' me a little whiskey. I'd go by there on a cold day and get me a little bottle of it—and my hawg huntin' would be over.

Me and my brother was hawg huntin' one time and found a bunch of hawgs, and I said, "Well, I'll be damned if here ain't a bunch of crazy hawgs." Dogs was a-bayin' 'em and they not payin' any 'tention to 'em. They's fallin' around there, and we looked over there and they'd turned a barrel of mash over and was eatin' it. They must not been in there over a hour 'cause there was lots of it there, and there was thirty, forty head of hawgs there, most of 'em was drunk. Why, we just walked all round 'em, and they paid no 'tention to us. Some of 'em layin' down. It was summertime and old hawgs was hungry, and they smelt that old mash, and got to rootin' and rarin' up on that barrel tryin' to get it, and turned it over.

We was up there in my hawg camp several years ago, didn't have any bridges or roads in there, just a wagon trail. We'd camp in there and gather hawgs, mark 'em, take about a week or ten days. We'd come out and rest up and go back again. But this time it went to rainin' and it rained, and rained, and rained. Next day that creek was half a mile wide. We stayed four days and was ready to come out. We'd butchered four or five hawgs and had nine live ones tied down in the two wagons. The only way we could come out was to swim it. We tied our wagon beds down. Ya know they'll float off if ya don't tie 'em down. But we had five hawgs in one wagon and one of my brothers drove off in the water and he got across. The other one started across, but his wagon bed floated off right in the middle of it. That water was swift! Dennis swum out in there but his horse got tangled up in some brush and he had to quit 'im. My older brother, Grady, swum out and cut him a-loose, but these hawgs was tied, all four feet tied together, so I swum out there, thought they was goin' to drown, but a hawg won't sink even with all four feet tied. You can't drown one of 'em even if he's hawg-tied. I didn't know that, but I experienced it right there. Ya see, the couplin' pin come loose from my brother's wagon—he didn't have the wagon bed tied on good—and the back part floated off, and the horses wallowed on out with the front wheels and the axle. If the wagon bed is tied down good, it'll drop down, but still float.

When a horse is swimmin' a wagon across a stream, you don't want to hook him up real short, because he swims with his legs way out behind him. Some horses, when you're ridin' 'em, just rare up and paw the water and lunge around, act like they don't want to swim, but if you just slip off the back of 'im, and grab 'im by the tail, he'll start swimmin' and go the shortest way across. I've swum these rivers and creeks, and sometimes be five hundred yards wide. That's a long ways for a horse to have to swim, and he will travel much faster if you slide off his back and grab his tail, you floatin'. When you get to land, if he's liable to kick, ya turn him a-loose as soon as you can stand up.

I've swam a horse out with two hawgs tied to the saddle and one to the horse's tail. You put a rope 'round a hawg's neck and a half hitch in his mouth and tie the other end to his hind feet—dead or alive. Then tie the rope to the horse's tail, and he'll come right on out. You can divide the hair of a horse's tail in two parts and just tie a square knot and put a rope through it, and the harder it pulls the tighter it gets. A horse never will quit pullin' as long as he has a weight tied to his tail.

You can ride a horse, with him swimmin', and hardly get wet, but a mule will swim with only his nose stickin' out.

I've got five dogs now. I breed cur dogs. I wouldn't have my gyp to get with an old shaggy town dog a-tall. I watch 'em and shut 'em up, and then I take 'em over in Liberty County to a friend over there that has a good line of dogs, and I breed to his dogs most of the time. You've got to keep extra dogs, 'cause sometimes they get killed and you'd run short, and we just couldn't get along without 'em.

All cur dogs have a dewclaw that no other dog has. They are

about two inches higher than his other claws, and they're on the inside of his leg. I ain't never seen no other dog that has 'em. There are other dogs that have 'em on the front feet, but these have 'em on the hind feet, too. That's the unusual thing.

I work my hawgs by myself now. Frank Hart is a retired doctor livin' in Beaumont, the only half brother I have livin', but I got a baby brother livin'. He never did hawg hunt much. Missed a lot to my way o' thinkin'.

Born 1909, interviewed 1971–1975.

Evie Brown

Introducing Evie Brown

We first went to see Mrs. Brown because we heard she had a blue pig, and, as one familiar with hogs, I had never seen a blue one. It happened that she had some shoats foraging not far from the house, and, with a little corn, she got them up close where we not only saw "Old Blue" but got a color slide of it. "I've seen 'em off and on ever since me and my husband married," she said.

"Something else you might not know: a duck won't eat corn if it's put in a circle so that each grain touches the next—so the circle's not broken. I guess they're superstitious or something, but they'll not eat a grain of it."

There were a few ducks at her place, and I said, "Mrs. Brown, I believe you, all right, but could we try it on these ducks out there so I can say I saw it with my own eyes?" She got the corn and we shelled enough to make a circle thirty inches in diameter. Then she tolled the ducks to the circle, but they wouldn't touch it. Finally, she scattered the grain with her foot, and they gobbled it up, as though they were starved.

I was curious about this but even more curious as to how she found out about it in the first place—just how would a person happen to learn that a duck wouldn't eat corn that formed a circle?

"My husband told me about it," she said, "and I know he knew it before we married in 1918, and he learned it from his daddy, and his daddy learned it before they left Alabama. If it's shelled corn, whole grains, as long as the circle ain't broken, they won't eat it."

It was not the unusual, however, but the commonplace, day-to-day events, that give flavor to Mrs. Brown's account of life in the Thicket. Whether it was coons in her fig trees, a panther in the cow lot, or a rattler at the doorstep, this warm-hearted, straight-shooting, frontier woman could handle the situation and ask no odds.

Mrs. Brown's husband died several years ago, and she and her son, Paul, live at the end of a road about halfway between Kountze and Saratoga. Paul is crippled but not incapacitated and, with his genial disposition, shares in the family responsibilities.

EVIE BROWN

My husband's daddy, Warren Brown, he wanted to raise hogs. That's how come him to work on the bear so much, 'cause the bear eat all his hogs up. We had lots of bear in here. He killed one with a big iron hoe once. He was goin' back to the garden spot, and the dogs was bayin' a young bear. His wife tried to talk him out of it. She said, "That bear will kill you, Warren Brown." He said, "No he won't, not with them two dogs hanging around his hind end." He just kept aimin' that old hoe until he got his aim just right, and he hit that bear right back of his head and killed him with that hoe—come up on him from behind. It was a young bear or he couldn't have done it so easy.

Later on he was workin' the garden and his wife and babies was out there to help him, and the dogs jumped a bear—about half grown. Bear was just walkin' along fightin' the dogs when they'd come close. They're quick and they can kill a dog with one slap. He said the bear was goin' to crucify his dogs; that's the remark he always made if they got to hurtin' his dogs. So he got his gun and killed it. That bear meat is good, and you can eat all that bear grease you want to and it won't make you sick. That's the truth.

Grandpa Brown said he had a little dog that was mean to come to him every time a bear would get after him. He wounded a bear once and the bear started after that little dog, and it come straight to him, and he laid down by a big log and that bear run right over him, chasin' that dog. They won't bother a dog unless he's fightin' 'im, but they'll slap a dog then, and crush him to death if they catch 'im.

I remember a story he told about a panther. He was drivin' by a neighbor's house early one mornin', just a shack, and there was a big panther on the roof diggin' a hole, pullin' the boards off to get into the house. He said he shot that panther and it fell through the roof, and the woman and kids was scared to death, had the cover pulled over their heads in bed.

A panther come here to the barn one night, and I woulda shot 'im but my husband made me let 'im alone. I had a young calf, just fresh born in that cow lot right out there, and I didn't have nothin' but a dim light and I couldn't see far, and my husband said, "Maybe it's just a big dog." He was sleepin' in that room there; he was in poor health then. And I says, "Honey, I know it's a panther; I done seen his long tail, and I seen him runnin' when he went under that tree there by my cow pen; he's after that little calf." I got my shotgun and went out that way, and he went up a tree, and my husband wouldn't let me go kill him. He said, "They're too bad to jump, and he's liable to jump on you." They can jump twenty or thirty feet. We didn't have a light on the place that we could see how to kill 'im, so he made me let 'im alone.

There wasn't nobody much livin' on this road then. We was the only one here at the end of the road—didn't have no close neighbors or nothin'. We had a pole road when we first come in here—lay poles across the road and throw dirt over 'em. It jolted you to death nearly, but we didn't bog down.

There was so many snakes here, why, if it hadn't been for our snake dogs, we'd been bit many a time. We had dogs trained to hunt snakes. I had a dog that was really supposed to be a squirrel dog, but I trained her for snakes, and she killed eight or nine snakes last year right around the house here—coral snakes, cottonmouth moccasins, rattlesnakes. We have a pond here, and sometimes she'd swim out in the pond and bring snakes to me, if they was swimmin' where she could get ahold of their heads. We always doctored a dog, if it got snake bit, with runnin' water. Put it in cold, runnin' water and hold it there, its foot or whatever part got bit. In about two or three hours you could always take it out and there'd be no swellin'—all be gone and the poison never bothered it. This same dog got bit four or five times last year by poison snakes, and one time by a big rattlesnake. The dog fell just like she was dead, but we picked her up and put her in the water and kept her there. In a little while she come to herself, the dog did, and she recovered completely. She would attack the snakes if they was crawlin', but if the snake was coiled up, she would bay it until some of us could get there to kill it. She was just a little dog, but real quick with them snakes. Most people would call her a regular feist, but her mother was a full-blooded squirrel dog, and she just naturally got started after snakes, and I'd kill 'em when she bayed 'em. She would take after 'em from then on and trail 'em, trail 'em a hundred yards, maybe, before she'd find the snake, trail 'em just like trailin' a deer. We'd get on its trail with a big hoe or something. I'd use the .410 if they was in the thicket where I couldn't get to them right away. She wasn't even a year old when she started showin' an interest in snakes. We'd know when she was after a snake 'cause she'd go along switchin' her tail.

Now I've had all my boys bit one time or 'nother, and my daughter-in-law been bit right here at the house. These copperheads and cottonmouth moccasins, terrible—everybody in my family been bit.

Paul said, "Copperhead bit me right here above the knee once. I was cleanin' out the yard, sittin' down, just like I was when you come up, and one crawled up my britches leg. Mama put me in water, turned cold water on me."

Water remedy is the best remedy on earth, 'cause a snake can very near kill you before you can get to a doctor to save your neck. And if you'll get in runnin' water and stay there two or three hours, I'll guarantee you, you'll never be sick from it, but do it real quick.

Cold water for snake bite was way back there in Grandpa Brown's record. An old lady he knew got rattlesnake bit and she was close to a runnin' stream of water, and she waded off into it tryin' to go to her children on the other side. She started turnin' blind, and she knew she wouldn't last but a few minutes. But as she was crossin' the creek, wadin' the water, she began feelin' better, so she just stood there and hollered over the hill for her children to come to her. She stayed in that runnin' water about two hours, and she got well. That was the first beginnin' of it.

I would o' got bit twice, I know, if it hadn't been for my dog. One was a ground rattler and the other was a copperhead. One coiled up under my fig limbs out there, and I had some butter beans runnin' on the line, and she always went ahead of me to the bean patch, pea patch, or wherever I went. I was pickin' butter beans off the fence, and the fig limbs hung down toward the ground, and she went to bayin' back under 'em, and I was about three feet away. "Uh, oh," I said, "Paul, she's found 'im. There's a snake under there. Bring me a hoe right quick and we won't disturb 'im." So Paul got the hoe and I killed the snake.

Another time, right beside my walk, in a flower bed, she was walkin' back and forth, and I'd done walked all around the snake and made him mad, I suppose. He was coiled up and struck at my light, and I said, "Uh, oh, Paul, I've found 'im." And caboom! I let 'im have it with the 20 gauge.

She'd kill any snake, didn't make no difference. I even taken a king snake away from her 'cause I didn't want her to kill the king snake. I let Paul carry it down and put it in the pond. The king snake will absolutely kill the other snakes, even poison snakes. We watched this king snake one day kill a snake and then swallow him. Paul said, "That snake is too big for the king snake to swallow," and he cut him half in two, and I'll declare if he didn't mess around and swallow that piece and go and pick up the back part of him and swallow it. That was a spotted king snake.

Well, finally this little old dog got with pups and I didn't know it, and she miscarried, and it set up infection and killed 'er. She was about three years old. I just lost her this spring. These other two, her puppies, already killed one snake apiece.

Before she got sick my son-in-law said, "I'd love to buy that dog." I said, "Well you live right here close to me, and why buy her, 'cause she'll keep the snakes cleaned up around your house, too, if the children ain't mean to her. You see she done rounded up your big coral snake right there by your house, and two big cottonmouth moccasins." There's been a lot of them want her but there was no sale for that dog. I wouldn't have sold that dog for a round hundred dollars of no man's money.

I had a brother-in-law got rattlesnake bit way up here on his leg, diamondback rattler hit him and he begged them to throw him in the river, but they didn't know the remedy. They poured a bottle of iodine on him, and Alice got scared and carried him to the doctor. And you know he was six long months gettin' over it—had to walk on crutches for weeks, and he's still got the scar. But it was six long months that he didn't walk on that leg, and he said, "I'll guarantee a thousand men can't hold me out of the water no more. If they'd throwed me in that river, I could've got hold of a bush or somethin' and laid there till I got all right."

Everybody had home remedies, passed from one to another, hard to get a doctor. You can take these little wild possum grapes, take 'em and boil 'em, and it's the best thing for a sick stomach there is. And these little green grapes, take 'em and squeeze the juice out of 'em and take about a tablespoonful of that juice and it'll break that diarrhea ever' time. I cured our grandson when he was nearly dyin' with it. You give him that about three times a day, and after you get him flushed off, then you start givin' him broken doses—smaller doses, see? That will check his bowels and clear up his stomach. It's good for old people or young people.

Used to long time ago, honey, we used herbs. This here rattan vine's as good a thing as ever was to cure fever on children, nearly any kind of fever. You boil it and drink the tea off'n it—boil the vines, cut it up in boilin' water, in the wintertime, anytime. We've used it on the children to break the fever lots of times, for malaria, too.

A nurse told me long years ago about vinegar and onion poultices. Children went barefooted so much they used to have stone bruises, and they used 'em on them stone bruises and carbuncles, and everywhere they had blood poison. Don't forget that. Keep a vinegar and onion poultice on a blood poison place and it starts to heal right now if you keep it hot. Try to keep it hot. I usually have me a little old pot or somethin' to keep it hot in. I boil onions in pure vinegar till they get tender, and then I put just a teenincy bit o' meal to make it stick together, kinda, and then I put it on risings of any kind, to draw 'em.

We had another dog, she was good for coons in my fig trees

and my plum trees. Coons eat every one of 'em comin' and goin'. They eat my chickens, too. Paul's killed several this year. I used to watch for 'em at night, and one time I told Paul, I said, "Son, I've got to have some rest; I'm goin' to turn the gun over to you." He went out there and sat flat on the ground—he can't stand up to do no good—and he shot that coon out of the chicken roost in them fig trees. Directly he said he heared another hen hollerin', and so he went out there and shot another coon. They eat up my plums somethin' awful. Plums and figs is the best coon bait there ever was.

I've had foxes come up here, and I've killed foxes right in my yard, tot'n' my chickens off after night, them red fox. One of 'em got out there one night and barked back at me, and I said, "I'll show you somethin'," and I went in the house and got the gun and shot 'im.

We have worlds of frogs 'round here, bullfrogs. My grandson caught frogs with his hands. Shine a bright light on 'em, reach down and grab 'em with his hands, put 'em in a corn sack. He'd spy another one, catch 'im the same way and put 'im in the sack. I believe he said he let one git away, but anyhow he kept catching 'em 'round that little pond right out front there till he caught thirteen big 'uns. I'm goin' to tell you right now, when them frogs was stretched out—front legs and all—they must o' been two feet long! Had great big old hams, and I eat all of it 'cept the guts and the head and the hide. I don't waste nothin' about a frog. You know you pay a price if you go buy 'em. And then my older boy, he went down here and caught nine the other night. He said, "Mama, I let a lot git away from me." I told Sam, that's my baby boy, to go down there and get that loud mouth. They keep me awake, sound like a bull a-bellerin'!

There was a big old alligator in my pond down there, been there for several years. Of course it was a violation of the law to kill 'em, but anyhow it was on my property, and I kept seein' him. He'd ease up to the top of the water, and I seen him stick his old head up, his old eyes, so I got the gun and let him have it. He tried to bail that pond out down there, thrash the water all out. It was about eight foot.

You can take a Jew's harp or a French harp and get out in a boat, out in the middle where there's a bunch of 'em, them 'gators stick their head up all 'round you when you play, come to you. You go to gruntin' like a hog, and I'll guarantee you, if they're used to eatin' hogs, they'll come right straight to you then.

Old man Bart Dark, he called up the law to kill a alligator that swallowed a kid one time, a girl. Her mother was down there washin' clothes, and the little girl, three or four years old, was right on the edge of the bank. That 'gator just come and slapped her in with his tail. That's the way they catch 'em. Bart Dark's daddy said he'd give fifty dollars to anybody to kill that alligator.

He had delivered that kid; he was a doctor. They searched and searched for that alligator and finally found him in a hole way back under the bank. It was about ten feet long, they said, and when they cut it open the child was still in his stomach.

I was born in Texas, right up here at Livingston. We stayed there till I was about two or three years old, then we moved to Brazos County and lived there till I married and come to Hardin County. My mother come from Arkansas, I believe. Papa's people all born and raised in Livingston, the McCaghrens. I was a McCaghren before I married. That's Irish.

I married Calvin Brown. Daniel Warren Brown was his daddy and D. S. Brown his grandpa. The Browns come from Alabama. They come in a wagon pulled by oxen, come over with a wagon and a dog following it. He come with the two oldest children, Gavin and Oliver, I believe it was, and the rest of 'em was born here.

Born 1902, interviewed 1964–1976.

Introducing Roscoe Crouch

At a time when most travelers were moving west, Roscoe Crouch headed east. At ten years of age, he left Los Angeles with his family in a wagon his father helped build and headed for Texas. Nine months later they arrived in Beaumont and, a few years later, settled in Saratoga, the heart of the Big Thicket. A lot of things happened during those few years. Roscoe Crouch finished his public schooling, attended barber college, cut hair in the logging camps on the edge of the Thicket, and finally set up shop back of the grocery store his daddy had opened in Saratoga. When his father died, Roscoe took over the grocery business and operated it until his death in 1973.

Saratoga was a quiet little settlement during these years, and Mr. Crouch had time to train and use his several dogs on occasional hunts. Dogs were used for just about everything, but Roscoe had a unique job for one of his curs. During prohibition days he developed a fondness for an occasional drink and, to avoid being caught, he kept a small flask tied around the neck of his dog. "I knew it was safe," he said, "because that cur wouldn't let nobody touch him." Friends say he had a habit of calling the dog every morning as soon as he got up.

Mr. Crouch was about six feet tall, medium build, large eyes, and deliberate of speech and movement. Few men of his time had a greater variety of experiences or recalled them more vividly.

ROSCOE CROUCH

I went to Bailey's Barber College at San Antone. I saved me up enough money workin' down at Port Arthur at the can factory to go to barber school. I wasn't but seventeen years old when I got out of there, and all those barber shops down there, they didn't recognize a college barber at all. They wanted you to serve three years. Well, I got down to Beaumont and tried to get a job there, and they'd just laugh at me. One old boy said, "I know where you can get a job, but you can't stay there." I said, "Why?" He says, "You'll find out." So it was down on a old floating barge, where they had gambling and bars—oh, everything there! Called it the Blue Goose. It was down on the other side of Port Arthur.

Ships landed about a mile from the Blue Goose and the sailors all come in there. Sometimes the place would be full of Norwegians; every kind of nationality on earth would be there. They'd get happy and a group of 'em make their own music. They didn't have no music boxes. They'd get off somewhere and sing, four or five groups of 'em singin' in their own language. It took nerve to stay there with 'em. Used to be a bunch there—Spanish ship, I think it was—and they used to amuse themselves with a game I never liked. They'd put on their oldest clothes and take knives, when they got along to a certain stage, drinkin', feelin' good, and they'd practice on one another with their knives, see how much clothes they could cut off the other one without cuttin' the skin— if you cut the hide, you lost. They'd put up a dollar or two for the winner. They was Spaniards, or some kind of bloodthirsty bunch.

The Blue Goose was a great big barge, covered over, of course. The owner's name was Al Younger. You've heard of the Younger brothers that was outlaws up in Missouri. Well, he was some relation to Cole Younger and that bunch. And he had a big Dutchman tend bar for him. He could handle two ordinary men. I've seen him take one in each hand, when they got too rough, and bring their heads together, throw them down on the floor. He was the main cheese runnin' the thing. His name was Charlie Myer.

Roscoe Crouch

This place had this barber shop that I run down there, just a boxed off little place for the barber chair. When I first went there the boys done lots of fightin', and it would make me nervous when I got to shavin' a man. Well, one old fella missed his boat—he was a tough fella—some kind of a mate on board ship. Ever' once in a while I'd buy him a glass of beer to keep them scrappers pushed out away from my chair. They had the bar and a place for those who worked there to stay at night. I stayed there. They put me with a Norwegian boy—he done somethin' 'round there in the kitchen. He made soup lots of times, and he'd holler out, "Hot soup," about one o'clock in the evenin'.

And this Younger—he was a good chef—he had a yawl boat where you could go right up one of those bayous through the marsh, and they'd get hundreds of ducks. We'd kill a big bunch of 'em, bring them back there, and he'd put all them dead heads that had nothin' to do, to pickin' ducks, then he'd have the Norwegian to cook 'em up and he'd put out a free lunch. Eat all the duck you wanted, didn't cost you nothin'.

So that was the way I got started barberin', was at the Blue Goose; got a year's experience there. Then I worked at those big sawmills on the edge of the Thicket—great big mills out in the woods, big camps out there. When I went out to the front, I just stayed there all day Sunday and worked on 'em. Had a whoppin' big mill there at a place they called Serrin; big outfit, belonged to Campbell Lumber Company.

The "front" is where they get the logs, cut them down, maybe ten, twelve miles out from the mill. I'd catch a ride out there on those log trams. Sometimes there'd be fifty to a hundred people. I remember one night I stayed out on Steepbank Creek, the front for Pineland, and they put me in a shed. Must have been twenty-five cots in there, and every one of those men seemed to have a individual jug. I drank a lot of coffee that night and had the big eye, couldn't sleep. Ever' little bit somebody'd take a drink from his jug—glunkety, glunk, glunk, just like a bunch of frogs. Temple Lumber Company operated Pineland. Them men didn't have any more sense than a ox, but they was tough. What I mean, them timberjacks could drink all night and work all day, just keep goin'. They didn't eat like people now, open up a can and make a meal on it. They eat what they cooked—beans and rice and all kinds of meat: venison, wild hogs, turkey, bear meat—hard eatin' like that, stuff they could work on.

Some of 'em didn't get their hair cut ever' three months. I've had them come in out of the woods Saturday night, whiskers a inch long, hair hangin' down, and all I had was a old smoky lamp to cut by. If he had a wart on his face, you cut that off too. You couldn't see it. Had a old bucket by the side of the barber chair, get your razor covered with that stuff and throw it in that bucket, dirt and everything that accumulated out there in the woods. I had a fast-cuttin' hone, and ever' time I shaved one of them birds, I honed my razor. Haircut was thirty-five cents, four bits for the job—shave and haircut. I had one old boy, he'd been out in them woods, I don't know how long; looked like a real old man to me. I guess I worked on that fella over a hour. When I got him all peeled out, he wasn't much older than me.

I come here to Saratoga in 1920. Railroad used to come in down the other end of town, and I lived down there. Put me up a little shop t'other end, more people down t'other end than there is up here now. My daddy was a groceryman at Saratoga. I was a groceryman there for years—after my daddy died.

In them days, when I come to Saratoga, there was lots of places in this country you couldn't get through—growed up in briars, vines, bushes, and everything else, but workin' your way around it in places you'd walk a good ways. I got tangled up in a place somewhere between here and Votaw when I was huntin' one day, and I didn't see any possible way of gettin' out, unless I went right back out the way I come in. There was a hog trail down underneath all that stuff, hogs had traveled it so long. So I got my gun in one hand and crawled along under there, and around a curve I met a dad-blamed snake, had his head up nearly to the top of the briars. He didn't seem to make any attempt to get out of the way, and I decided I'd shoot. I had a shotgun and when I turned it loose in there, I never heard such a racket, all hemmed up that way. I killed the snake, but I bet the leaves fell for ten minutes. I guess I crawled four or five hundred yards before I got out of that stuff. A hog would have been worse than a bear to meet in there, 'cause he'd o' charged you, and you couldn't have got out of the way.

I was born in Los Angeles, California. My folks was North Carolinians, and my father and mother went out there, and they happened to be there when I's born. My daddy had been in the produce and mining business. He was energetic and worked hard, but finally lost everything. He wanted to see Texas. So he had him a wagon built, built a-purpose for the trip. It was a Cadillac, what the Cadillac is to the Ford, ahead of the other wagons, built longer and had a platform on each side for barrels of water—big vinegar barrels full of water on each side. It had a regular bow-shaped top, but it was made out of two-inch lumber. Had a floor up there for the kids to sleep on, and then my mother slept in the bottom of it. The shed was slanted two ways. It was covered with some kind of tarpaulin stuff that they had in them days. There was three kids. I was the oldest, and I sat on the seat with my father, rode shotgun. I was ten years old.

I'll never forget the day we left Los Angeles. We'd been preparin' for a long time, and the mornin' we left, the neighbors all come out, neighbor women 'round there; there was all different nationalities in that block we lived on. I don't think there was any two of the same nationality. I remember when I got in a tight or somethin', I was liable to talk in four or five different languages—learned it from the kids, you know. These neighbors, they was all out there, some of them made out like they was cryin'. I don't know whether they was or not. But I kept lookin' back, and when we finally made a curve in the road, that's the last I ever seen of them.

We come on, hit the desert—crossed it—and got in with a old prospector who was goin' part of the way. He knew the way by mountains he could see way off in the distance, knew the general direction to take. You couldn't tell where the road was, 'cause first time there come a sandstorm, it'd cover up the tracks. Just sand, you know. Seems to me it took us nearly two weeks to cross the desert, but surely it wasn't that long. We traveled by night, moonshine. Hot as the dickens in that desert. On this side of the desert there wasn't anything except cactus, some sagebrush, and later on, mesquite. One day we saw a animal ahead of us, off to the side, and when we got up close to it, we saw it was a mountain lion, a catamount, panther—they're all about the same. This old prospector had two donkeys, one to ride and one a pack animal, and this catamount lit on top of the one he was leadin'. You never saw such fightin', kickin', bitin' in all your life as that donkey did. He run him off. Them donkeys could fight!

One night I woke up and the wagon was stopped. I raised the curtain and looked out, and I bet there was a hundred Indians sittin' 'round our wagon. My daddy was out makin' coffee and passin' it around. They was friendly Indians.

This old prospector knew of a place called Cameron Lake, said we could fill up our barrels there. Well, we got there, but a year or two before, a bunch of cowboys, thieves or somethin', undertook to push a herd of cattle through there. They was nearly dead for water, and when they smelled this lake, they run in there and bogged down, and they couldn't get out, and they was still in there, just the hide and bones. Well, we just had to fill up our barrels anyhow, but my mother would always boil drinkin' water for us, and we didn't catch nothin'. I've seen the water so hot in them barrels it was like stickin' your finger in a kettle.

When we hit the Pecos, the Rio Grande River had been up and it backed the Pecos River up. We camped there three days to let the river go down. My father was restless, and he finally decided to drive into it. So he got a lot of poles off the mesquite and stuff, made a kind of runway down into the water, and we hit it and got nearly across, but then the couplin' pin come out. The water was runnin' over the bed of the wagon, but my daddy stayed with the horses, and when he got out on the bank, as luck would have it, a bunch of cowboys showed up there. I guess there was fifteen or twenty of 'em. They seen what shape we was in, and they rode out in the river and throwed their ropes 'round enough of the wagon to pull it out. They wrapped their ropes 'round the saddle horns, and they pulled the rest of the wagon out. The front wheels was gone with the tongue, but they got their ropes 'round the bed of the wagon and just pulled it out. Didn't take 'em long. Then they helped get it fixed up, and we come on.

Where we crossed the Devil's River, the Indians was fishin'. They take hair out of a horse's tail, plait it and form a loop, a lasso. It would stay open, you know. These fish be feedin', and he'd sneak up there, and slip this down behind the gills and yank him out of there. Didn't use no hook. They was experts at it.

One time we hit the plains country somewhere, cliff on one side, rocky country. Kids used to get out sometimes and walk beside the wagon. My sister was five years younger than me. I guess she was fifty feet behind the wagon, and I was behind her, and one of them catamounts come down out of those rocks and crossed between me and her. He looked at her, just looked at her a little bit, like a big dog or somethin', and kept goin'.

Crossin' the mountains, we come down one place where the road had been blasted, and it was just like steps. We had all the wheels locked, and was usin' four head of horses then. We dropped from one rock to another, just slide off, drop down, just comin' down like steps. We started at daylight, and my father said that night, he figured we made about seven or eight miles. I remember one place it was just like a shelf, one side you could see the tops of the bushes way down there, and the other side was just like a wall. There was no way of passin' one another, but they did have holes in the wall here and there. They sent me ahead, in case we met the stage, we could get in a place where we could pass. But that wasn't a very long distance through there. Dad had all kinds of brakes on that wagon. Underneath he had hard rubber bumpers. Instead of comin' all the way down on the springs, it would hit the rubber bumper first.

Didn't meet many people. Only thing we seen was Indians and Mexicans. We did meet a couple o' white fellas in a buggy. They had the news from where they'd come from, and we knew it from the western part. That's the only way we had of gettin' news. We probably stopped there a couple o' hours and talked. One thing they did say, they'd been eatin' quail. Said they'd heard you couldn't eat one every day for thirty days. That impressed me. They was still eatin' on 'em.

It was hard on the horses. We carried grain along for 'em to eat. That western country had mostly barley. When we hit the plains, that mesquite grass was just as rich as grain. We'd give the horses a handful of grain, hobble them at night, and they'd eat that grass for two or three hours and lay down and sleep. They stayed in good shape. We arrived down here with two head.

My father traded along the road, different places. He got hold of a horse that had been in the cavalry, had "U.S.A." branded on him. We started with four head, mostly buckskin. Those big Norman horses, they wouldn't last any longer than a snowball in Halifax in that desert. We had one rattail mare my father said was the toughest animal he ever seen, could stand more work. Had no hair on its tail, born that way. It was what you call a rattail mare. She come all the way. When my father got to Port Arthur he sold the wagon to a travelin' show.

On the trip we lived on game a lot. We had flour and Mama would cook bread, and we'd get those little cottontail rabbits. Those little western rabbits was just as fine eatin' as you ever seen when they're young. And there was plenty of birds. We'd camp anywhere around a waterhole, and game would come in there late of a evenin'. I know we always had plenty to eat, whatever it was.

Took us nine months from the time we left Los Angeles till we got down to Beaumont. We come through El Paso, Austin, San Antone, on down here. My father heard Gates was goin' to build a mansion at Port Arthur, and he was a pretty good carpenter. John W. Gates, bet-a-million Gates, they used to call him. He was the one founded Port Arthur, him and Stillwell—started it off there with that Gulf refinery. I expect I'm the only man left alive went huntin' with him. One day, after he got the mansion pretty well built, why he took me huntin' with him, shootin' prairie jacksnipes. I carried the game, he'd do the shootin'. He come from up north somewhere and decided to start a little refinery there at Port Arthur, later Gulf refinery. They also built an export pier way out in Sabine Lake. You could wade out in Sabine Lake a mile before it got deep enough for anything much to float. They built the pier so small boats could come up there to load and unload.

When they built the mansion, it was out on the prairie, good walk from Port Arthur. Last time I was down there in 1919, I couldn't tell where it was, what had become of it, everything had built up so much. I imagine it's still there.

1879–1967, interviewed 1966–1967.

Introducing Hardy Farmer

The three years Hardy Farmer spent in the Big Thicket formed a dramatic interlude in his life as a rancher on the Edwards Plateau, 350 miles to the west. During the prolonged drought in 1917, he moved his cattle from the short grass of the higher, drier, limestone country to the open range of the Big Thicket and stayed there until 1921.

After more than half a century, old timers in the Thicket remembered him well, and they mentioned his name with respect. "Did you ever get to know Hardy Farmer?" they would say, or, "You should have known Hardy Farmer." They never said why, but it was obvious he had made an impression.

We finally decided to visit him at his home in Junction, Texas, and found him reading the paper on his shady lawn at nine o'clock in the morning. During his active years he was possibly five feet ten inches tall and weighed about 180 pounds.

He greeted us cordially. He and Mrs. Farmer had turned the operation of the ranch over to their only child, a married daughter, who was born while they were in Hardin County.

"Mr. Farmer," I said, "We have come to get your impressions of the Big Thicket." Mrs. Farmer said, "Excuse me. Let me leave before he expresses himself." It was an appropriate anticipation.

Life would have been no more baffling had he spent those three years in a foreign country. "Everything was just the opposite, just backwards from anything I was ever used to," he said. He couldn't understand why they valued a dog in the Thicket more than a horse was valued on the range, and he didn't like a country where a cow would get poor on grass belly high—"not enough strength to support the hair on her hide." The contrasts could not have been sharper.

He liked the people—most of them—and talked about Carl Richardson, the Hooks brothers (Bud and Ben), Carter Hart, the McNeelys, and many others. Time after time, in speaking of people he had known, he would say, "He was one of the finest men I ever knew."

Hardy Farmer never once returned to the Big Thicket, but he continued his subscription to the Kountze News till he died in 1974. People there must have liked him, too, for a carload of them attended the funeral of this man who had been gone for over fifty years.

When we started to leave his home in Junction, I said, "Well, Mr. Farmer, we will be heading back to the Thicket." His quick rejoinder was, "I don't envy you the trip."

HARDY FARMER

We had a seven-year drouth here, and I went down to the Thicket with my cattle, shipped 'em by rail, about eight hundred head. I took them up to Waggoner's and just turned them loose. They nearly starved to death in spite of everything I could do. I ordered a carload of [cottonseed] cake, and we done fairly well with them the first year. My brother wrote me we hadn't had any rain and not to ship 'em back.

I didn't think much of that country. It was completely different from the country I'd been raised in. It was boggy and I didn't like it at all. I lost about half my cattle, just about half of 'em. They bogged down and just everything happened; they stole 'em, bunches of 'em. It was pretty bad, and I just couldn't help it. I got into those bogs down in there, had to have my horse pulled out of them. He'd be down, half buried in that mud and slime! They'd just take him by the tail and pull him 'round and 'round till he could get up. I don't like that country a bit.

Alligators, mosquitoes, and ticks! I've killed many a alligator down there. Used to come up in the shade down there, and I had a high-powered rifle, and I'd just shoot their heads off, shoot them right back of the neck. They weren't very large, about six or seven feet long. We found a big one at Village Creek one day. The Mexican and I were looking for my cattle on a real hot day, and when we came to Village Creek, we decided to swim. When we got to the other side we saw a big alligator in the water, and the Mexican wouldn't swim back for his clothes. He walked four miles upstream naked—and he was a modest man—to cross over on a bridge, and then back. I swam back and waited for him. They told me alligators don't bother you much, there wasn't much danger in them. But the Mexican walked eight miles without a stitch of clothes on because he didn't believe it. He was a smart old man. His name was Abel Pruneda—Avel in Spanish. He went out there with me and stayed with me the whole time.

You couldn't lose that Mexican. He knew where he was all the

Hardy Farmer

time. I'd just follow him. I've been so lost, looking for my cattle, I wouldn't recognize my own house. I couldn't have lived there without that Mexican. He just got around and get the neighbors to do things, easier than anyone I ever saw, just that type of personality. Aztec Indian is what he was. Even the women there fell for him. I don't know how old he was, but he was gray as a rat. He was born at St. Ignacio.

As much as it rained there, you could die of thirst in the summer, if you got lost. Good gosh, I've drunk out of cow tracks there, out in those woods—yeah, get down and drink out of a cow track; damn scum, brush it off with my hat. Oh gosh! I told Carl Richardson I never did want to go back there, never again as long as I live. It was simply awful. I can't express it. I liked the people. They were fine people. Some were sorry, steal your cattle or do just anything on earth, but most of 'em were fine people. Carl Richardson, Bud Hooks, the McNeelys, Carter Hart, were as good friends as I ever had. Bud Hooks told me one day—I had a big western saddle and a six-shooter and I started to go west toward the Trinity after my cattle—and he said, "Let me tell you something, if I was you, I wouldn't go up there. Those fellows up there with those little stills might shoot you." And I said, "Well, by golly, I don't think that much of my cattle." I just let them go.

I never saw so many dogs in my life. Old man Allums had twelve, and he could put his hands up to his mouth, that way, and sound just like a horn. He was an old friend of mine. He's dead and gone now. Everybody had dogs. I didn't think much of them. They thought more of a dog down there than we do of a horse out here. I killed one once and it was pretty bad. Fellow over at Batson owned a dog and he came over there, got to followin' me. And an old friend of mine had a bunch of sheep there, and I was riding out to the range there, and this dog got after those sheep, and killed a big lamb. I got down and cut his throat. That's the way I kill dogs, just cut their throat. About a week afterwards old man Hooks came to me and said, "What went with that dog that was follerin' you?" And I said, "Well, I hate to tell you." After that, though, I told him the whole story, rode down there purposely to tell him what I had done to the dog. I said, "The dog's up there"; and he said, "Don't say anything about it. That fellow wouldn't take a hundred dollars for that dog." I wouldn't have given a nickel for him! He had violated one of the highest laws of the range, and that was the only thing to do, was to kill him, so I just cut his throat. His owner wouldn't have been pleased, but he never did find it out as far as I know, because I never told it till now.

We had a pretty bad fire while I was there. I was trying to save a little piece of ground for my cattle, and there was a dirt road there, and this horse that I rode, I had to hold him by the bridle to get on him, but this time I ran to him—that fire shootin' over my head—and I ran for that horse, and just caught the horn of the saddle, and clung to him and rode him out of that fire, just hanging on the horn and the stirrup. It's a wonder he hadn't killed me. Those people down there set that fire. They claim it's better country if they burn it off. Oh, it was awful! Usually that horse wouldn't stand for me, but this time I ran to him and the old horse just stood there. I guess I was just careless. I could hear that roar and the fire comin'. But I just thought I could work a little bit longer. I was tryin' to work it where that fire would stop at the road.

An old friend of ours down there had a lumberyard. He said, "I'll just send the lumber out there and you can build any kind of house you want." The old Mexican was a pretty good carpenter. By gollies we built us some kind of a little old house, one room; had the harness and saddles in one corner, bed in another corner, and cooked in one corner, somethin' else in the other corner. There wasn't any livingroom. Mrs. Farmer cooked over the fireplace. Mary, our only child, was born while we were there. She lives on the ranch; she's runnin' the ranch now.

I had the measles while we were there. That old Mexican had to go to Silsbee on horseback for a doctor. He cared for me just like I was a baby.

That's the darndest country in the world to get through. I can still feel myself pulling that brush out of the way so I could take another step. Cattle couldn't make it through them places, and they were liable to bog down if they went around them. Golly, I thought all my cattle would bog down. I started to load a bunch of steers one time, there at Kountze, and you know it rained so much that those cattle bogged down, big steers bogged down in the railroad lot, fixin' to load 'em. Cut my finger off that time.

Once I was drivin' on one of those rough trails, lookin' back to see if I could recognize a cow—I thought it was my cow—and I hit a stump. I went right through that windshield. I got up and drove that old crazy car—it would just wind every way—drove it down to a friend of mine, McNeely's, and she come out and she said, "My goodness, Mr. Farmer, what's the matter with ya?" And I said, "Well, I just had a helluva time." Cut my hand, and had a cut across the forehead. That blood made me look terrible, but there wasn't much the matter with me after she washed me. That was near McNeely's. He lived on Village Creek, Clarence Mc-Neely. That was the county clerk's father.

A friend told me one day—we were riding out there in the woods—he told me, I got too many children, and I'll just give you Billy. I said, "All right, when I get ready to go home I'll get him. I'll send him down here every year to see you. I'll educate him." We were pretty well fixed at that time. I went there to get him and his wife said, "Why, that sonavabitch! Why hell no, I'm not goin' to give you that boy! He don't have no right to give my boy away!" By golly she just got on the pack, she was on the fight. It was my friend's stepson. Billy was about five or six years old. He was the cutest little fellow I ever saw. If you see him, tell him I remember him mighty well. By golly, I sure did want that little boy—barefooted, didn't have much clothes. I ate there one day. I thought they had knives and forks all around, but by gollies, they didn't. I was the only fellow had a knife and fork. They just used their fingers. Bacon and potatoes, that's all we had, and cornbread. They ate a lot of game, killed game all the time. All they lived on was game, wild hogs, and potatoes. They raised sweet potatoes. A lot different from our diet out here. It was all changed, all different, just backwards, doggone!

In a way they took the law in their own hands down there, and did just as they pleased. I never lived among a bunch of people that did just as they pleased as much as those people did. They were just simply outlaws, that's all. They didn't care a thing in the world about the law, if they could get by with it. They were lawless in every way, anyway to violate the law! I never saw such a bunch of people in my life. I never have!

By golly, we had several close calls down there. We found a mound of ashes with a hand sticking out. It hadn't burned; it fell out of the fire. The finger joints were all in there in the hand. And the old Mexican said, "Shhhh, shhhh; don't say anything about it," and I never did till I came out here, never did say a word about that. Oh, there had been a helluva fire there—those pine knots, you know, they had piled them up. I don't remember exactly where it was, but it was right out from Kountze there. I wouldn't want to tell about it—not in that country.

Old man Hooks told me one day that he shot at a fellow up there. Said he never was so glad of missin' a man; said he was a good old man, but he was tryin' to kill his brother. It was up at Woodville, I believe, and he was a fine shot. He says, "I don't know why I missed that old feller, but I did. Shot at him about five times." That was Bud. He was the finest man I ever met, I believe. I didn't know Ben very well. I never met a nicer man than Bud Hooks. Bud Hooks made enough money, but didn't care a thing in the world about it. He was a bear hunter. They tell me that he caught a bear by the tail one time to keep it from killing his dog, and he killed it with a knife.

I knew Leak Bevil. I used to stay in his office about half the time. He came up here one time, years later, and he said, "You don't know me." And I says, "The hell I don't. I'd know your hide if it was stretched on a fence post." I know the way he walks. Leak was a pretty rough hombre. He borrowed a pistol from me one night, went up there to clean up on a bunch of fellows at Woodville, but wasn't anything happened. I was always sorry that I let him have my pistol.

They hung a nigger there in the courthouse one time. I was

well acquainted with the sheriff. I forgit his name now. He said,
"Be sure to come back, Hardy, we're goin' to hang that nigger in a minute." And I just rode off. I didn't want to see a nigger hung. I didn't want to see it. They built a scaffold right in the courthouse. He was condemned to be hung. It was legal.

Those cattle they had down there, they didn't even look like cattle. We took Herefords down there, all Herefords. Those little old cattle down there were the sorriest little things I ever saw. By god, their big bulls wouldn't weigh over five hundred pounds. They were a mixture of everything. I never saw such a mixture. They didn't care. It didn't matter just so's they could raise a calf. Those little old bulls used to try to follow me, follow my cattle when I was drivin' 'em in the woods. I got so I'd go back there and rope them, turn their heads down and stomp their horns in the ground. They'd kick there for a good while, but directly they'd get loose. I was a mighty strong man then, about thirty-five—eighty-seven now. That's been a helluva long time ago.

Old Bud Hooks kept me from being indicted by the grand jury one time—for drivin' cattle off the range. That was when I got to whipping those little bulls, taking their heads and stomping them in the ground. They was going to get me, but he was on the grand jury, and I knew they wouldn't indict me. Those nesters up there turned me in, said I was drivin' the cattle off the range. It's against the law to drive cattle off the range. Those durn cattle were follerin' me. I sure as hell wasn't drivin' 'em. I hated for my cattle to have to associate with those scrawny, sorry, no-good things. Just couldn't keep 'em from it.

To get them up into a group, we had a bunch of cow punchers from down there, a bunch of niggers. That's where old man Bud Hooks came in so handy. He hired a bunch of niggers for me. I'd never worked a nigger.

Take a fellow out of this western country and put him down in there, and every old nester in there hated me. They wanted that range to themselves. Oh, boy, I couldn't have lived down there without that Mexican. He was just a lot of company. We got back with half our cattle. The others were lost or stolen or bogged down or somethin'. I don't know what the hell went with 'em.

1883–1974, interviewed 1968.

James Addison Moye

Introducing James Addison Moye

Addie Moye does not tell a story; he relates incidents, and nearly all of them are humorous. He is not a person with a collection of stories he tells from time to time, but, during our long conversations, he recalled events that he had not thought of, it seemed, in three quarters of a century. He remembered them vividly, however, and was occasionally overcome with laughter as he told them. One gets the feeling that Addie missed very little of the fun and mischief that young men engaged in.

He worked hard most of his life in logging camps and sawmills. He is about five feet ten inches and probably never weighed over 160 pounds. "Hard work won't hurt a man," he says, "unless he gets too much on his back." At present, he lives with his daughter and son-in-law, Mr. and Mrs. Allen Stockholm.

Addie likes music and had just returned from an all-day singing fifty miles away when we first met him. He was ninety-five years old but had made the hundred-mile trip alone, driving his own car. He is active and alert.

The fiddle is Addie's favorite musical instrument. In fact, it was the favorite of most people, the most popular instrument in the Thicket. The fiddlers afforded music at the dances, log rollings, and just plain home entertainment. There were all kinds of fiddles, made from gourds, cigar boxes, pine, and other materials. Some of them were made of good material and with painstaking care. Dolph Fillingim comments as follows: "My daddy made several fiddles. He used thin strips of maple around the edge, about three inches wide. Made the back from holly. It was hard and rebuked the sound and sent it up. He dressed it off, give it the violin shape with hand tools. He used sweet bay for the neck. The fingerboard was made out of pine, and the top was soft pine, gave the fiddle a mellow, soft tone. He bought strings. You could buy steel strings or catgut."

Regardless of the "make," however, no other music would tempt Addie Moye so quickly to a shindig five miles away on a rainy night after cross-loading on a logging tram all day.

JAMES ADDISON ("ADDIE") MOYE

I grew up around Dallardville, Polk County, close to the Indian Village. My father's name was Tom Moye and my mother was Ellen Davis. The Davises come from Mississippi and the Moyes from Alabama. Grandpa Brighton Moye, they called him Tom, settled on Hickory Creek, and papa was born there, but later they moved down to Big Sandy. They was all raised there.

I remember grandpa had a big dance at his house. Him and his boys had made some cane beer. They danced all night long; sometimes the sun was up when they quit dancin' and playin' the fiddle. You know when they're a-boilin' syrup, they have skimmers, and they skim off all that foam that boils up on top and throw it in a barrel. After a while it ferments, and you can draw it off down there just like the Lord made that wine out of cold water. And it will kick you down; I can witness that. Best beer you ever drank!

There was eight of us boys and five girls in papa's family, and it was sort of like a fella I stayed all night with way up the country one time by the name of Little. He had a big family, and I said, "Mr. Little, how can you make a livin' for all this big family?" He says, "Every Little helps." That's the way it was with us. We all worked hard.

Mama had a wash place on a little spring branch about one hundred yards from the house, and I'd help her when she washed the clothes on Saturday. Three little bears hung around there all summer, and I'd say, "Mama, those bears goin' to come here and get us." She said, "I'll throw hot water on 'em."

One time I went to stay all night with one of my uncles. He had three boys and he raised 'em a-batchin'. He told the boys, "Down there by that foot log across the creek, I saw tracks of that old cat that's been a-catchin' my chickens. I'm goin' to set a steel trap on this end of the log, so don't go down there." Well, next mornin' we ran down there and the bobcat was in the trap. My uncle cut a long switch out of ironwood, and he handed the old shotgun to his oldest boy, said, "Don't shoot him yet. I'm gonna whip him thirty minutes before I kill 'im." The boy stood there and his papa went to whippin' that cat, had the hair a-flyin', and he rolled and he jumped as far as he could, and his foot slipped out of the trap, and the boy shot and missed, and the bobcat left the country. He said they never saw him 'round there again.

Brown Wiggins' daddy was haulin' some cotton one time, great big oxen, and camped at Bluehead Pond. Dunny and George Moye was already camped there, and they was a-layin' there asleep on a little piece of duckin'. One of those yoke of oxen took a fright and run over them two old men and just stepped everywhere only on 'em, and they hung the old man's suspenders and tore 'em off. He got up a-runnin', and they had to go catch 'im.

Papa used to haul our cotton to Woodville, and he'd buy a year's rations. I remember if we'd play out of matches we'd have to keep a fire goin' on a log or a stump, or somewhere.

When coal oil would play out, we'd go out to a rich pine log or stump, get splinters a foot long or more and light the end of 'em. Somebody would have to hold the light to eat supper by, always et after dark. One time when it was my turn to hold the light, the hot tar run down my arm, and I throwed that light down in a hurry! It made plenty of light, smoked a whole lot, soot get all over everything.

We used to go to the singin' conventions, and I took two girls up there one time, hitched Old Bald to the buggy. It lasted three days, and we was comin' back from the campgrounds, old dirt roads, and it rained worse than it did this evenin', put Toodlum Creek level with the banks, and we had to go through it with Old Bald. Them two girls got out and said, "We'll wade that thing, or swim it; we're afraid to go through there with the buggy." I said, "I'll stand up in the seat and try to hold the buggy bed down and drive across. If you all want to wade it, go ahead." That old horse would jump and lunge and swim, but that buggy floated. Mary and Ada waded that creek, put their clothes on their heads; they just left on their panties. I nearly die when I think of that. They was sure good singers.

Bill Longley, from Jesse James' bunch, they robbed a train up in Iowa or somewhere, and Bill Longley got down in this country and come to grandpa's place and asked could he stay all night there. He wouldn't let anyone touch his horse, and he had two big guns on 'im, and a belt full of cartridges, and he stayed all night at grandpa's. Next morning grandpa said, "I'm goin' to have a hog killin' today, Longley, won't you stay all day with us?" He said, "Yes, I haven't been in a hog killin' in a long time; let me shoot 'em." And when they went out to the hog pen Longley pulled out them pistols and shot seven hogs before grandpa could stop 'im, shootin' with both guns.

Burgess Wiggins could really play a fiddle, and he played at all the dances. We was at a dance at Bill Madera's once and Jim Collins had his fiddle there, and him and Bill Madera had a fight, and Jim got mad and went home and took his fiddle. I jumped on my horse and went down to Pete Wiggins's and borrowed his fiddle. He said, "Well, Addie, if old Burgess is there and a-playin', he'll break it; you'll have to pay for it if he does." I says, "All right, I'll pay for it." And Burgess broke it and I paid for it. He was settin' in the window and got too drunk and fell out, broke the neck off'n the fiddle. But, boy, he was a good fiddler! Everybody wanted him to play at all the dances, but he liked to dance, too; and sometimes he'd put a big bandage on his hand, like he hurt it, so he wouldn't have to play.

We was comin' home from church one night, always had a quart of whiskey, especially Jim Moye, my cousin. Jim Youngblood and Tom Williford was in the bunch. We had to cross at the old water mill and me and Ed went through the mill house with our girls, but they crossed over the millpond on a board that they had been using to wheelbarrow dirt across to mend the dam. Jim Moye stopped to take a drink and that board broke, and they all went to the bottom, eight feet of water, but Jim held to the bottle. They got out, drippin' wet, and we went to Uncle Tom's. The preacher was there, ruint the whole thing.

Tom Moye had a bunch of fat hogs 'cross Hickory Creek, and the creek got up and the sloughs got so full that he couldn't get over there to look after them. Just as soon as the creek went down, he rode a horse across and went to a branch down there where a fire was burnin', and a barrel had been buried there to pour hot water in to scald the hogs, and he tracked the wagon right up to Tom Lindsey's house, little wagon with two wheels. When he come back Uncle George said, "Did you find your hogs?" He said, "No, but I found where they went." Tom Lindsey got hold of it, and two or three men eggin' Tom Lindsey on, sayin', "If you don't kill Tom Moye, I'll always believe you stole his hogs." Tom Moye was at a log rollin', and it was just about 11:30. Tom Lindsey rode up and hitched his little mule side of a fence out there and come over where the log rollers was, and he said, "Tom Moye, did you say I stole your hogs?" And he had a loaded quirt in his hand wrapped around his arm and a iron pin in the end of it to make it heavy. I don't know just all the words that went between 'em, but he hit Tom with that loaded quirt and mashed his skull in, and Tom grabbed a hand spike to hit Tom Lindsey, and Dave Hendrix and Henry Teakles caught his lick, but he hit him anyway and skinned his head down one side. Both of them caught his lick or he'd a-killed Tom Lindsey. Tom [Lindsey] staggered off about nine foot and said, "You hit me with that spike and I'll shoot you," and he pulled a pistol out and killed him. Tom Lindsey's wife said, "You stole Tom Moye's hogs and then killed him, and I won't live with you another day." He went to the pen for eight years.

When he got out and come back to Saratogie his right arm was just shakin', and I asked dad, "What's wrong with old man Tom's hand, shakin' all the time?" He said, "That's the hand he shot Tom Moye with," and that stayed with me. He was a mean man, Tom Lindsey was. The Lindseys was all good men but Tom.

Post office used to be in people's houses, and when Jim Jones died, his son Willie and his daughter, Fannie, run the Dallardville post office. Two fellers, Will Johnson and a Bailey boy, come down there to rob them one night. They beat Willie over the head and went and got all the money he had in the house. When they was caught they went to get Yank Collins to defend them, and Yank said, "No, sir, I wouldn't defend you at all, beating up them two old people down there." One of them went up for five years, but I don't remember about the other one.

Ida Hadley was old man Tom Cravey's girl, and she married a fella in Beaumont by the name of Paul Hadley. Jake Giles, the sheriff in Jefferson County, went after Paul. I don't remember the charges. He was livin' way up above Nacogdoches, and he went up there and arrested him and brought him back. Old Jake Giles dozed off, and Ida slipped his gun out and killed him on the passenger train. They pulled that string in the coach and the engine stopped, and they lit out. They caught 'em, put Ida Hadley in jail up at Kountze. I went with the sheriff to feed the prisoners one morning and stuck a plate in to her and she commenced doin' that at me [putting her hand above her head and pulling down], like she was pullin' the string. I knew her before she married Paul Hadley. That was the prettiest girl ever was.

I was raised in the woods; loggin' front's all I ever knew. One time Uncle John Salter—he married my mama's sister, Aunt Susan, and run the woods gang there at Warren—he give me a job haulin' water for the crew. I was drivin' a old ox hitched to a cart with the water barrel on it. I'd haul water from a spring out there to the loadin' crew and teamsters, and I'd tie that old ox, old Rowdy, to a tree back of the skidway where the men could come and get a drink. Well, this tram engine come along and shot fire out of the smokestack and set the woods afire and burnt up old Rowdy. They was burnin' pine knots, and boy you couldn't ride on that flat car behind the engine, you'd be covered up with big coals of fire comin' out of that smokestack. One fella got a coal down his shoe there and if you ever seen dancin', he done it. We called it the fire dance. Uncle John fired me. Lost my job and didn't even get any of the barbecue; but he hired me back a few days later. They didn't care about losing the ox. They'd weigh up the bacon a little heavier in the company store and go up on flour a little bit till the ox was paid for. They'd all say, "Look out for bacon and flour to go up."

They burned pine knots for fuel, lots of 'em. Annie Moye married Bud Hendrix, and him and his brother Cornell sold pine knots and rich lighter pine to the mills, good burnin' heart pine. In the virgin longleaf you could see a long way, no undergrowth, just big, tall pine trees. The longleaf is nearly all heart, just a narrow strip of sapwood on the outside. Trees died from old age sometimes, and when they fell they wouldn't rot for ages and ages 'cause they had so much turpentine. When limbs broke off up there at the top they'd have turpentine knots and they'd use 'em for flares, and hunters used 'em a lot for night huntin'. Bud and Cornell just go through the woods pickin' up pine knots and heart pine and sell it to the railroad for firing the boiler. A lot of people did that, cut the tree hearts up in short pieces, make huge stacks along the tram line.

They had turpentine crews—that was another outfit—and they'd come ahead of the timber cutters, maybe a year ahead, draining the trees they were goin' to cut. They'd chop two to four boxes in a tree, depending on the size, and set a tray in that chipped out place. A tray would hold nearly a gallon, and they'd take the ax and skin the tree for two or three feet above, and the turpentine would drain into the box. Then they'd come along with a two-wheel cart with four barrels on it, pulled by a mule or ox, and pitch them trays in the barrels and put new ones in there. The resin was so thick you couldn't empty over two-thirds of it, so they pitched pan and all in the barrel. It didn't seem to hurt the timber.

They wouldn't let Negroes stay on the Warren tram. That was one place they couldn't work them, crew run 'em off. Old Young and Brough was runnin' that mill and they didn't have no niggers, crew tarred and feathered them. Old Brough come out on the caboose one mornin' and said, "You all run my niggers away," and got to fussin' with the men. They grabbed him—he was owner of the mill—and hollered, "Bring the tar barrel and the feathers." And boy, he had to beg to get loose. They didn't tar and feather old Brough, but they scared him to death.

Old man Copley, he was a surveyor, lived between Saratogie and Kountze. He'd say, "I'm goin' to step up to Caney Head." It was about twenty miles. Or he'd say, "I believe I'll step down to Beaumont." He could outwalk a horse. He'd step down to Caney Head or Beaumont or Old Hardin before he'd hook up to his buggy. Copley was taller than long Tom Moye, seven feet tall nearly. He'd walk twenty mile just as fast as he could walk. You couldn't keep up with him in the woods.

Old Judge Hightower used to hunt bear a lot, but he was the judge of the court up at Livingston when I was a boy. A young fella had drowned a man he went a-fishin' with over there on the

Trinity River. He got two dollars and a half off of him, and a big plug of tobacco. He fixed a rock on 'im to hold him on the bottom, and rolled 'im in the river. He got caught on a big fishhook down stream, a feller pulled him up, and they traced it to this boy that went fishing with the old man. It was just like a detective story. I sat there and listened to them lawyers argue that case, and they give him ninety-nine years in the pen. They wouldn't hang him because he was a boy, a minor. And that old Judge Hightower would work that skin on his head, and he could move his ears like a hound dog, scared me to death. And the way he'd drink his whiskey! He'd cut a hole in a lemon and fill it full of whiskey, and he'd drink that, do it in court, anytime. He always had a little flask in his pocket to fill up the lemon, and I would think he was just suckin' lemon juice for a cold or something. I got big enough to sit on the jury, and I liked to watch old Judge Hightower wag his ears and suck that lemon. There's been more murder trials in Hardin County than any county ever I heard of.

V. A. "Yank" Collins, a Hardin County attorney, once said, "I never saw Judge Pedigo, Judge Hobby, or Judge Hightower consume more than three days trying a case. The rules of practice and procedure have varied but little in all the life of our Texas judiciary, but those old courts did not allow lawyers to talk half a day about nothing and then take another half a day to discuss the case with cocounsel or witnesses, nor consume three days in writing and excepting to the charge.

"The court usually wrote its own charge and it was prepared by the time the evidence was closed. The most important murder trial I ever heard in Hardin County was the trial of J. F. Redding for killing Ezra Green about 1878. I listened attentively to the case all the way through, and it was tried in three days."

Born 1880, interviewed 1975–1976.

Introducing Bill Willie Gilder

Bill Willie Gilder lives in the Haynes settlement, which was owned by a slaveholder before the Civil War. When the slaves were freed, he offered to give the land to the slaves when he died if they would stay on and help him work the land. They stayed and got the land, and Bill Willie bought his place from some of the heirs.

We visited him one Saturday afternoon in the fall of the year. He received us warmly but with mixed feelings, I'm sure, as his radio was about to broadcast a Southern Methodist University football game and Gordon Gilder, his grandson, was a backfield sensation on its team.

Quickly I suggested we come back some other time. "Tomorrow," he said, "Tomorrow, after church."

As we sat in his yard and talked the next day, the wonderful aroma of collard greens cooking interrupted our conversation. "That smells wonderful," I said; "nothing smells much better." "I guess so," he said, "but it don't 'specially start my appetite no more. I eat so many collard greens during the Depression, I had to wrap my ankles to keep the cut worms off; but they's good food, you betcha."

"I practically raised Gordon," he said, "me and my wife. He stayed with us, and you might say we raised him, just like my own boy. I think that's where he got that speed—from me. I used to be fast, could outrun most anything when I was young."

Cecil Overstreet, who has known Bill Willie since boyhood, agrees. "When Bill Willie was young, he was very athletic," he said. "He could throw a baseball plumb out of sight. He could take two rocks, take one in each hand, take two steps and throw both of them out of sight, together. Throw them with one hand as well as the other. And he was the best bird shot I ever saw. He could kill five birds on a rise with a pump gun, shooting them individually. During the Depression nobody had any money, shotgun shells were forty-nine cents a box, and Bill Willie said, 'If you buy some shells, I'll kill us some quail.' There are twenty-five shells in a box and he got twenty-three quail and a hawk, and had one shell left, and everything he shot, he shot flyin'. He'd train bird dogs for people in Beaumont and they'd give him a dog now and then. I gave him a pair, myself. He babied me when I was young and I've babied him ever since."

Bill Willie earned his living as a nursery man. He learned the business from a teacher he liked a great deal, Mr. D. P. Reagan, while they both worked for Griffin's nursery, south of Kountze. "Mr. Reagan was a good teacher, one of the best," he said. "He told me there would always be a need for a good 'tree man.' "

A few years ago Texas had two pecan trees for every person in the state, and, if it is not true today, it is not Bill Willie's fault. He is an expert "tree man" and has budded more pecan trees than any other man in that part of the state. He has worked for himself for many years and, even yet, does an occasional job for an old friend.

BILL WILLIE GILDER

So far as I know I'm the onliest boy child my father had. I guess that's the reason they call me Son. I named myself. I was maybe eight or ten years old and I told them, "My name is Bill Willie." I sign it "B. W. Gilder" to make it short. My father was Jack Gilder—he come up from out of Tyler County. He worked at Old Nona, Nona Mills, died November 18, 1918, of flu. I was born at Old Nona.

Nona is about two miles from here, and I used to run from here to school up there. We had one room and one teacher and twenty-five children. I got to the seventh grade; that's all we had. There wasn't any high school. I had the best teachers in the country. The first one was a man, J. N. Perkins, and the next one was a woman, Miss Foley, and they was strict! I'd study my lesson by a coal oil lamp, get down in front of the chimney. Someone told me if I'd sleep with my books under my head at night, that'd make you learn your lesson. I'd study my lesson real hard before I went to bed and then I'd take my books and put them under my pillow, and I wouldn't move offa there. I believe it helped.

I married Luberta Haynes. We had three children: Willie B. Gilder, Bill Willie, Jr., and Fern Lucille.

My first job was with the Griffin Nursery, about three miles south of Kountze. It was owned by W. G. and W. C. Griffin, and I believe they come from Florida. They got old man D. P. Reagan out of Alabama to come and teach buddin' and graftin'. He told me it was a job I could learn how to do and there would always be a demand for it as long as there was people livin' in the United States—buildin' homes and havin' pretty yards and things—and he said there would always be a demand for a fella that knowed somethin' about buddin' and graftin' and propagatin' plants. He was a born tree man.

Lots o' people, includin' me, thought they was goin' to make a lot o' money off'n satsuma. Griffin convinced the people they could make lots o' money. He wanted to sell the trees. The satsuma is budded on a wild plant. The seed cost a dollar a

Bill Willie Gilder

pound. You can bud lime, lemon, grapefruit, cumquat, orange, satsuma, and tangerine—that's the citrus fruit. I budded fifty-six hundred oranges for a fella by the name of Bruce Watts. There was a big freeze, man—big snow on the ground, ice an' stuff— jus' killed 'em all out. They jus' lost heart over it.

Griffin planted a lot of pecans. We planted nine fifty-five-gallon wooden barrels of pecans. You'd graft to the seedlin'. They weren't really paper shell. The Russell and the Sly was just about the thinnest shell you could find.

I grafted for lots of people. We planted them pecan trees where Mr. Bush is along in 1918. They're still there. They're huge. A pecan tree don't bear every year. Maybe every other year, and then you got to keep 'em cultivated. A pecan tree needs workin', tendin' to. I don't have the leastest idea how many pecan trees I've grafted. Good gracious alive! I used to graft five to six hundred a day, and I worked at it till about 1928, when the nursery went out of business. I worked about thirty years around Sour Lake. Them people there love their pecan trees. I done a bunch of graftin' for Mr. Bud Hooks and Mr. Ben Hooks, too.

Gordon Gilder, the grandson I raised till he went to SMU, was a good athlete. Now that Kountze-Huntsville high school game, whooooo, man alive! I think that was the best game we ever had, right there! Gordon run one touchdown that they nullified—call it back on 'im. Pretty soon he made another touchdown, a long one, and they called it back! Then he run a hundred yards, clean through the whole team! I told my wife, "I do believe if I could put just one feather on 'im, he'd fly." Gordon called me after the SMU game last year. He said he run a ninety-six-yard touchdown. He said he was runnin' along, thought he was runnin' as fast as he could go, and somebody kind o' brushed him, and he said he commenced runnin' then shore 'nuff. Like when a wild hog gets after a man, he don't run just as fast as he can—he run as fast as he has to! He taken some of that after me. I believe I was just about the fastest thing been through this part of the country. We didn't have nothin' to clock us, but we had a little old gray horse, and we'd turn that horse's head north and I'd get back this-a-way and you'd say go; by the time you could turn that horse around and catch up with me, I'd crossed the line down there ahead of 'im.

I used to go to the hunting camps and cook. I used to cook for Mr. Ray Gay and Lester Gay and Jeff Overstreet and Mr. McKim, Dr. Anderson; oh, I just used to have a big time. I tell you I never cared much about killin' a deer, just like shootin' a beef, I figured. I'd rather shoot one quail than ten deer. I hunted with jus' about ever' fella in this part of the country. Bird huntin', whooooo! If I missed a bird it worried me all night. I jus' didn't see how I done it.

I learned to shoot 'round in these woods here. I was keepin'

some dogs for C. E. Walter, a banker out of Beaumont. I went
down there and got two pointers, one of them named Rip and
one of them named Rap, and I brought them up here and trained
'em for him and he give me five hundred shells.

I used to hunt with a doctor out of Port Arthur, Dr. S. G. Ellis;
he was a dentist, and I hunted with Dr. McCall. Of course long in
there white people didn't think colored people ought to kill birds;
that was too big a sport, cost too much, shells was high. Colored
fellow he couldn't get the shells, too expensive, and then you
know he jus' wasn't qualified to do that; that was white man's job.
But everyone I ever went with, I made him play catch-up. Jus' as
the bird'd get jus' above the dogs, you know, I'd kill 'im. I practiced that, and the more you practice anything, you begin to get
perfect at it. Everyone I ever went out with, I made him play
catch-up. He have to ask me to let him shoot first.

I owned pointers and setters. One of my neighbors give me
one pointer, then I raised one or two. Old Jack, the one I called
Smokehouse, was the best pointer I ever had, and he was a
bobtailed dog. You could take him out in the tree swamps and
he'd tree a squirrel for you, bark; and then when you comin' out,
birds be comin' back out into the piney woods to roost, you
know, and he'd point quail then, and we'd kill a mess of birds
comin' out. Named him Smokehouse 'cause he was a meat dog,
helped us get our meat.

You know we had a old part bird dog and she had pups, and
the little cats started to suck. That bird dog was shaggy, and
maybe it was 'cause it was kinda cold, and they got to sleepin'
with the dog, and I guess they got the idea they wanted some
milk. No use goin' huntin' for their mama for milk and it right
there. Dog was named Speck. Pups and kittens slept together,
nursed together. They all got along good.

We had a regular old hog dog, old brindle cur dog, I thought
was just as good as ever went in the woods for a bunch of hogs;
and we trained him to go get the calf every mornin'. You know,
when we milk the cow at night we used to turn the calf out. This
dog was named Brownie, and I carried him with me a time or two
and made him run the calf back home, and all you had to do
after that was let him out and say "Get the calf, Brownie," and it
wouldn't be long before he be comin' back with 'im.

They're good watchdogs too. We had one, you couldn't get no
farther than the gate. Had to keep a good fence, and when you
come to the gate, brother, you holler. Please don't come in the
yard, 'cause he'd bite you shore.

We had a feist named Buttercup, and we thought it was the
best squirrel dog in the world. When we'd go squirrel huntin',
he'd tree a squirrel, and wouldn't be but just a minute till he have
'nother one treed. You know, he'd tree 'em just about as fast as
you could kill 'em. Sometimes I see him barkin' at the squirrel

and the squirrel be barkin' at him. I used to go down here to this creek before breakfast and I'd kill four squirrels and come back to the house and dress 'em, and we'd have 'em for breakfast.

These fox squirrels, lots of 'em so tough you can't hardly cook 'em no other way than parboil 'em with rice or make dumplin's out of it. Then sometimes you find these young cat squirrels, they gooood, fried, 'specially in hard times. Durin' the Depression I bootlegged squirrel—sell 'em for two bits apiece. We had our own hogs and cows—fished a whole lot. We eat birds, squirrels, and rabbits and ducks. Oh, man! ducks was plentiful, these big old green heads. We didn't go hungry.

Born 1899, interviewed 1969–1976.

Introducing Floyd Warren

When we first met Floyd Warren he had sixty-five dogs that would not hunt a thing on earth but bobcats. Floyd trained them that way, for bobcats are his specialty. He has hunted over thousands of acres and is welcome to hunt anywhere because his dogs hunt nothing but cats, and man is their only enemy.

A bobcat will lead the dogs through the roughest terrain in the Thicket, but Floyd follows, cutting his way through the matted undergrowth, or crawling underneath. He is crippled in one leg but can outwalk anyone on a cat hunt. His interest is shared by his wife, Fran. They met on a hunt when she came from Philadelphia to visit her sister near Beaumont, and they have been hunting together ever since.

Few people know the nature of a bobcat like Floyd, and he learned it on the ground. He comes by it naturally as his daddy and granddaddy were cat hunters, too.

It requires training and discipline for a dog to stay on a cat trail, but Floyd knows how to train them; and, if he finds one occasionally that "trashes" on him, he gets rid of it.

In the beginning it was with great difficulty that the Warrens literally cut their way into the Thicket and settled on a little ridge between Black Creek and Pine Island Bayou, but its appeal to each generation would make it even more difficult to leave. The grandchildren and great grandchildren still live in the shadow of the original homestead.

FLOYD WARREN

I'd rather hunt bobcat, wildcat, than anything else. It takes a better and smarter dog to be a cat dog. A cat is harder to trail because he don't have the scent a fox has, and a fox can't pull the tricks a bobcat can. Sometimes he'll double back on his same track, back and forth, and he'll go in a tree, and won't stay there. Lots of tree dogs will just hang up on that tree instead of circling and picking his trail up. And the cat will jump over to other trees and come down. He's more like a coon than a fox, but a coon don't dodge like a cat. A coon won't run long on the ground before he'll tree. Nine out of ten times a cat will just run it out on the ground until a dog catches him. He goes in the roughest country he can find and makes it hard on the dogs.

Used to when we had lots of hogs, a cat would go miles to go through a bunch of hogs and get the hogs to rallying, and they'd get the dogs off their trail, but now we don't have many hogs. Now they'll hunt up deer; they'll go through deer to try to switch the dogs off. The deer has a stronger scent than a cat. He'll do this to anything he can switch the dogs off on. They're smart. If a bobcat has kittens, and they're going to catch her and she knows it, she'll go through the kittens to try to pull the dogs off of her to save her life. I've run an old cat two or three hours and when the dogs are just about to catch her, well, as a last chance, she'd go through her bed, and lots of times the dogs are switched off on her bed. I'd go and get the kittens and then go back again and run the old cat again and catch her. We've brought the kittens home that she went through. Most dogs will smell around her bed a while where the scent is so strong before they get back on her trail. I had one old cat that went to her kittens and right there she stood till the dogs got there, and tried to fight them off. The dogs run in on her, and they had a awful fight. She run from them, and they caught her again and killed her.

To hunt cat it takes a dog that will hit a trail and stick with it, won't switch on different game, even if a deer gets up beside him. They got to really like what they're runnin', and I think they get this quality by huntin' cat, and they need to hunt often. I try to

Floyd Warren

hunt two or three times a week, keep my dogs in good shape. The amount of game that's caught with them is what makes them good.

I generally hunt early in the morning, when there's a little moisture. I go three or four o'clock in the morning. When it gets dry, sometimes I go at night—have to go earlier when it's dry and hot.

I like to hear the dogs runnin'; there's nothin' like it. They bark different on a cat than they do on anything else. A dog that has a chop on a deer trail will howl when he gets on a cat trail. Of course my dogs don't run nothin' but cat. It's most fun just before they catch him, and they've got the body scent. When he gets real hot and gets real tired he puts off more scent, then the dogs run him faster, by body scent. Then they start changin' their voice; they're runnin' to catch 'im, they're runnin' for blood. They get more and more excited, scream and raise all kinds of fuss. Sometimes you think they've done caught 'im. He's stinking so loud, the dogs just scream. It's awfully pretty to hear them just before they catch the cat. They squeal like people were beatin' 'em with sticks. They just go wild.

Usually dogs will tree a cat in twenty minutes to an hour and a half. If he goes over that he is usually runnin' on the ground. The dogs knock the wind out of 'im after runnin' 'im hard for about an hour or so, and if he don't get a break where he can get his wind back, he can't climb good. He can run longer, if the dogs don't crowd 'im, than a fox, but if the dogs crowd 'im and knock his wind, he can't run long.

A cat can wear a bunch of dogs out if he gets to trottin'; if they don't knock his wind, a cat can trot all day. A cat is faster than a fox for a short ways, but for long runnin' the fox has the wind. If you jump a cat in the early part of the night, maybe that cat hasn't had anything to eat all day, so naturally he can run faster than if he had just eat a rabbit. If he's full, he can't hold out as long. That way, sometimes they give you a hard race. You know how rabbits will get along side of a old loggin' road just about sunup and graze? Well, these cats will walk the old roads, huntin' rabbits. About five or six o'clock in the mornin' you can pick up a cat followin' a old road better than anywhere else, some old loggin' road.

Most cat hunters go out for the dogs to catch 'em. If a dog catches 'em, okay, but I don't shoot 'em. I hardly ever shoot one. If they climb a tree why I jump them out and let the dogs run them again. Sometimes I shoot up there by him and scare 'im out, or I climb up there by him and take a switch and slap him a time or two. He'll slap back at you. If you don't crowd him too close, he'll usually jump out.

I see the fight at the finish might near the biggest part of the time. I usually get in there when they start dodgin' close. When the cat is winded, he'll start runnin' and squattin', runnin' and squattin', and the dogs overrun him. He'll run like this a hundred yards, sometimes fifty, when he gets his wind knocked. The dogs go on him as soon as they get there. Sometimes there's one or two dogs not quite as gritty as some of them. They'll stand back until the pack gets there, then they'll go in on 'im and just roll 'im up. Four or five of them grab him at the same time. I've had two or three dogs chewed up bad, and I had one dog the cat hit on the backbone and almost broke 'im down in the back. We had to carry him out of the woods.

I believe the grittiest dog I ever had was a old July-Trigg. It was a good-blooded dog, registered on both sides. She went in a hollow log with a cat. When she come out she was really tore up, but she run that old cat out, and she jumped over all the other dogs to get to 'im, she was so mad. You can seldom find a single dog that could kill a cat. They're vicious fighters, cats are.

I had one old dog go in a log and kill a cat in it, a Walker and Redbone hound crossed. I still have that old dog. It was a big old log, gum tree. They run in that log, and I think the cat never did turn 'round. The dog killed 'im, and we had to pull them both out of the log.

All hunting clubs want the cats killed on account they eat up the little deer, and they eat squirrels, and they eat up the little pigs in the woods. Cats like bottom country, thickets, and that's where they range. Cats stay 'round sloughs a lot. They just like bottom country. You can see their signs.

I hardly ever sell a cat dog. Sometimes I'll sell a young dog that I got started pretty good. If one goes ahead and makes what I want, why I keep 'im. But coon dogs, deer dogs, squirrel dogs, stuff like that, I sell 'em. Cat dogs is too hard to make. I've been offered some good prices for 'em, but I never sold. A fellow up at Jasper offered me a thousand dollars for one dog. He'd have to like the dog, strictly a cat dog.

I usually start trainin' 'em around a year old. A good cat dog will be three or four years old, sometimes five, before they're tops. A cat dog can work till they're seven or eight years old; they don't have the speed, but still they're good for check dogs, check on your younger dogs you're trainin'. If your young dog starts something, your old dog will go to 'im, and if he don't bark and comes back, you'll know they're "trashing" and you get after them with a stick. That's the way to break them from runnin' trash. You get after a young dog a time or two, if you're lucky enough to catch 'im and switch 'im, it will break 'im. Usually I just blow my horn, and if it is a good young dog, why with two or three toots on the horn, it will come on and follow the old dog. If it is something I don't want, the old dog will come back before I blow. If he's on a cat, he won't come back, just stay with it. You have to have the old dogs; they do more toward trainin' than I do.

I've got 'round sixty dogs, most of 'em hounds. Most of 'em are to hunt bobcats, a few deer dogs, coon, squirrel, and stock dogs. You can use a stock dog for a deer dog; it's your cur. They can't cold-trail like a hound, but they're good runnin' dogs, tree dogs. If a dog will lead them, jump it hot, they're a good-runnin', fast dog and they'll fight a cat. The Walker hound makes a real good cat dog, but they can't trail like potlickers: the Bluetick, Black-and-Tan, Redbone, all cold-blooded dogs. I have more Walkers than anything. I like them crossed for cat huntin', a mixture of all of it.

We have the brown bobcat and then the lynx, spotted cat. The little brown cat is meaner than the spotted cat. He fights harder when caught. They're both bobtailed. The spotted one gets the biggest.

We had five cats once. We caught them and my wife made pets out of 'em, just like house cats, caught 'em before their eyes were open. She raised 'em on a bottle, and we had one that stayed in the house with us. If it got out in the yard, it would run under the house, didn't really know what to do when it got outside. All five of them tamed, but the tomcat made the best pet. I had one female, and she was mean when I fed her. Finally I took her up to the pasture and turned her loose, and I didn't hunt 'round there for a couple o' years, gave her a chance to raise some kittens. I'd caught them out pretty close.

I had two sow cats that I caught, out here in a cage, and I was wantin' a tomcat to see if they would breed in captivity. I treed one up the road here, a big old tomcat, run him about two hours. The dogs was about to catch 'im and he went up a hollow tree, a big hollow, the openin' about three or four feet off the ground. When he went up that hollow, I run up there and put my back and shoulder just right to get in front of that hollow. I had a boy with me and told 'im, "Go get the cage and I'll keep old tom in this tree." His wind was knocked out of 'im, you know. He stayed there I guess about five minutes, and he lost his rest and fell. Boy, he come and hit me right in the middle of the back, and when he did, well, I just fell down, you know, and give him plenty of room, and boy, he tuk to the woods! Them dogs ran him about five minutes and caught him and killed him.

About a week after that I jumped a big tom over here in our pasture, and we run him about two hours and he got to runnin' back and forth across an old trail. I had the whole pack on 'im. I had a small cotton rope, and I decided I'd just get it and when he come across the road I'd catch 'im, but before I did, I called all the dogs off 'im but two. You know he had the wind knocked out of 'im. He'd run and squat and run and squat, and he'd whip back across that road. I got the dogs all caught but two, and he come across that road and I popped that rope 'round his neck, and when he hit the end of that little rope, boy, he squatted and he lunged to jump on me, and when he did them hounds tuk 'im by each hind leg, and we jumped on 'im and tied 'im hog-fashion and brought 'im home. He was a big old tomcat. While they was fightin' 'im we tuk some heavy coats and throwed over 'im and got on top of 'im and helt the dogs off, and tied 'im up. They didn't hurt 'im 't-all.

We kept 'im about a year, and I turned 'im and both females out right here. The place I had wasn't big enough for 'em to mate. He was about five years old. He was a big old cat. You can estimate their age sorta like a dog, according to their teeth, and the way they're grayed around the mouth. One in the prime of his life, four or five years old, well, he's usually bigger and fatter than an old cat; you know, his teeth start to gettin' bad on 'im. His life is about the same as a dog, go from seven to twelve years old. Ever' now and then a dog will get fifteen, sixteen. Cat is about the same; about seven, eight years old is average.

Man is the cat's only enemy. I just like to run 'em; I don't really like to destroy 'em. But the hounds, they catch 'em. But there's always a few that's going to get away no matter what kind of hounds you got; they're that smart. I've got the only cat dogs that I know of.

My daddy was a cat hunter, hunted just like I do, all the time. He'd rather cat hunt than deer hunt.

We used to hunt alligators. They're sluggish just before they go into hibernation, get sluggish in cold weather and you can catch 'em easy; but hot summertime, boy, they're real active then. It's against the law to kill a alligator now.

We went out with Rodney and Tolbert once and they caught a fifteen-foot one. They find their hole and one of them straddles the hole and waits, and the other one takes a long stick, a fishhook on the end of a stick, you know, and he works it down in that hole, and the alligator will get to fightin' at it, and sometime you can just tease 'em out. The guy up over the hole, when the alligator's front feet comes out, he mounts 'im, and the other one ties his feet up over his back. Then they put a stick in his mouth and tie the mouth shut, and then they start workin' 'im on out till the back feet come out of the hole, and they tie them up over his back and bring 'im on out. His tail can still flip, but he's on his belly and his feet ain't down there to give him a good toehold, so then they tie his tail. You know they got little ridges on the tail, the big ones, and they tie a rope in between them ridges and put the rope 'round to his mouth-rope and sort of get 'im in a half circle, and he's helpless. Rodney usually done the pokin' and Tolbert done the mountin'. They'd try to cover the eyes. They're not so bad when they can't see. Alligator doesn't have any power with his jaws when they're closed, but when they're open he can clamp down with a lot of power. They worked without sayin' a word.

There's some down here on Pine Island. The little ones, they'll grunt, and then the old 'gator will come to them. It's sorta like a puppy dog gruntin'. Them little ones, they'll holler when they get separated out there in the bayou. They got a funny racket they make.

We got several little ones out of a big mud hole once and took 'em home. The old mama is mean when you bother the little ones, and they can move fast. Daddy said never run from them straight, but turn, and turn, and turn. They have to slow down to turn—flop that tail around.

The eggs look more like a turkey egg than anything. They all don't hatch at the same time. Sometimes they have sixty, seventy eggs. I've seen twenty, thirty of them at one time, already hatched out, in the same hole. They hatch out on top of those dry banks. They take limbs and stuff, build it up sorta like a old goose will, put those limbs over the nest, sometimes grass, pretty close to the water. We took ten, twelve eggs from a nest one time and hatched 'em here at the house.

Daddy was whippin' a old gator once, popping 'im with his long whip. He said every time he'd pop him that 'gator would swell up like a lizard, and directly he whipped that tail 'round there and jumped at 'im, and dad said he missed his horse's front leg not more'n a foot.

Born 1924, interviewed 1972–1975.

Introducing Pearl Wiggins

Pearl Wiggins lives alone only a short distance from the banks of the Trinity River, a few miles north of Romayor. If I don't find her home I look for someone with a fishing pole headed for the pond, or the lake, or the river, on her 303 acres. Fishing is her favorite recreation, although in her refrigerator one is as apt to find squirrel as fish, or duck, in season. Her .22 rifle is her favorite for squirrel hunting, but last year she took up her .410 because her eyesight was not so good. Her aim is still steady.

Mrs. Wiggins was one of four children, three girls and a boy. Her brother died at eighteen, and she was her father's "son" after that, working the cattle, securing the boats when the river was on the rise, penning wild hogs, fighting off the wolves, or whatever was required. She has lived in this immediate vicinity all her life.

Strange circumstances brought Pearl Wiggins' grandparents together in Texas. They both came from Tennessee, near Memphis. John F. Carr, her grandfather, liked to gamble, but his desire exceeded his skill, and during his late teens he ran up numerous gambling debts which his daddy had to pay off. This continued until his daddy had enough of it and packed him up and sent him to Texas—him and a Negro servant.

John Carr was attracted to a girl that lived some distance from his home in Memphis, but, when he went to see her, he learned that the family had moved and no one knew where. So he later came to Texas, learned surveying, and settled on the western edge of the Thicket near the Trinity River. On a surveying trip, miles through the woods, he came upon a newly built log cabin in a small clearing, and, believe it or not, it was the home of the girl he knew in Tennessee, and her family. They married and settled near Williams Creek, where later he owned the old Carr-Smithfield landing for steamboats plying the Trinity between Anahuac and Dallas. This ended his carefree gambling days, and he became an outstanding citizen.

Mrs. Wiggins still lives on the old family homestead of her parents, Bob Jones and Carrie Carr Jones.

PEARL WIGGINS

My grandfather, John Carr, had the mill just below here. The grist mill, where they ground corn, and the cotton gin were east of here about a mile, on Williams Creek. You couldn't get to it now to save your life, it's grown up so thick. That old grindstone there, it came from the steam mill just under this hill. Grandfather had slaves and they worked at the mill, and they stayed with him, thought lots of him. He treated them well and had nice little houses for all of them.

He also had the stagecoach stop on the route from Anahuac to Nacogdoches. It was a two-story house made out of logs that fit tightly, and the servants' quarters were under the same roof but separated from the main house, and that part was one story. This was all laid out for a townsite, but the railroad came to Livingston and everyone flew.

Up the river he had a ferry. The river wasn't like it is now. That dam up there holds it. It gets so low now you can't go no place. It got to where you couldn't cross the river in a skiff, hardly.

When I was a small child, Livingston was the closest settlement. I regard Ace as part of the Big Thicket, but not the Indian Village, or Livingston. It's too far north. The Thicket was where no one lived then, and it was wild country, beautiful, sparkling creeks—and wolves! Why, wolves, they came right to my house. We had goats, and my daughter had a pet. The yard gate was every bit as close as this one here, twenty feet, and that pet goat stayed inside the yard, of course. That's where she kept it, and those wolves would come to that gate trying to get that goat, and they did catch others out in the pen, lots of times. Oh, they were bad! I don't get to hear them howl anymore. Oooh! You know that's the saddest noise! But I love to hear them howl.

I've had wolves jump across my horse's neck trying to get a puppy I had in my lap. My husband and I had gone out here on the creek to fish, and we carried the puppy and the squirrel dog. We tied our horses, and there was a hole not farther than forty

Pearl Wiggins

feet from the horses. We got up there and I was fixing to throw my hook in, and my husband said, "Oh my goodness, Pearl, let's run! They're going to get the puppy!" And I guess there was twenty-five wolves, and the dogs had got under the horses and the horses were kicking to keep the wolves off. The horses were tied, but they were just a-dancing and a-kicking at the wolves. We got on the horses and took the dogs up in our laps and rode off. The wolves gave ground when we got up there, gave enough ground that we could get to the horses and get the dogs and be safe. It was a little trail and it was so thick we had to bend the limbs back, and those wolves were jumping between our horses, and one jumped over the neck of my horse, trying to get the dog. They hate dogs, I reckon.

Hunting was good. We used to have so many blackbirds coming over, they'd just cover the sky, and so did the pigeons, and so did the ducks. Ducks would come down here to this pond, just cover it. Mama said so many wild pigeons used to come they'd just break the branches off the trees, there'd be so many of them.

The Indians used to come down here, the Alabama Indians, and hunt with grandpa, and they'd bring in bear meat and wild turkey. Whenever we'd want some wild meat, papa would say, "Well, Carrie, are we without fresh meat?" He'd get his gun and ride off and in about an hour he'd come back with a deer, or whatever we wanted. Papa would kill a beef and divide it amongst the neighbors, and they did the same. No refrigeration, but of course they'd jerk the meat and put some down in brine, but we had fresh meat nearly all the time. Mama always kept a ham cooked.

The Black-and-Tan hounds are the prettiest hound, according to my way of thinking. They have long ears, kind o' narrow with a little curl. They're good for fox hunting. Papa would run fox at night, but they didn't kill the fox, just shake him out of the tree and let the hounds get after him again. He'd go fox hunting just to hear those hounds, and I've sat up many a night listening to them. They'd just ride off with the hounds, you didn't have to go far until you jumped a fox.

In the canebrake we had panther, bear, rattlesnakes, everything. The cane grows up real tall and you can make fishing poles of it. The switch cane, the young cane, comes up, and you didn't have to feed a cow, or if you had a bunch of horses, you didn't have to feed them winter or summer. They stayed fat as could be on switch cane. Big oak trees grew in that bottom, too, and daddy had a thousand head of hogs—fed on those acorns—and almost that many cows. We sold them on foot. It was open range. Some of them were stolen, but there was plenty for everybody. Daddy built pens for the hogs out in the woods and baited them with corn for a few days. You see they'd make a chute, made it of logs, made it strong, and made a wide "V" up where the hogs went in. Away out there they put corn along and then they put it in the pen to toll them in. We shipped our hogs and cattle.

I like to hunt, but I didn't get to do any for two years. They dumped the post office on my front porch. The old Carr-Smithfield landing was where steamboats used to land as they went up and down the Trinity. I remember the last one that ran. Well, they discontinued the Smithfield post office and it was moved far away. There was an old gentleman by the name of A. C. Emanuel. He had got to be pretty old, but he loved to read and he liked to take his daily paper, so he carried a paper around, and everyone signed to have a post office here, and he was appointed postmaster. Then they had to name it so they decided to name it Ace, after his initials. Well, after he died, they dumped the post office on my porch, and I kept it for them for two years, trying to get rid of it all the time. I told them I didn't want it. "Well, you're the proper person to take care of it, the only person who will know," they said. And they honestly didn't bring it in the house. All the mail, everything, was dumped on my porch. Well there was nothing to do but fix a place to keep the things separate; so I built a little room on the porch, cut a hole down there and fixed where they could put their letters in, and I took care of the mail. And I told the inspector, "I want to get rid of this just as soon as I can." He said, "Well we're going to swear you in in the mornin', and we'll get you out of here just as quick as we can."

It took two years for me to get rid of that post office. When they were making the road through here, I would have to get up at eleven o'clock and go and let the boys that were working on the road get their mail, because they couldn't get it in the daytime, when the mail came in. It was a terror! And people came in to mail packages, and I just couldn't keep regular hours. Two years of it! About the time we got it to where we had regular hours, you know, my nephew took it—Gordon Munson. He lives right down here at this little store. So they've had it ever since, over thirty years. Back then, they paid me just cancellation. In December I got one hundred twenty-five dollars. That was all these cards going off, you know, and packages, and oh that was money! I wouldn't have done it again for anything. Couldn't go fishing! Couldn't go hunting! Couldn't do anything!

I hunted with my brother, when he was alive, and with my daddy, and I've gone alone lots of times. In the last few years, since I've been a widow, I'd go with different ones. Mrs. White and I went hunting one night, and she'll never forget it. We killed five coons out of one tree—adult coons, down in my pasture. It was an oak tree, and they were after those acorns. The dog found them, and we had the pleasure of getting them out. She took them home. I don't know, I think she gave them to her neighbors; they ate them, but I can't. I mainly fish now.

1897–1976, interviewed 1969–1975.

P. O. Eason

Introducing P. O. Eason

It would be hard to say whether Phil Eason was a preacher who hunted, or a hunter who preached. He has spent his life doing both. If there is any story he tells more passionately than that of matching wits with a turkey gobbler in a pin oak glade, it is when he was converted and got the Holy Ghost in a little Pentecostal church in the Big Thicket. Sometimes he will ponder a short verse of Scripture for a week to garner the Lord's deepest meaning. His daddy was a preacher and so was his sister.

Phil Eason knows the lore and the lure of the woods as a keen observer who has spent his life there. Like most Big Thicket people, he hunted many different things for food, but it was the wild gobbler that thrilled him most. He had rather get a turkey than a deer. It was a solitary sport, no dogs, no companions. He went alone, riding his horse deep in the woods, sometimes miles, to spend the night by a campfire near his hunting ground. Long before daylight he would leave his horse and campfire behind and move cautiously to the turkey range.

To Phil Eason, though, a hunt is never just a hunt. Going into the woods is in itself an aesthetic experience. From years of close observation he has developed an uncommon sensitivity to the surroundings in which he has spent his life. In talking with him one comes to the conclusion that, as much as hunting, he enjoyed sleeping by a campfire or sitting under a tree exulting in the sights, sounds, or solitude of the forest.

There was one exception. Mr. Eason met his wife, Amber, when she came to teach in the settlement, and they recall the times that young folk in the community would go as a group on a possum or coon hunt at night. Hunting, of course, was secondary on these occasions.

The Easons live at their deep Thicket home where Phil was raised and where he and Amber raised their own family—a small clearing surrounded by deep woods not a hundred feet from the house. It is interesting to speculate on the thinking and the feelings of a person who hacks his way through an unmarked wilderness and brings his oxcart to a stop in this isolated spot and calls it home.

Chronic illness in recent years has slowed down Phil's hunting, but has not stopped it. "I can get my limit of squirrels from my porch," he said, "and I have eaten as much squirrel meat as any other kind." Three days after leaving the hospital with orders to rest he was on a deer stand waiting for a buck, but it would be hard to imagine Phil Eason sitting in a rocking chair during deer season.

P. O. (PHIL) EASON

O f course we got pleasure out of hunting, but my greatest pleasure was being in the woods, and a lot of it was being out alone at times, next to nature. I was out there in the purest of nature. There was no contamination of anything, just God's creation was out there—over me at night and around me—owls a-hollering, and I've had packs of wolves come right up and scratch within fifty yards of my camp. They've been close enough at night that I'd hear them snap and snarl at one another. I never had any fear of anything like that. I never even thought about being bothered by wolves—wouldn't thought no more about one of them hurting me than I would one of my dogs.

Along about four o'clock in the morning it begins to break day to the creatures of the swamp. Owls will holler all during the night, but they go wild just before daybreak, and I've heard wildcats holler and scream around me, and occasionally a panther, but I never did think a panther would hurt anybody unless you were trying to hurt him.

I've heard all my life that a panther screams like a woman, but three years ago, I was sitting on a deer stand one morning before daylight, my 30/30 across my lap, backed up against a stump before daylight, couldn't see my hand in front of me, and as I was sitting there, a panther—he couldn't have been over fifty yards from me—he screamed, and if there is any comparison to be made to the way it sounds, you could just say you step on a cat's tail and he screams. Just enlarge that about fifty times, and you've got the sound the panther makes, the same kind of scream. It was so close it just pierced my ears nearly. Though I never was afraid of a panther, I don't believe a leaf rustled that I didn't hear for the next thirty minutes. I couldn't have concentrated on anything right then. But there is a thrill in that. I don't know how to explain it, but there is a thrill in it for me. Just the sound of that panther—just to know I had heard that panther and to know he was there.

When I went out to camp that way, my mother—that's when I

was a boy—would make me up some biscuit dough and put it down in some flour, and I'd take it in my saddle pocket, and maybe some sweet potatoes and fat back in the other. I'd kill me a squirrel before I got in my turkey hunting grounds and dress it before I camped. I'd never shoot a gun nor even break a stick after I got in the turkey range, because you can scare an old gobbler in the evening and he won't say a thing in the world next morning. He won't gobble before he comes down off the roost. They have extremely good hearing and the best eyesight of nearly anything in the woods, superior to anything I know of.

After I got my fire built I'd get me a green forked stick and put that squirrel right up in front of the fire and just cook it gradually. Put a thick slice of that fat back just above him and that grease would drip on it, and when I got him cooked, I had a dish fit for a king. And I'd pinch off a piece of that dough and just start stretching it and wrapping it around a stick, about the size of my thumb, as far as it would go, then I'd put it by the fire and turn it until it got brown. It made a delicious hot roll to eat with my squirrel. I'd get a oak stick if I could. There's some sticks, persimmon, for instance, that in the heat of the fire would cause the sap to come out and ruin the taste of your bread.

I usually camped by myself. I loved to hunt by myself. That would give me a chance to meditate and to think. I liked to have certain periods of time to be alone. I started to hunt just when I was big enough to follow my brothers to the woods, but after I was about sixteen, I usually went alone.

I didn't have any fear of the animals. It was our opinion that if you didn't interfere with them, they wouldn't interfere with you. The human scent would run a bear off, and a panther is not apt to come around unless you have some fresh meat. I've heard almost every sound in the world at night, but I'd been taught to believe that wild animals wouldn't come up to a fire, and as far as I know it's true. Even so, I slept light and was aware of any movement at night.

I've stayed out when ice was on the ground with nothing but a saddle blanket. I made a practice of trying to find a low place in the ground on cold nights, and build a log heap in there and set it afire early in the evening and let it burn down before night, burn down till it was just a bed of coals. I'd get me a long limb and rake the coals out, and the ground would stay warm all night. I'd rake leaves in there, and throw my saddle blanket over me, and sleep warm.

Back where we hunted, it was virgin timber. We have a little of it left across Pine Island Bayou—what we call Red Oak Woods back there, never been disturbed, virgin timber. But when we said "Thicket," we meant thicket! Briars and brush, possum haw, bamboo, rattan, white bay, just everything; you just had to cut your way through. And in the baygall country, you'd just go from one tussock to another, and bog to your knees if you stepped in between. There's places we call hurricane places, where timber had all been blowed down, and it would naturally grow up thick. Sometimes it would rain for three or four days and get the ground real wet, and then the wind would start blowing. We sometimes had what we called hurricanes in those days. It blew straight through, not like a cyclone. When the ground got real wet, especially in the hardwood country, a lot of trees blew over. Most hardwood doesn't have a taproot; it just has runner roots, and the hurricane wind would blow them over when they got big.

I usually started hunting turkey in February. I'd ride or walk the woods out until I located the turkey signs. You could find where they had scratched. I've heard people talk about turkey roosts, but I never found a turkey roost in the Big Thicket in my life. I'd find where they'd scratched, show up good in these dreens where the leaves was washed away; you could see the bare ground, see where they'd walked. When I'd find this fresh turkey sign, I knew they were in that territory.

They range over a big area. They may be here a week or two and then three or four miles over yonder. In the spring of the year, mating time, those old gobblers just go through the woods. They'll be here tonight, and tomorrow night they'll be three miles away. Through the winter, turkey go in a group. After the old hen hatches her young, they go in a group until mating time again; and then the young gobblers begin to separate off and go from one bunch to another. If there's an old gobbler in the bunch, which there usually is, why he'll whip these young gobblers, and they'll begin to move out. If there happens to be two old gobblers, why the one that's the best man, he stays with that little bunch, and the other one has to hunt himself another bunch of hens. But they never get in large groups where two or three families get together. They don't group up like crows.

Seems to me I've seen as high as fifteen or twenty turkeys in a bunch, but an old turkey hen will sometimes hatch off as high as twenty at one setting. But after the armadillos come into this country our turkeys began to thin out. You know along creek banks, where the turtles dig holes and lay their eggs, I've seen the old shells there just scattered all over the place where those armadillos dug them up; you could always see armadillo tracks. They'll root up snake eggs and eat them, too.

There have been mornings I've woke up and maybe hear a turkey gobble from my camp, and I broke ice on ponds of water and waded them to go to the turkey. I don't know why I've lived as long as I have, because I've waded ice water that way and then have to set down by a tree, sit there and call to this turkey. Nine times out of ten, that turkey wouldn't gobble again till daybreak, then I'd call him to me. I wouldn't try to cross a big baygall, but back in this country is what we call hog-wallow country; it's holes and mounds, because in years past the timber had blown down and the roots had pulled up big mounds of clay. The trees finally rotted and left just a mound of dirt, and where the root pulled up, this left holes in the ground, and every one of those holes would be full of water in wet weather. If you'd tried to go around all the water, you never would get to the turkey.

The best time of day to get a turkey is from four o'clock on to daybreak—I mean to get to him. You had to have daylight to shoot him, but I did kill one at four o'clock in the morning once, shot him in the tree, moonlighted him.

After I set up camp, I'd sometimes go to the turkey range and I'd set down on a log, or against a tree, and every once in a while I'd yelp. Maybe I wouldn't get any hearing out of a gobbler, might not answer me that evening at all, but whenever he located the place he was going to roost, when he hit that roost up there, he'd gobble three or four times before he settled down for the night; so lots of times I'd know where my turkey was next morning. Before daylight I'd go easing off over there and get close as I could without scaring him off, and stop and wait for him to gobble before daylight. When he's real fat in the early spring, he can't gobble as loud as he can later, when he's thinner from traveling. I wouldn't try to get any closer than a hundred yards of one, because he detects the least little noise, even the noise of your feet. A turkey can hear a tremendous long ways. If he gobbled before daylight, I'd try to slip up under him, but if I couldn't, then I'd back up against a tree and yelp a few times—not much, just enough to get him to answer. Sometimes I could call him up close enough for a shot if it was daylight.

I didn't have a watch in them days, but I could tell when it was time to move out, because the owls know when the day begins to break before you do. Along about four o'clock in the morning, every owl in the woods starts just raring; they'd just jar the ground there'd be so many of 'em, just go wild! You never heard such a racket in your life as they'd be making. You could tell it was fixing to come daylight. I knowed it was time to make my coffee. If I was close to turkey country, I'd just back off from camp, careful not to make any noise, and when those owls began to kind o' die down, those old gobblers would start gobbling.

I'd find a place to sit down and lean back against a tree and I'd yelp, try to call him to me. I preferred peach leaves to anything I ever used. Some people use a turkey box to call 'em, but you can make a miss-lick that don't sound just right and they'll know it. It was much easier for me to yelp with a peach leaf, just double the leaf up and put it up between my lips, and blow the top part of the leaf, not the bottom part. I can make almost any kind of a call, bird call, on a leaf after I practice awhile.

All through the winter, back in the thicket where there's hardwood timber, leaves would be four and five inches deep. I

could go out there on those hammocks and scratch around and
always find a certain little plant that grew under those leaves, and it would be green the year 'round. It's something similar to the turkey berry. It had long narrow leaves on it, four or five inches long, and I'd get out there and scratch around until I found one, and it was good for calling turkey to you; and we could get switch cane any time. It's good for calling, too.

Lot of folks try to find someplace where they can hide to kill a turkey, but you don't want to hide. If a turkey is coming from the west, you want to get on the west side of the tree, sit right down in front of it, where he's coming right to you, because you blend with the tree. I've had them walk up to within 150 feet of me.

I sat down against a tree one morning, Big Pine Island Bayou was right in front of me, and I yelped a little and a gobbler on the other side came up there and walked up and down the creek a time or two, and I could've shot it, but I didn't want to have to wade the creek to get it. When he went behind some brush I grabbed my leaf and gave two or three yelps, and he just rose up, flew over, and lit about thirty steps from me, and of course that was all there was to that one.

Those old gobblers are smart. That's why I liked to turkey hunt, because when you killed an old white-headed gobbler, you could just pat yourself on the back, because you had accomplished something! They were smart! You had to know how to yelp for one and how to sit for one. And when I'd call them that way, sound like a turkey hen and get them coming to me, you could hear them strutting, hit the ground with that wing and go brrrrrumb, sound just like a drum, like someone rolling a barrel; and when one got that close to me, I'd always be setting with my knees up and my gun right over my knees, in my hand. Sometimes in the spring of the year it would be warm weather, and the mosquitoes would be awful bad, and I've had mosquitoes cover my face up, and I wouldn't even slap them off. I've set that way until I'd almost take a nervous breakdown waiting for that turkey to come, because I knew I couldn't move. I couldn't do that for any other animal in the Thicket.

A young turkey is different. Almost as sure as you found a young gobbler at all you could call him to you, because he was hunting company. Something else about them, when you yelp, they know exactly where you're at, and they will come just as straight to you as they can, just about run over you, half yelping and gobbling, trying to come back to the bunch. I've watched them come when they were just as far away as I could see one, look like he wasn't much bigger than a crow, and they'd come just as straight to me as they could. They can distinguish direction perfectly.

I shoot a turkey in the head if it's close enough. My favorite gun was always the twelve-gauge shotgun. I've hunted with shotguns, rifles, different gauges, and in my boyhood I hunted with what we called the old single-barreled Long Tom, but my favorite was always the twelve-gauge shotgun.

I knew one old gobbler that had a range of twenty miles. Maybe you'd hear him this morning down close to Menard Creek, and next morning you could find him over in the telephone box country. If he found hens, he might stay several days. We got to where we knew him well, we knew his track, but he'd been shot at so many times you couldn't call him up at all. I know he was better than four years old, because he got in a steel trap I had on a log four years before and damaged his middle toe on one foot, and I could always tell his track. Four years later I killed that turkey. He had a great big old knot on that middle toe.

We had pin oak back in the thicket, small pin oak acorns, and turkey would eat them just like a chicken would eat corn. I've seen where they'd go down in these little old dreens and wade those dreens and catch crawfish. They'd get fat during the winter, when we had a good acorn crop. They could swallow a big white oak acorn, but they preferred those pin oak and red oak acorns, the smaller ones. They just loved dogwood berries. They'd be just as fat as they could be in the spring of the year. They'd eat any kind of berries: gooseberries and huckleberries, and in the spring of the year there was lots of wild mulberry. Turkeys mostly prefer the low, hardwood country, but they'll come out on the hammocks and make their nests on higher ground, and raise their young.

You know a turkey is a peculiar thing. If he flies up and lights out yonder and you run out there to him, why he'll set there and look at you until you stop, and then he'll fly. Not every time, but nearly, they'll sit right there on that limb until you stop, and then they'll do their flying.

I never thought anything about getting lost. Until I got to be old I thought a fellow was a sissy if he took a compass into the woods with him. Maybe I was just born that way, but every minute and hour that I wasn't at work, why, I was in the woods. But I could go in strange country and come out, too. On clear nights I'd pick those seven stars for a guide; some people call them the Little Dipper, but we called them Seven Stars. The tail of that Seven Stars always points east, so I could go by that. If it happened to be cloudy I could watch this hardwood timber. There's a moss that grows on the north side of a hardwood tree that doesn't grow on the south side.

We have lots of haws here, and in the fall the red haw and the black haw trees would be just loaded. I used to stop when I was a boy and eat a bait of those. They were real sweet after the frost fell. I got the habit of eating just a little bit of every kind of berry that I found in the woods, and I've eat those turkey berries, too.

They don't have too much taste, and they're real seedy, but I'd eat them.

I was born and raised in this Thicket. My father came back in here and took up 152 acres of land. It was about a mile east of Indian Springs, which was on Big Pine Island Bayou. We had about as much bayou south of us as we did west. After my father and mother died, I took over the place and raised my own family in these woods.

To preempt land back in those days, people would go in there and get a surveyor to run us out 160 acres and make land marks, establish corners, you know, and if they lived on it ten years, it became their land. If they didn't have but a house and lived there, why it was their land; but naturally we cleared some land and grew mostly corn and sweet potatoes and sugar cane. There was a syrup mill up here at Thicket. Of course we had hogs and cattle in the woods. We'd have our own cornmeal all the time. I was never real bad about eating cornbread, myself. Since I've gotten old I eat lots of it, but I'd eat a cold biscuit before I'd touch a piece of cornbread.

I was the only boy in our family. My mother had three sons during her earlier marriage, but my half-brothers were practically grown when I was a young boy. I had three sisters and a younger brother, but he was accidentally killed by another small boy playing with a gun that was not supposed to be loaded.

Most families were superstitious in one way or another and mine was no exception. There were strange noises in our house several weeks before my little brother was killed. Along in the middle of the day it would sound as if somebody had thrown a bucket of rocks up on top of the house and they would roll down the roof. We looked but we couldn't find any rocks or anything else that could have made the noise. My mother always believed this was a warning. The house was covered with old-fashioned tar paper without any felt, so on hot summer days, it would stick to the lumber under it. As it grew hotter it would begin to expand, pull loose in places. We learned later that this caused the noises. I would like to state here that I am not superstitious, because where there is a sound or apparition there is a reasonable answer, and I have always been able to find it; however, there have been times when my hair would almost stand on end while I was trying to figure it out.

As a boy I dreaded wash day worse than anything else. We didn't mind the work, but there was no getting through with it. We had to stay around and be handy. We'd build the fire around the wash pots, draw water with an old bucket to fill 'em up, and then fill two or three tubs of water. And we had to do the battling. Dad got a big cypress block out of the woods, about 2-1/2 feet in diameter and 3 feet high, and put it close to the wash pot. Mother would lift the clothes out of the pot after they'd boiled. She'd use a long, smooth stick, and lay the clothes on that block, and they'd have two or three of us kids around there battling them clothes. One of us give out, and the other would battle a while. We used something like a long paddle to battle with, wide on one end with a smooth handle, and we'd beat them clothes to get the dirt out before mother washed them in the tub. We had a bored well, and we drew water out of it with a bucket 3 feet long and 6 inches in diameter. Sometimes that water had to be carried 50 to 75 yards to fill up those tubs and the wash pot.

Cane harvest was about the most exciting time of the year for the boys and girls, and even mother would hitch a ride on dad's wagonload of cane and go to the cane mill. We'd drink all the cane juice we wanted. When the cane grinding was over and the syrup was made, there would usually be a party and a candy-pulling at the home of one of the neighbors. All the young people, and a good many of the older folks, would be there. Some would come from so far away they would have to stay the night. They'd clean an old cast-iron wash pot, then fill it with syrup. We built a fire under it and cooked it down till it got thick and started to scorch, or burn. Then a boy and girl would take out as much as they could handle between them and begin to pull it. They'd use a little butter or hog lard on their hands to keep the syrup from sticking, and the syrup would cool off and become brittle, and make good candy.

When I was a boy we would have parties and all meet at some family's house and play games until late at night. There would always be refreshments. The neighbors lived maybe three miles apart, just dim wagon roads connecting them. Now these parties would be in full swing until twelve or one o'clock, and then everybody would get ready to go home. If the boys had brought the girls to the party they would then walk home with them. This was the best part of the get-together, and it was a most pleasant distance we traveled. But it was different coming back down that dark, lonesome road all alone. Mind you there were plenty of wolves, bobcats, panthers, and rattlesnakes, and you never knew if something was slipping along behind you or not. If you have never been out in the Big Thicket at night, you don't know what a dark night can be like. We didn't know what a flashlight was. We had the old kerosene lantern in those days, but what young man would carry a lantern in one hand while piloting a young lady home with the other? We'd rather take a chance on being caught by a panther or bit by a rattlesnake. Of course this was the courage we had while escorting the young lady home, but when you started back and heard animals in the bushes, and so dark you couldn't see the ground in front of you, it was something else. Many nights a pack of wolves serenaded me with their lonesome howl, and it would make my hair stand up, give me goose pimples all over. The confidence I had around my campfire, with my gun in my hands or at my side, the belief that a wild animal wouldn't attack a human, this all left me on those dark nights as I walked through the woods, unarmed and without a light.

Sometimes we'd go possum hunting, and one or two of the older folks would go along as chaperones. We'd take one or two kerosene lanterns, and an ax, but we wouldn't get more than started good before someone would get tired and we'd find logs for all of us to sit on. Then we'd build a big fire, and sing, and tell stories, and just talk. My wife was with me on one of these hunts during our courtship.

We'd have several varmint dogs, and my old dog, Trooper, would always bring back to me anything I killed or he caught. The girls had just started a song, "Oh Willie, My Darling," when the dogs struck a fight with a varmint. While we were singing away, here come old Trooper with a skunk in his mouth, right between the logs. We didn't have time to get up, but I've never seen so many heels in the air at one time in my life as we rolled backwards over those logs.

We had a large kitchen built separate from the rest of the house, and it had a large fireplace built out of clay and moss. They would mix water with the clay until it was a stiff mud, then take a large ball of the mud and flatten it out, place a handful of Spanish moss on it, and fold the mud back over the moss. This was what we call a mudcat. You would be surprised how many of these mudcat, or Big Thicket brick, it took to make a chimney. Nearly all the homes had an iron bar in the fireplace to hang pots on for cooking. We would get up at four o'clock in the morning, go out to the old kitchen, build a fire, and put water on to boil for coffee. The boys and girls of the family did this because dad was getting those last few minutes of rest. When he got up he would have to go to work, maybe to the woods where he worked in mud and water all day, many times getting home after dark. Or maybe he would have the mule harnessed and ready to start plowing by daylight. The job of building the fire in the kitchen rotated among the boys and girls, and there was a real commotion when pa or ma called out for the wrong one.

We used fine wood ashes and scrubbed the chairs till they would be almost white. We would take the same kind of ashes and wet them till it made a soft paste, and use it to dress down the front of the old fireplaces, and when it dried it looked almost like plaster.

We'd use a mop made out of shucks to scrub the floors, bore holds in a board and put shucks through 'em and cut 'em off even, then put a handle on it and it would last a long time. We'd mix sand and lye soap together and it made them floors shine.

My father was a minister, but I was a long ways from being a minister, I'll guarantee you that. I had gotten so wicked that I wouldn't even go in a church house.

I was converted one night at a service in Saratoga. I was outside talking with the boys and didn't intend to go in the church. They'd leave the windows open, you know, and people would stand around on the outside. I walked around behind the church house and—I don't know whether you believe in things like that or not—but something got ahold of me, and I got under deep conviction. I couldn't tell you to save my life what that preacher said that night, what his sermon was. I don't know, but I've always said I am glad that church house had a back door, because I was on the back side, and I found myself going in that door, and the next thing I knew I was at the altar praying and asking God to forgive me of my sins. That was an Assembly of God Church. I'm an Assembly of God minister. Most of my preaching has been in this section. I've been in different places, but most of my evangelistic work has been done down in East Texas.

My wife was born on the edge of the Thicket and came down into our country to teach school, and we fell in love and got married. We have two boys and four girls. Our oldest boy died at fourteen.

The Thicket has been my life. I've hunted just about every animal in the woods, but it wasn't just the hunting. I just enjoy being in the woods. There's hardly a time of the year you won't find flowers in bloom, and in the spring it's just a sight when the haws and the sweet bay and magnolias, and berries and jasmine and wild plum and dogwood are in bloom. My favorite is the wild honeysuckle.

I got out of the hospital Friday and took a walk in the woods Saturday, just back of the house here. Of course, I was just about dead when I got back. The doctor told me to stay inside, but I can get a couple of squirrels for dinner without leaving my backyard. They bark at my puppy dog I got tied back there. And I'd be surprised if I couldn't jump a deer a quarter of a mile from the house. I'm not able to walk much yet, but my boy's going to take me to a deer stand in the morning. Doc wouldn't like it but I don't think it'll hurt me. If I die, I'll die happy.

Born 1901, interviewed 1968–1975.

Epilogue

The stories in this book are complete in themselves, but each one describes life in the Thicket from a different point of view. Together they present a segment of history by the people who made it.

Several of the persons who told these stories were ninety-five to one hundred years old, and their grandparents were the first white settlers in this pristine wilderness. They were adventuresome people, attracted to the area despite the unusual hardships it imposed. The same is true of their offspring. It is not unusual to find the great-grandchildren still living on the original family homestead. It is doubtful if the young people of any area have remained closer to the land and traditions of their forefathers. They live close to nature every day but have never lost their sensitivity to the beauty of the commonplace things in their surroundings. We never talked to an old-timer whose favorite flower was not the wild honeysuckle, and several of them had bouquets in the house, though they were growing wild a hundred feet away.

Of course the Big Thicket of today is vastly different from what it was in the beginning. Modern machinery has cut roads through parts that formerly could not have been traversed. The virgin stands of longleaf pine, which Thicket people called "open country" because it had no underbrush, have been cut out except for a few remnants. The bear, long the dominant animal of the Thicket, is only an occasional visitor now, and wild hogs, since the days of the open range, are harder to find. Developments on the periphery are increasing.

What is left, however, is still the Thicket, much as it always was. Panthers are heard occasionally; bobcats, fox, and deer are still common, and the smaller animals abound. When we first went down there we stopped at an old house on one of the newer roads and asked an old lady on the front porch, "Where is the Big Thicket?" Her terse reply was "Just leave the road."

We are familiar with East Texas, but Kountze is the only town where we have been privileged to see dogs chase a fox across a man's front yard and to look out of our trailer window and watch a pileated woodpecker get his breakfast from a sweetgum tree.

Of primary interest to outsiders is the plant life of the Thicket. Many of the plants are rare, and others are found in unusual plant communities. The first person to suggest the preservation of a portion of this land was R. E. Jackson, a conductor on the Santa Fe that ran through a part of the Thicket. In 1938, H. B. Parks and V. L. Cory, of Texas A&M University, completed a biological survey of the area which documented its scientific value. Since that time, state and national interest has resulted in the preservation of 85 thousand acres. With the integrity of the Thicket's biological aspects thus assured, there is natural concern for the preservation of its unique customs and culture. These may, indeed, be endangered, but years of face-to-face exchanges with these people tell us that the mark of Big Thicket pioneers is indelible.

Early cabin